WILLIAM CONGREVE

by

MAXIMILLIAN E. NOVAK

William Congreve is generally acknowledged to have been the greatest comic dramatist of the Restoration, England's greatest period of comedy. Working in a comic mode which had been thoroughly established for almost thirty years, Congreve took advantage of comic formulas previously used by Dryden, Etherege, Wycherly and Otway in order to make comedy at once more artful and more meaningful. In spite of his debt to his predecessors, Congreve was more obviously a writer belonging to a brief historical period between the Glorious Revolution of 1688 and the end of the century, when the attacks of the Societies for Reformation of Manners and the efforts of Jeremy Collier put an end to the rare combination of wit, imagination, and moral intelligence with which playwrights of the time had been exploring contemporary life and manners—particularly problems of love and marriage.

Restoration comedies, including Congreve's, have been attacked for their immorality and, more recently, for their failure to deal with their society in any direct or socially significant way. Instead of defending Congreve against these misplaced attacks, this present study describes his achievements as a writer—what he did and what he failed to do. Like most Restoration dramatists, Congreve had a hard-headed attitude toward sex, though he was not hard-hearted about true love. He spoke of himself, with some truth, as a satirist of contemporary society. But his real concern was with art—the art of the novella, poetry, tragedy, and, most of all, the art of comedy.

thors Series

man, Editor

NA UNIVERSITY

Congreve

 112

William Congreve

By MAXIMILLIAN E. NOVAK

WILLIAM CONGREVE

Library of Congress Catalog Card Number: 73-125258

FOR MY PARENTS
GEORGE AND ELSIE NOVAK

Preface

Probably the most important recent development in criticism and scholarship on Restoration drama has been the tendency to treat each dramatist separately and to realize that the forty years between the return of Charles II to the English throne and the end of the century cannot be considered as monolithic and static. Clifford Leech has written of William Congreve as a product of the end of the century, and, more recently, Arthur Scouten has suggested that the comedies of the 1690's have a distinct, indeed, a unique texture. In this study, I have attempted to treat Congreve and his plays specifically in terms of English art and society after the Glorious Revolution of 1688. For the most part, this book is concerned with explication and close examination of Congreve's writings, but I have always tried to keep in mind the specific context of that last decade of the seventeenth century in which a brilliant style of comedy flourished.

Though Congreve inherited social, critical, and philosophic of the seventeenth f ideas to assume ie same under a English queen as ind James II with hey saw so beau- The libertinism of l the end of the of Rochester, who art and life that comedy. And if ise tradition, one that produced the er in the century. rne were still vital ed in the thought writings of that nedies must com- vhen he was bor- nes—from earlier a to his decade.

ABOUT THE AUTHOR

Professor of English at UCLA, Maximilian E. Novak has written extensively on Restoration drama and eighteenth-century fiction, including two books, *Economics and the Fiction of Daniel Defoe* (1962) and *Defoe and the Nature of Man* (1963). He is an editor of the Augustan Reprint Society and a general editor of a new edition of Defoe's writings. His edition of three plays of John Dryden will appear in 1970 as volume ten of The California Edition of *The Works of John Dryden*.

In quoting Congreve throughout my text, I have relied on Bonamy Dobrée's edition, which was based on the collected edition of 1710. I feel that this represents Congreve's mature deliberation about the way he wanted his plays to appear in a permanent literary form, and it is as a writer of great comedies that endure as literature that I am mainly concerned with Congreve. I have eliminated italics in all quotations, except where they seemed to indicate some specific emphasis, since what was merely a printer's convention of Congreve's day is often a barrier today to a correct reading of a speech or poem. Footnotes have been kept to a minimum because of limited space, and I trust that the bibliography will be used to supplement the notes.

Even without footnotes, my indebtedness to previous critics and scholars should be perfectly apparent. I have drawn most of my facts about Congreve from Professor Hodges's excellent biography, and much of my initial critical impetus and inspiration came from Professors Thomas Fujimura, Dale Underwood, and Norman Holland. I have benefited from conversations with Arthur Scouten, Lucyle Hook, John Barnard, Stoddard Lincoln, and the late Herbert Davis and his wife, though I am not at all certain that any of them would approve of some of my conclusions. Sections of my book have appeared in somewhat different form in *College English, Criticism,* and *Essays in Criticism,* and I want to thank the editors of these journals for their permission to reproduce some of the same material. I would also like to thank the librarians of the William Andrews Clark Memorial Library for their untiring help and my wife, Estelle, for her criticism, assistance, and patience.

University of California,   MAXIMILLIAN E. NOVAK
Los Angeles

Contents

Chronology

1670   William Congreve born on Sunday, January 24, to William Congreve, of the Congreve family of Staffordshire, and Mary Browning, daughter of Walter Browning of Norfolk. He was baptized on February 10.

1674   Congreve's father receives a lieutenant's commission in Ireland and moves his wife and son to Youghal, where he remains for five years. Congreve receives his earliest schooling there.

1678   Congreve's father transferred to Carrickfergus, another seaport on the northeastern coast of Ireland.

1681   Enters school at Kilkenney where his lifelong friend, Joseph Keally, and Jonathan Swift are scholars.

1686   Enters Trinity College Dublin on April 5, where he is under the tutelage of St. George Ashe, Swift's tutor.

1688   William of Orange lands in England on November 5. Congreve leaves Trinity College for England and a visit to Stretton Manor.

1689   Spends the spring and summer at Stretton Manor and may have begun *The Old Batchelor.*

1691   Enters the Middle Temple on March 17 to study law. Begins to frequent Will's Coffee House and becomes a friend of the Wits. *Incognita* licensed December 22.

1692   Publishes *Incognita* on February 18, and also the eleventh satire of Juvenal in Dryden's edition of the satires of *Juvenal and Persius* in October. Gives two songs and three odes to Charles Gildon for publication in a *Miscellany of Original Poems. The Old Batchelor* revised by John Dryden, Thomas Southerne, and Arthur Maynwaring. Congreve given a six-month pass to the theater.

1693   Reprints the Odes in *Examen Poeticum* along with translations from Homer's *Iliad.* Improves his friendship with Dryden. *The Old Batchelor* performed in March with a continual run of fourteen nights. *The Double Dealer* appears in December. Begins his acquaintance with actress Anne Bracegirdle. Writes *To Mr. Dryden on the Translation of Persius,* song from Southerne's *The Maid's Last Prayer,* and Prologue to George Powell's *A Very Good Wife.*

1694   Writes Song from Dryden's *Love Triumphant,* set by Henry Purcell; *Prologue to the Queen; To Cynthia.*

1695 *Love for Love* produced at opening of new company at Lincoln's Inn Fields on April 30. Writes an ode on the death of Queen Mary and another *To the King, On the Taking of Namure; Concerning Humour in Comedy,* Prologue to *Pyrrhus* by Hopkins, Prologue to *The Husband His own Cuckold* by John Dryden, Jr., and *Epilogue to Oroonoko.* Congreve receives a government sinecure as one of the commissioners for Licensing Hackney Coaches.

1697 *The Mourning Bride* performed February 27. *The Birth of the Muse* written.

1698 Jeremy Collier attacks Congreve and the morality of the contemporary stage in *A Short View of the Immorality and Profaneness of the English Stage.* Congreve replies in *Amendments of Mr. Collier's False and Imperfect Citations.* Writes Song from *Orpheus Britannicus.*

1700 *The Way of the World* produced on March 12. Dryden dies, May 1. Congreve travels on the Continent.

1701 Congreve's libretto, *The Judgment of Paris,* performed at Dorset Garden.

1703 "Verses Sacred to the Memory of Grace Lady Getkin" and "A Poem in Praise of the Author" both published in *Misery Virtues Whetstone.* Congreve writes a song for Nicholas Rowe's *The Fair Penitent. The Tears of Amaryllis for Amyntas* and *A Hymn to Harmony* published. Congreve meets Henrietta, Duchess of Marlborough.

1704 Joins with William Walsh and Sir John Vanbrugh on *Squire Trelooby,* a translation of Molière's *Monsieur de Pourceaugnac.* Appointed with Vanbrugh as head of a new theater in the Haymarket with funds from the Kit-Kat Club. Contributes poems to "Dryden's Miscellany," including *Pious Selinda* and *Prologue to the Princess. Prologue to the Court on the Queen's Birth-Day.*

1705 Becomes Commissioner for Wines. Gives up share in Haymarket Theatre.

1706 Moves to Surrey Street off the Strand, where he resides throughout his life. Publishes *Discourse on the Pindarique Ode* and *Pindarique Ode Humbly Offer'd to the Queen.*

1707 Writes *Semele.*

1709 Painted by Sir Godfrey Kneller as one of the Kit-Kat Club.

1710 Swift visits Congreve and finds him nearly blind. First Collection of Poems and Plays published by Jacob Tonson. Publishes *Poems Upon Several Occasions.* Translation of Ovid's *Art of Love,* Book III published.

1711 Writes *Tatler* No. 292, February 17.

1712 Complains to his friend Joseph Keally of his failing eyesight.

1713 Richard Steele dedicates *Poetical Miscellanies* to him.

1714   Made Secretary to the Island of Jamaica December 17, an office which gives him an adequate income for the rest of his life. Made Searcher of Customs November 14. Friendship with Scriblerians: Alexander Pope, Jonathan Swift, John Arbuthnot, and John Gay. Fall of Tories and death of Queen Anne.

1716   Steele dedicates Joseph Addison's *The Drummer* to Congreve and asks him to settle dispute over Addison's authorship. Corresponds with Lady Mary Wortley Montagu.

1717   Visits Richard Boyle's villa. Home to recuperate from illnesses. Edits and writes introduction to Dryden's *Dramatick Works.* Translation of Ovid's *Metamorphoses,* Book X published.

1719   Writes to Giles Jacob welcoming his visit and agreeing to give him an account of his life and writings for Jacob's *Poetical Register.*

1720   Pope dedicates *Iliad* to Congreve. Writes *An Impossible Thing* and *The Peasant in Search of his Heifer.*

1722   Visits Bath for his health.

1723   Duchess of Marlborough gives birth to a daughter, Mary, undoubtedly Congreve's. Sponsors concert with Duchess of Marlborough.

1726   Visited by Voltaire.

1729   Writes *Letter to Viscount Cobham.* Dies January 19.

1732   *The Daily Post,* July 15, reports that a careless servant of the Duchess of Marlborough broke a wax statue of Congreve while bringing it downstairs.

CHAPTER 1

Congreve: the Myth, the Man and the Milieu

PROFESSOR John C. Hodges, in his comprehensive and detailed biography, protested against a reference to William Congreve as "the man of mystery." To his contemporaries, Hodges points out, Congreve was a familiar and well-known figure. "Dryden found him a personable young law student who could ably assist either in the translating of Juvenal or in the making of a contract with Tonson," writes Hodges. "Swift passed many a pleasant evening with this 'very agreeable companion.' Lady Mary Wortley Montagu declared Congreve the wittiest of all her acquaintances. Pope believed him 'most honest hearted,' and Steele praised his congeniality in no uncertain terms." Unquestionably, Congreve was a delightful companion, but this is hardly enough to say about such an interesting literary figure. Though his contemporaries unquestionably knew him well, the fact is that we do not.

I *The Myth*

Because there is so little to go on, the myths which grew up about Congreve have more solidity, if not more truth, than anything we can glean from his letters or the remarks of his companions. What made him such a delightful personality? Lady Mary wrote, "I never knew anybody that had so much wit as Congreve." But she also testified that "he was so far from loving Pope's Rhyme, both that & his Conversation were perpetual jokes to him, exceeding despicable in his Opinion, & he often made us laugh in talking of them being particularly pleasant on that subject." Professor Sherburn conjectures that "Lady Mary, in an obvious rage, is doubtless exaggerating"; but, after all, if Congreve was a wit, he had to have something to be witty about; and few subjects are so diverting as the weaknesses of friends.[1] In his letters Congreve finds fault with the writings of Swift, Nicholas Rowe, and Colley Cibber. Nevertheless, he managed to be a friend of John Dennis and Pope, of Kit-Kat and Scriblerian, and of Whig and Tory. He seemed almost deliberate in cultivating the friendship of deadly enemies.

Then there is the myth that his mistress, Henrietta, Duchess of Marlborough, had a statue made of Congreve after his death with which she conversed. The report of this incident in *Biographia Brittanica* is among the more imaginative:

The Lady, commonly known by the name of the young Duchess of Marlborough, had a veneration for the memory of Mr. Congreve which seemed nearly to approach madness. Common fame reports, that she had his figure made in wax after his death, talked to it as if it had been alive, placed it at tables with her, took great care to help it with different sorts of food, had an imaginary sore on its leg regularly dressed; and to complete all, consulted Physicians with relation to its health. These things are usually ranked under the appelation of whim; But whenever a person act thus absurdly, the best excuse is insanity.

Henrietta was far from insane; and, as far as one can tell, she did have a statue of some kind, and she was not alone in her liking for Congreve. Swift actually persuaded his friend, Mrs. Barber, to omit a satiric attack on Congreve from one of her works, and his other friends also worked hard to spare him pain and to help him to preferment and literary success. When they wanted someone to act as a peacemaker, they asked for his aid; and of these Dryden, John Dennis, and Thomas Southerne head the list. He was one of those men whom everyone esteems, admires, and respects; and at least one woman came close to worshiping his image.

Yet Voltaire found Congreve vain and pretentious. His main fault, wrote the young *philosophe* was his "entertaining too mean an Idea of his first Profession, (that of a Writer) tho' 'twas to this he ow'd his Fame and Fortune. He spoke of his Works as of Trifles that were beneath him; and hinted to me in our first Conversation, that I should visit him upon no other Foot than that of a Gentleman, who led a Life of Plainness and Simplicity. I answer'd, that had he been so unfortunate as to be a mere Gentleman I should never have come to see him; and I was very much disgusted at so unseasonable a Peace of Vanity." When Voltaire visited him, Congreve was old and ailing. He may have felt some irritation at the intrusion of Voltaire on his quiet and private life, but everything suggests that he behaved with a kind of Olympian indifference which his friends had long grown to accept and which must have seemed odd to the brilliant Frenchman whose dream was to build a reputation through writing.

Congreve was obviously wearing the mask of the retired gentleman, the disciple of Horace, whose retirement was not to the country but within the city he loved where he could be a part of the civilization which only a few capitals in eighteenth-century Europe could afford. But Voltaire wanted to speak with the writer of England's most "witty and regular" comedies, not with a retired gentleman. He probably felt, not without justification, that the French carried off that pose better than most Englishmen. One sympathizes with Voltaire's disgust, though surely he missed the point: few writers were so vain as Congreve, but his real vanity concerned his writing. Perhaps Voltaire would have discovered that fact had he chosen to level his wit against the artist rather than the man. Congreve had received adulation from no less a person than John Dryden, the greatest writer in England; and he was not to be flattered by a visit from a young Frenchman of little reputation.

However Congreve may have received Dryden's panegyric, there is no question that adverse criticism irritated him beyond endurance. He did *not* rush on to the stage to berate the audience for its failure to appreciate *The Way of the World*, but whoever invented that story must have thought it a credible fiction, true to the myth of Congreve's character. In his own criticism there is an unmistakable arrogance; more than Addison, Congreve gave some imaginary senate laws in every pronouncement he made on literature. Jeremy Collier clearly infuriated him, but it would be a mistake to think that the churchman caused him to lose his sense of criticism as well as his sense of humor. Confronted by Collier's insulting attack in 1698 on his art and morals, Congreve is willing to admit an occasional lapse in moral propriety, but he would admit to none as an artist. Voltaire should have realized that, though Congreve took himself very seriously as a writer, he was much less serious about himself as a man.

His letters provide ample evidence to support this view. Congreve reveals not only the sense of humor that we would expect of a great comic playwright but also that rare ability to laugh at himself—at his tendency to become fat, and even at his bad eyesight and sickness. He also reveals a deep sensibility and strong emotions, as in his letter to his friend Joseph Keally on the occasion of his father's death:

I know you are no stranger to sentiments of tender and natural affection, which will make my concern very intelligible to you, though it may seem unaccountable to the generality, who are of another make. I am pretty well recovered of a very severe fit, which has lasted **a** month. I think to go abroad for air to-morrow; and by degrees depend upon time to cure what reasoning and reflection seldom effect. I had written to you sooner than any body; but the fulness and violence of my fit was such, that it disabled me. I thank you for your usquebaugh, whether ever it arrives or not, but am more pleased that you give me hopes of seeing you this summer: I hope your resolution will continue.[2]

Here is one part of Congreve, which made him so excellent a companion—a warm love of friends, deep feeling, and an infirmity which seemed to win sympathy from all who knew him. Congreve, we must recall, was a writer of pastorals as well as comedies; he was, in fact, like Shaftesbury's ideal man of the eighteenth century, a combination of humor and sensibility. He apparently wrote his first play, *The Old Batchelor,* under a tree and revised it in an equally romantic setting, "before a black mountain nodding over me and a whole river in cascade falling so near me that even I can distinctly see it." He may have viewed this scene with the eye of Horace and Virgil rather than Wordsworth, but the sensibility Congreve expressed for the English countryside and his use of natural setting for inspiration anticipate a century of enthusiastic appreciation of nature. Congreve also could evoke a romantic nostalgia for his boyhood prowess when he spoke of his sickness. "As to my gout I am pretty well," he wrote to Joseph Keally, "but shall never jump one-and-twenty feet at one jump upon North-hall Common."

If Congreve was a man of sensibility, he was also a lover of the civilized life; and we must remember that the play that Congreve was writing in such a romantic setting was a sophisticated comedy of London life. And the remark about the usquebaugh and his gout reminds us of Congreve's weakness for good food and wine. The Horatian pose of the lover of life and devourer of its feast for the senses has its basis in Congreve's genuine tendency to gluttony. The buttery books at his college reveal that he ordered six times the amount of wine, beer, and snacks that Swift had in his penurious career at Trinity College, Dublin; and, to a certain extent, Congreve may be seen as a model libertine, not as the wild rake of Thomas Shadwell's version of the Don Juan myth, but a genteel epicurean living up to the ideal of a gentleman as set forth by Sir William Temple and St. Evremond. Gout may run in the best of families, but surely Congreve courted the illness which eventually destroyed him. "He had the misfortune to squander away a very good constitution in his younger days; and I think a man of sense and merit like him is bound in conscience to preserve his health for the sake of his friends, as well as himself," wrote Swift with the extraordinary clarity of vision and deliberate consideration of human self-interest which distinguish him.

Swift could not forgive either the loss of such a genial companion or the pain which Congreve's death caused him. And no wonder, for if Congreve's sickness could wring pity from the Dean, his wit could provoke laughter, and who is a better companion than one who makes us laugh. Swift tells us that on one occasion when he dined with Congreve he "laughed till six"; and, when he was not in Congreve's presence, he could experience the same amusement from his plays. "I saw a volume of Congreve's Plays in my room, that Patrick had taken to read," he writes, "and I looked into it, and in mere loitering read it till twelve, like an owl and a fool: if ever I do so again; never saw the like. . . ." To Denis, Congreve composed one of those letters which one could only dream of receiving. Writing from Cambridge, he disparages the country in general and life at Tunbridge Wells in particular:

After all this, I must tell you, there is a great deal of Company at *Tunbridge;* and some very agreeable; but the greater part is of that sort, who at home converse only with their Relations; and consequently when they come abroad, have few Acquaintances, but such as they bring with them. But were the Company better, or worse, I would have you expect no Characters from me; for I profess my self an enemy to Distraction; and who is there, that can justly merit Commendation? I have a mind to write to you, without the pretence of any manner of News, as I might recommend you to some new Acquaintance that I have made here, and think very well worth the keeping; I mean Idleness and a good Stomach. You would not think how People Eat here; every Body has the Appetite of an *Oastrich,* and as they drink Steel in the Morning, so I believe at Noon they could digest Iron.[3]

He follows with the suggestion that the water at the spa is not conducive to writing and proposes a play based on the introduction of this *"Anti-Hypocrene"* into the drink at Will's Coffee House, the gathering place of Dryden and his circle of poets. Admittedly, such a letter is more for posterity than for a close friend. That so few of this kind survive suggest that most of Congreve's letters were like those to his Irish friend, Joseph Keally—personal and warm.

Yet even these are hardly revelations of the inner workings of Congreve's soul; there are no confessions. Indeed, the bulk of what Professor Hodges calls "strictly personal" correspondence is full of externals—news of politics, accounts of extraordinary events like the storm of 1703, and witty gossip about friends. We miss Swift's baby talk to Stella or the intimate glimpses we have into the life of Samuel Pepys. It is possible then to agree with Professor Hodges concerning Congreve's reality for his contemporaries, while agreeing with F. W. Bateson's contention that the Congreve we know has very little to do with the writer of comedies. He was something of a wit and a "very agreeable companion"; the rest of the man is in his art, and that, like Shakespeare's, has a quality of both intense personal involvement and complete anonymity.

II   *Early Years: 1670-1700*

"It was said by himself that he owed his nativity to England, and by everybody else that he was born in Ireland," wrote Dr. Johnson in lamenting the pride and falsehood common to authors. The general observation is true enough, but the facts are wrong. Congreve was born on January 24, 1670, at Bardsey in Yorkshire, the son of William Congreve and Mary Browning; and he was baptized seventeen days later.[4] His father was a second son of Richard Congreve, a squire of Stretton Hall in Staffordshire, a supporter of Charles II, and the possessor of an estate of six hundred pounds a year. The Congreves were members of the gentry who dominated the country politically, economically, and socially in a rigidly stratified society. Social mobility existed, but it was notable and more common in the cities and large towns than in the country. Bardsey, the village in which Congreve was born, was part of the estate of Sir John Lewis, who had his main estate nearby at Ledstone Park.

Though Congreve's enemies preferred to believe that his account of his birth was so much pretense, it separated him in a very real sense from the mass of writers, hacks of little learning and low birth, to whom he could show contempt as an artist and as a gentleman. The poet Matthew Prior was often derided as the son of a wine drawer, and Alexander Pope was sometimes insulted for being the son of a tradesman. If genuine ability as a writer might sometimes provide the same kind of social mobility afforded by the army and the church, Congreve always had the comfort of being able to think of himself as a gentleman who wrote, rather than as a member of London's Grub Street.

Shortly after the birth of their son, the Congreves moved from Bardsey Grange to London, where they buried their only other child, Elizabeth, on September 28, 1672; and, after working briefly at purchasing horses for the Duke of York on the Continent, Lieutenant Congreve received an army commission on March 19, 1674, to serve in Ireland. When he was four years old, William Congreve accompanied his parents to the garrison at the seaport at Youghal, and five years later to another post at Carrickfergus. We know nothing about his early schooling, but a good deal is known about the curriculum of the school at Kilkenny, where his father joined the regiment of the Duke of Ormond in 1681. At this school Swift received his early training, and it was one of the great institutions in the British Isles.

Under the protection of the wealthy and powerful Duke of Ormond, Kilkenny College was attended by from fifty to sixty boys between the ages of nine and fifteen.[5] Congreve was almost twelve when he entered, and his studies were directed by two excellent masters, Henry Ryder and Edward Hinton, the first from Trinity College, Cambridge, the second from Oxford. By modern standards, the training was amazingly comprehensive and rigid in teaching morality and the Classical languages. Students assembled for morning prayers at seven in the morning in winter and at six during spring and summer. They spent the rest of the day in the classroom until five o'clock with the exception of a two-hour break, half an hour of which was devoted to reciting the catechism. The curriculum included reading, writing, and speaking Latin in the fifth form; parsing and construction in the fourth; and in the third the scholars began Greek, while continuing their work on the standard authors, Caesar, Cicero, and Terence. In the first form, Hebrew might be added. A knowledge of oratory was inculcated through spoken exercises.

For all this scholarly drudgery, there were compensations. Thursday and Saturday were half-days, and there were short vacations during Easter, Whitsun, and Christmas. Congreve waxed nostalgic over the games, and Swift commented on "the delicious holidays, the Saturday afternoon, and the charming custards in a blind alley; I never considered the confinement ten hours a day, to nouns and verbs, the terror of the rod, the bloody noses, and broken shins." At this school Congreve is reported to have written his first poem, one about the death of the headmaster's magpie; and here he made some lasting friendships. Swift left Kilkenny half a year after Congreve entered, and the acquaintance between the older boy and the new student could not have been profound; but Congreve found in the corpulent Joseph Keally both an eating companion and a fast friend.[6]

Congreve's biographer imagines him to have been a studious young man, already nearsighted, learning his Greek thoroughly under the direction of Edward Hinton and attending local performances of plays by townsmen and the visiting Dublin players from Smock Alley. "There is every reason to believe that before Dr. Hinton wrote into his register, 'William Congreve of the first Class Entered the University of Dublin, April Ao. 1686,'" writes Professor Hodges, "that youth had already become a student of the stage." Of these conjectures, the only certain one is that Congreve learned his Greek thoroughly enough to receive encouragement from Dryden to translate all of Homer. The portrait painted of him at this time shows a young gentleman with a heart-shaped face, pointed chin, and an elegant taste in dress. In this artist's conception there is less of the myopic scholar than of the future wit.

At Trinity College Dublin, Congreve, then sixteen, shared the same tutor as Swift, who once remarked, "Never a Bishop in England with half the wit of St. George Ashe." Not all of those graduating from Kilkenny went to college; some became merchants, gardeners, and attorneys; but those that did manage to join the three-hundred-odd students there had the benefit of learning from scholars who were interested in the exciting new ideas of the Royal Society and of the new science. Admittedly, Ashe's contributions to science were not the kind that would inspire questioning students like Swift: they included an account of a man whose finger tip bled periodically and of a girl in Ireland who had horns growning out of her body, exactly the kind of science Swift was later to attack; but the spirit of investigation was genuine enough. It is not without its amusing side that two of England's most brilliant wits were tutored by a man who once launched into a praise of mathematics and an attack upon "an impudent sort of adversaries, the railleurs and wits," and upon that laughter which was "the easiest and slenderest fruit of witt" because "it proceeds from the observation of the deformity of things, whereas there is a nobler and more masculine pleasure which is raised from beholding their orders and beauty." Congreve was to echo a similar sentiment in his attack on farce, but he never became a convert to science. He shirked his science lectures but hardly missed a class in Greek.

As at Kilkenny, the method of study was rigorous. The medium of study was Latin, tutors were seen daily, and lectures were read out of books. The undergraduate had to listen carefully, take notes, and then expand them into a Latin commentary every week for inspection by the lecturer. They also had to prepare a Latin theme every week upon special subjects, attend lectures on Greek, and declaim twice a week on a subject taken from morality or politics. The final year was devoted to logic; Aristotle was read in the second and fourth year; and religion and morality, so much a part of the training at Kilkenny, were by no means neglected, with daily disputation of theology, a chapel service, prayers in the morning and afternoon, and discussion of biblical texts on Sunday and Friday.

Yet here again, life was far from unpleasant. Outside the walls was Dublin, called by Narcissus Marsh, a provost of the college, a "lewd and debauch'd town." It is inevitable that someone as urbane as Congreve must have been fascinated by the first genuine city he had encountered. Swift was accused of "notorious neglect of duties, and frequenting the town"; and other offenders were punished for climbing the walls, which were ordered to be built three feet higher during Congreve's last year there. Like every college at Oxford and Cambridge today, Trinity College must have had a secret and delightfully dangerous route to freedom.

Professor Hodges maintains that Congreve would have made his way to the theater at Smock Alley, but records of performances are sparse. All performances may have been stopped by February, 1687, when Tyrconnel assumed the Lord Lieutenancy in the turmoil preceding the fall of James II. A clue to some of the plays Congreve might have seen is provided by a manuscript at Harvard University, which lists prologues to some of the plays performed at this period. Included are Jonson's *Volpone*, Brome's *The Jovial Crew*, Otway's *The Atheist*, Dryden and Lee's *Oedipus*, Southerne's *The Mother in Fashion*, and Durfey's *The Boarding School*. On the whole, preference was given to older plays, as is indicated by the complaint of one prologue writer:

> You are of late such Antiquaries grown
> That no regard's to Modern writers shown,
> Fletcher, & Johnson only will go down.
> Their works, like Medalls, doe their value raise
> Ev'n from their Imperfections and Decayes.[7]

The writer then suggested that the audience preferred the fools in older plays because they did not identify themselves with those of the past. Certainly, Congreve was well grounded in the older theater; and performances of Dryden, Southerne, and Durfey could have made a stronger impression on him had he seen them staged.

Nevertheless, Dryden's complaint that *The Old Batchelor* lacked "the fashionable cut of the town" suggests that he considered it the work of a writer unfamiliar with the stage. Congreve may well have learned most of his early craft from writings on dramatic theory. Professor Hodges suggests that Congreve purchased François Hedelin's *Whole Art of the Stage*, a volume of Horace, and Dryden's *Essay of Dramatic Poesy* while still at Trinity College; and, while the evidence depends merely on the publishing date of 1684, Congreve's familiarity with French classical criticism is obvious from his earliest critical statement, the preface to *Incognita*; and certainly Dryden and Hedelin are likely sources for his ideas. It is sufficient to conjecture that Congreve was probably more interested in the theater than most young gentlemen of his time and that before coming to London he had read more plays than he had seen.

That event occurred suddenly—and before he could take a degree from Trinity College—as a result of confusion preceding the Glorious Revolution. After an impressive start, the hold of King James upon the loyalty of the English diminished rapidly. In spite of repeated professions of loyalty and absolute obedience which appears in *The London Gazette* after James's proclamation of liberty of conscience for Dissenter and Catholic alike, the nation was alienated from the throne by a fear of a return of Catholic repression. In Ireland, Tyrconnel was establishing a Catholic hierarchy and a Catholic army from which Congreve's father was excluded. Some time in 1688 the young Congreve joined the exodus of refugees from what was expected to be a general massacre of Protestants. When William of Orange arrived at Torbay, the same nation which had been extravagant in its oaths of fidelity to King James accepted the new monarch and his English queen with relief, if not with gratitude.

To the Tories, William III remained Hogen Mogen, the Dutch usurper; but to Whigs like Congreve, he was a hero, an opponent of French tyranny and the living representative of opposition to France and Louis XIV. The Whig theory of the Revolution as the final triumph of the rule of law and property was accepted even by men as inherently conservative as Swift; and, though some historians have argued that the Glorious Revolution brought with it a triumph of mediocrity and middle-class values, it also gave the nation a new stability. Congreve remained a Whig at heart, even when he was employed by the Tories; and one explanation for his startling and brilliant early career may be found in a milieu favorable to a young romantic talent—a milieu full of new hope, excitement, and change.

The revolution brought with it not only a heroic king but also the first English queen since Elizabeth I. Mary II became the focus of literary attention; and, if there were *précieuse* elements in English literature during the reigns of her two predecessors, this tone, plus a distinct feminine orientation, is notable throughout the 1690's. Peter Motteux remarked in his *Gentleman's Journal* that his *"miscellany* is not only the Gentleman's but the *Lady's Journal,"* a comment which he repeated in an issue written mainly by women. Motteux defended the abilities of women and in a review praised Nahum Tate's *A Present for the Ladies* (1693), which claimed that women were as intelligent as men and capable of a role in literature and politics:

One of the blindest Prejudices is, that which makes Men prefer themselves to Women: Should a Woman pretend to preach, or command an Army, it would be a piece of Extravagance with relation to our Manners; yet if we rightly examine the thing, we will find that this only proceeds from Custom, which we persuade our selves to be very well grounded, because it hath always been the same, and that Men are in actual possession. As for Women, they stick to the Lot which hath been prescribed to them, and confine themselves to their private condition, supposing it to be their natural state; so that things being settled in that manner, by the mutual consent of both Parties, this Order seems to us rather established by Nature, and an universal Consent, than by the Usurpation of Men.

Motteux proposed that women should be removed from the "narrow Sphere of domestic management," and such advanced arguments of this kind were suggested shortly after by Mary Astell and Daniel Defoe.[8]

The importance of Queen Mary's influence on the literature of the times has been underestimated. Bishop Burnet, in his *Essay on the Memory of the Late Queen,* testifies to her love of poetry; but he adds that, if she was "tender of Poetry," she also "had a particular Concern in the Defilement, or rather the Prostitution of the Muses."[9] Before Mary came to the throne, there had been occasional complaints from playwrights about the displeasure felt by the women in the audience at the bawdiness of Restoration drama and their demands for scenes of love and *tendresse;* but after 1688 the trend was apparent. The evidence for this change has been traced carefully by John Harrington Smith;[10] even Dryden, in his dedication to *Cleomenes* (1692),

notes that "Some have told me, That many of fair Sex complain
for want of tender Scenes, and soft Expressions of Love." Though
Mary was influential in starting the Societies for Reformation
of Manners which attempted to exert a moral reform of contemporary life and, incidentally, literature, there has probably
been too much stress on the moral objections of the feminine
audience. What women spectators wanted most of all was a
literature which had the qualities of the French romances, and
they disliked the bawdiness and satire which pleased Charles
II and his court.

How well did Congreve suit this new audience? Kathleen
Lynch[11] has shown to what extent he was influenced by the
précieuse tradition, but perhaps the evidence for the continuance
of the platonic versus the anti-platonic literary dialectic is
deceptive: it was always present, but it came to efflorescence in
the 1690's. With the new *préciosité*, Congreve was clearly sympathetic as his admiration for Sir John Suckling demonstrates; with
the new moral flavor of the times, Congreve had little sympathy.
Henry Higden, in his preface to *The Wary Widow* (1693),
complained that the success of *The Old Batchelor* ("the Baudy
Bachelor") showed that "the nicest Ladies may be brought . . . to
stand the fire of a smutty Jest and never flinch."[12] It is plain that
Congreve encountered somewhat more flinching than he expected,
but then he was a wit and a libertine, and like the older dramatists
of the Restoration, he could not see why wit was incompatible
with an idealistic approach to true love. From the publication of
his novel *Incognita* in 1692, with its *précieuse* imagery of hearts
and cupids, to 1707 and the characters of Cupid in his opera,
Semele, Congreve was eminently a man formed by the love
traditions of the 1690's and the court of an English queen.

Little is known of Congreve during his early years in England.
He was in Staffordshire at Stretton Manor during the spring and
summer of 1689, and there he met Katherine Leveson, to whom
he dedicated *Incognita*, and here he may also have begun *The
Old Batchelor*. His father, whose fortunes improved with those of
William III, departed in 1690 for Ireland to become the chief
agent for Richard Boyle, Earl of Cork and Burlington, leaving his
son in London to enroll on March 17, 1691, in the Middle Temple
to study law. Congreve's career as a law student, which is re-
counted by Giles Jacob, is likely to have been given to the
contemporary biographer by Congreve himself. "Mr. *Congreve*,"
he writes, "was of too delicate a Taste, had Wit of too fine a turn
to be long pleas'd with a crabbed unpalatable Study; in which the

laborious dull plodding Fellow generally excells the more sprightly and vivacious Wit; This concurring with his natural Inclination to Poetry, diverted him from the Bar to the declining Stage, which then stood in need of such a Support; and from whence the Town justly receiv'd him as *Rome's* other Hope."[13] At the Middle Temple, Congreve had the opportunity of meeting many men whose interests were more literary than legal; indeed, many of the best comic dramatists of the Restoration had found their start at the inns of court—Sir George Etherege, William Wycherley, Thomas Shadwell, and Thomas Southerne. Here Congreve met the future Whig pamphleteer, Walter Moyle, and doubtless it was not long before he had joined the wits who sat at Dryden's feet in Will's Coffee House.

A young man with a knowledge of the law must have been a useful person to know, and Congreve helped to arrange the legal aspect of the literary relationship between Dryden and Jacob Tonson. But, above all, Congreve must have recommended himself as a wit and as a promising writer. *Incognita* was finished by 1691, and the next year brought Congreve his first taste of success. He published three odes of Horace and two songs in a miscellany, he had *The Old Batchelor* accepted for production, and he contributed to Dryden's edition of Juvenal and Persius a translation of Juvenal's eleventh satire, an attack on Congreve's own vice—gluttony. It is important that Congreve made his early reputation as a translator of the Classics, for to the Augustan critic nothing distinguished the true poet from the hack so much as his capacity to translate and incorporate lines from Virgil or Horace in his verse.

Also important are the poems Congreve selected to translate. The odes of Horace are filled with a love of nature and the country, and in the following year Congreve demonstrated his sensibility in a translation from the *Iliad* of the laments of Priam, Hecuba, Andromache, and Helen over the body of Hector which appeared in Dryden's *Miscellany;* and Dryden significantly praised Congreve's contribution:

I cannot forbear to tell your Lordship, that there are two fragments of Homer Translated in this *Miscellany;* one by Congreve, (whom I cannot mention without the Honour which is due to his excellent Parts, and that entire Affection which I bear him;) and the other is by my self. Both the Subjects are pathetical; and I am sure my Friend has added to the Tenderness which he found in the Original; and without Flatery, surpass'd his Author. Yet I must needs say this in reference to Homer, that he is much more capable of exciting the Manly Passions, than those of Grief and Pity.

Dryden declares that Congreve is not only the ideal man to translate Homer—a task Pope later undertook and dedicated to Congreve—but that he is the master of the "pathetical" and of "Tenderness." In short, Congreve possessed the very talents which a rococo age demanded.

The success predicted by Dryden came to Congreve with the performance of *The Old Batchelor* in March, 1693. The play ran for an astounding fourteen days, and it was in its third printing before the end of the month. Like Byron, Congreve may be said to have awoke to find himself famous. Some of the critics complained that Congreve was merely a creation of Dryden—a publicity stunt; but Motteux echoed the opinion of most: "The success of Mr. Congreve's *Old Batchelor* has been so extraordinary, that I can tell you nothing new of that Comedy; you have doubtless read it before this, since it has been printed thrice, and indeed the Wit which is diffus'd through it, makes it lose but few of those charms in the Perusal, which yield such pleasure in the Representation."[14]

Admittedly, part of the play's success was owing to the magnificent cast; the greatest actor of the age, Thomas Betterton, as the Old Batchelor; Dogget, the brilliant comic, as Fondlewife; and the two great women of the stage, Mrs. Barry, the licentious or heavy actress, and Mrs. Bracegirdle as Araminta, the virtuous and witty ingenue. Plays were then written with the players in mind; and, whether Congreve was inspired to create the role for Mrs. Bracegirdle or whether seeing her in it inspired him, Congreve apparently fell deeply in love with her. She had a reputation for virtue at a time when many actresses were little short of courtesans. For example, Mrs. Barry had been trained by the libertine and poet, the Earl of Rochester; and she was famous for forgetting the faces of the men she slept with shortly after parting from them. During the reign of Charles II, the actresses were the "King's Ladies" in more ways than one.

But "that Romantick Virgin," Mrs. Bracegirdle, was another matter. She had been reared in the family of Betterton, and she had appeared on the stage at least as early as age sixteen. Her freshness and innocence were welcomed by the audience; and, in spite of disparaging remarks to the contrary, there appeared little evidence to counter her pose of virginity. "Scarce an Audience saw her," wrote Colley Cibber, "that were less than half of them Lovers"; and he suggested that the heroes of both Congreve and Rowe were always pleading their authors' passions for Anne. She was described by Aston as having "dark-brown Hair and Eye-brows, black sparkling Eyes, and a fresh blushy Complexion; and whenever she exerted herself, had an involuntary Flushing in her Breast, Neck and Face, having continually a chearful Aspect, and a fine Set of even white Teeth." She must have presented that most appealing picture: innocence in the midst of corruption.

Her beauty inspired Lord Mohun, probably at the time that *The Old Batchelor* was in rehearsal, to attempt an abduction —an incident detailed in a manuscript in the British Museum.[15] After the first effort failed, Anne escaped into the theater; the great actor, William Mountford, who created the role of the gentlemanly wit which distinguishes the comedies of the 1690's from earlier ones, came out to protect her, and entered the Horse Shoe Tavern with his sword drawn. Captain Hill, one of Lord Mohun's companions, engaged in a duel with Mountford in the middle of the street, and the actor fell with the words, "he has killed me." If Congreve did not die defending Anne's virtue, he may well have suffered the fate of the rest of her admirers— to love without hope. The author of *Animadversions on Mr. Congreve's Late Answer to Mr. Collier* described Congreve as sitting in a side box "ogling his Dear Bracilla with sneaking looks under his Hat."

To her, Congreve probably wrote a number of his poems, including the witty description of his hopeless love:

> Pious Selinda goes to Pray'rs,
>   If I but ask the Favour;
> And yet the tender Fool's in Tears,
>   When she believes I'll leave her.
> Wou'd I were free from this Restraint,
>   Or else had hopes to win her;
> Wou'd she cou'd make of me a Saint,
>   Or I of her a Sinner.[16]

Whether, as Professor Hodges assumes, Anne was "kind" to Congreve, belongs to the realm of romance and conjecture. If some of his poems may be regarded as autobiographical, they show situations of waiting for love and finally achieving it. The magnificent song, "False though she be to me and Love," has all the conviction of Thomas Wyatt's "They Flee from Me"; but we could just as well credit this Congreve poem either to the poetical imagination or to other affairs. It is difficult to imagine the witty Congreve as a celibate (he does once compare himself to a Carthusian), but there is no evidence to support either an affair or the suggestion of one poet that he married Anne after a long liaison.

Congreve left London for the quiet of the country after the success of his first play. Motteux, in his notice on *The Old Batchelor*, stated that the next play was already finished. Congreve was only twenty-three and the future looked full of promise, but all was not well. His eyes were weak, and he was in a health spa, Tunbridge Wells, in August when he wrote to Tonson, his printer, complaining of "a continual heat in the palms of my hands" and of his plans to try the waters at Epsom. Invalidism is one way of explaining why he preferred to live quietly and privately; and, in passing through London, he avoided everyone he knew. The statement he was to make to Joseph Keally in 1708, "Ease and quiet is what I hunt after. If I have not ambition, I have other passions more easily gratified," was apparently also true for the young dramatist.

Congreve developed some cause for dissatisfaction with the world, for his second play was not so successful as the first. Dryden wrote to William Walsh:

His Double Dealer is much censur'd by the greater part of the Town: and is defended onely by the best Judges, who, you know, are commonly the fewest. Yet it gets ground daily, and has already been acted Eight times. The Women think he has exposed their Bitchery too much; and the Gentlemen, are offended with him; for the discovery of their Follyes: and the way of their Intrigues, under the notion of Friendship to their Ladyes Husbands. My verses, which you will find before it, were written before the play was acted. But I neither altered them nor do I alter my opinion of the play. . . .

Congreve's dedication to the printed version reveals a very angry man, but the play, which ran for eight performances, can hardly be considered a failure. Like Dryden, Congreve appealed to the opinion of the best critics; and he had Dryden's poem with its comparison between Congreve and Shakespeare to promote him. Other poets followed Dryden in hailing Congreve's genius; Swift, in a poem which Congreve probably never saw, wrote:

> Thus I look down with mercy on the age,
> By hopes my Congreve will reform the stage;

> For never did poetic mine before
> Produce a richer vein or cleaner ore.

And Motteux printed a poem by William Dove that pronounced
Congreve to be one of those poets who are of the "prophetic
Line," whose genius would make him the greatest writer in
Europe:

> Sure thy Soul acts in a divided State,
> Free from thy Body, and exempt from Fate!
> Go on, great Youth, but as thou hast begun,
> The Prize thou'lt merit e're thy Race is run.[17]

About a month after the first run of *The Double Dealer* the
Queen ordered a special performance, and by 1702 the anonymous author of the *Comparison between the Two Stages* singled
it out as his finest play.

Congreve's next play, *Love for Love*, was probably ready by
the end of 1694, but, as Colley Cibber points out, it was held
up by a quarrel between the actors of the Theatre Royal and
the ignorant and greedy owners of the monopoly. Betterton
appealed to the Earl of Dorset and eventually to the king, who
"consider'd them as the only subjects whom he had not yet
delivered from arbitrary power," and promised them his support.
On March 25, 1695, King William issued a separate license to
Betterton, who took most of the best players—Mrs. Barry, Mrs.
Bracegirdle, John Bowman, Joseph Williams, Cave Underhill,
Thomas Dogget, William Bowen, Mrs. Susanna Verbruggen,
Mrs. Elinor Leigh, and George Bright—to a new theater at
Lincoln's Inn Fields. On April 30, 1695, they opened with *Love
for Love*—an enormous success. Charles Gildon noted that
every performer was applauded "for a considerable time"
before he spoke and that any play would have been welcomed
under such circumstances; but, as he admitted, "yet all this got
it not more than it really deserv'd."

As a direct result of the success of *Love for Love* Congreve
was given a full share in the new company based on his pro-
viding a new play every year "if his health permitted." This
agreement must have resulted in a considerable addition to
Congreve's income. Though he was depicted as growing rich on
government sinecures by writers like William Thackeray ("commissionership of hackney-coaches—a post in the Custom house—
a place in the Pipe-office, and all for writing a comedy!"), Congreve actually had no official post until his appointment as Com-

missioner of Hackney Coaches on June 6, 1695; and it was
probably awarded him not for his comedies but for his promise
as a propagandist for William III's regime. Before this date,
Congreve had written a panegyric to the queen on the occasions
of her witnessing *The Old Batchelor* and of her death (January
28, 1695), a pastoral elegy. He may well have seemed to the
court the ideal political poet to support William III that Dryden
had been previously for Charles II and James II. Several months
following his appointment, Congreve published *To the King
on the Taking of Namure* with its lavish praise of King William's
heroic deeds:

> Not the wing'd Perseus with Petrifick Shield
> Of Gorgon's Head, to more amazement charm'd his Foe.
>   Nor, when on soaring Horse he flew, to aid
>   And save from Monsters Rage, the Beauteous Maid;
>   Or more Heroick was the Deed:
>   Or she to surer Chains decreed,
>   Then was *Namure;* 'till now by *William* freed.

>   (II, 213)

Whatever utility a poet might be to any government, Congreve
surely was. His *Mourning Bride* was eventually to create a Whig
myth of rebellion against a tyrant as an antidote to the Tory
myth which Dryden spent some thirty years creating.

The *Mourning Bride,* Congreve's next major work, did not
appear until February 27, 1697. During the preceding year,
more or less a blank in Congreve's biography, he apparently
had visited Ireland with his fellow dramatist Thomas Southerne to
receive a master of arts degree in February, and he had probably
also visited his parents. Perhaps contact with Southerne, a writer
of successful tragedies, to whose *Oroonoko* Congreve had contributed a prologue in December, 1695, may have inspired him
to try his hand at what most critics of the age considered a
higher dramatic form. The prospect of Congreve's turning to
tragedy must have been ominous; Swift reports the typical
comments of a coffee-house wit, who

> Said, how a late report your friends had vex'd,
> Who heard you meant to write heroics next;
> For, tragedy, he knew, would lose you quite,
> And told you so at Will's but t'other night.

Congreve, who ignored the warnings, wrote what Charles Gildon
described as "the greatest Success, not only of all Mr. *Congreve's;*

but indeed of all the Plays that ever I can remember on the English Stage." Richard Blackmore praised it for its morality as well as its literary merit as "the most perfect *Tragedy* that has been wrote in this Age."[18]

Such encomiums must have pleased Congreve, who, smarting still under accusations of immorality in *The Double Dealer*, made a special plea to the "tender Hearts" of the women in the audience. But he soon had new cause for grief; in April, 1698, Jeremy Collier made Congreve a main target of attack in his *Short View of the Immorality and Profaneness of the English Stage*. Congreve replied three months later with his *Amendments of Mr. Collier's False and Imperfect Citations*; and, though the literary implications of the "Collier controversy" are discussed in the next chapter, it should be noted that Congreve's reply reveals much about his general attitudes. His answer was witty and clear, but he failed to understand that the real issue was emotional rather than intellectual; and he was betrayed by his attitude toward Collier, whom he regarded as a fanatical nonjuring, Jacobite clergyman, who was beneath contempt politically, intellectually, and socially.

If Collier's attack suited the ends of the Societies for Reformation of Manners, Congreve would have said that it revealed no manners at all. There is no reason to think that Congreve was, as Cibber put it, "too hurt" to reply effectively; within his own critical terms, he did reply effectively, for he held the not uncommon theory that good art cannot be immoral. A stage which brought out preadolescent girls to recite prologues and epilogues that promised future sexual availability was certainly a challenge to Congreve's theory and provided a rich field for the moralists. If Congreve did not settle the problem, it should be pointed out that trials over censorship in modern times suggest that it may never be settled.

Tired of being drawn into quarrels with "Knaves and Fools," Congreve turned to writing his last great comedy, *The Way of the World*. A few days after the first performance on March 5, 1700, Dryden wrote to a friend, "Congreve's new play has had but moderate success, though it deserves much better." The play was by no means a failure, but there must have been many in the audience who, like Ramble in the *Comparison between the Two Stages*, being told that Congreve worked for two years on the play, would have replied, "I have known a better writ in a Month."[19] Once more Congreve was accused of being too satirical, of having too much dialogue and not enough plot.

Congreve could only write, "That it succeeded on the Stage, was almost beyond my Expectation; for but little of it was prepar'd for that general Taste which seems to be predominant in the Pallats of our Audience" (I, 336). Having tasted success so early, Congreve probably had no desire to write additional failures. One of the characters in the *Comparisons between the Two Stages* refrains from criticizing *The Way of the World* in deference to the fact that its author was "done with the stage."

III *Later Years: 1701-1729*

Congreve's literary career does not end in 1700, convenient as such a date may be for literary scholars. Dryden died at the beginning of May in that year after writing a masque condemning the previous century for self-interest and deceit and announcing that it was "time to begin anew." And perhaps Congreve would have begun anew if his health during his remaining twenty-nine years had permitted. He was continually visiting health spas, and his letters tell of his gout and growing blindness. But there are many puzzles. If he stopped writing comedies for the stage, he surely might have tried his hand at another *Mourning Bride*. Had his genius faded? How often does such a lyrical talent, whether in poetry or drama, extend beyond the age of thirty? Since Congreve was not a man to dash off a play, it would have been much simpler for a man of weak constitution to write lighter pieces, works which would not require a prolonged effort of will and ego. In fact, Congreve did not stop writing; he merely quit writing with such intensity.

Some sense of relaxation of effort may be evident in his trip to the Continent in the late summer and early fall of 1700 with Charles Mein and Jacob Tonson. After returning, the first project he turned to was an opera; and in 1701 his libretto, *The Judgment of Paris,* was performed at Dorset Garden. A competition had been held for the music, and an announcement appeared in the *London Gazette* offering a prize of two hundred pounds for the best music. A year later, on March 21, 1701, the competition began with the music of John Eccles; and Congreve expressed some of his excitement in a letter to Joseph Keally:

Indeed, I don't think any one place in the world can shew such an assembly. The number of performers, besides the verse-singers, was 85. The front of the stage was all built into a concave with deal boards; all which were faced with tin, to increase and throw forward the sound. It was all hung with sconces of wax-candles, besides the common branches of lights usual in the play-houses. The boxes and pit were all thrown into one; so that all sat in common and the whole was crammed with beauties and beaux, not one scrub being admitted. The place where formerly the music used to play, between the pit and the stage, was turned into White's chocalate-house; the whole family being transplanted thither with chocalate, cool'd drinks, ratafie, Pontacq, etc. . . .[20]

The occasion appears to have been very much like a modern music festival; and, if Congreve may have felt like Paris in choosing Venus, who was acted and sung by Anne Bracegirdle to "a miracle," he also could not have been unflattered to have had his libretto set to music by the best composers in England.

That Congreve should have taken delight in a form which many critics detested may seen strange. The professional critics, John Dennis and Charles Gildon, raged at opera's threat to the legitimate theater; and Pope's *Dunciad* envisioned the world as collapsing into chaos to the sound of an aria. Opera was considered sound without sense, or as Congreve himself stated in his epilogue to the *Italian Pastoral*: "To Sound and Show at first we make pretence,/ In time we may regale you with some Sense,/ But that, at present were too great Expence" (II, 271). Some poets, like Dryden, tried to create an English opera, but the failure of such experiments was detailed by the English translator of François Raguenet's *Comparison between the French and Italian Operas* (1709), who concluded that opera ought always to be sung in Italian.[21] But Congreve was interested in ballads and songs throughout his career; some of his verses were set by the great Henry Purcell. Congreve also contributed songs to a number of plays and to a collection of songs, *Orpheus Britannicus*, in 1698; and, as late as 1722, he was sponsoring a concert with the Duchess of Marlborough.

How pleasant it must have been for Congreve to have written the part of Venus for Anne and to have had Paris sing:

> All Loves Darts are in thy Eyes,
> And Harmony falls from thy Tongue
> Forbear, O Goddess of Desire,
> Thus my ravish'd Soul to move,
> Forbear to fan the raging Fire,
> And be propitious to my Love.
>   (II, 194-95)

How pleasant, after all the criticism leveled at him, to have written in a form which had for its ideal spectacle and music

and a poetry modeled upon the demands of music; for, as
Dryden pointed out, a good libretto and good poetry might be
two very different matters. Congreve tried his hand at this once
again with *Semele,* which was in rehearsal in 1707 with music
by John Eccles and which was later used by George Frederick
Handel. In some sense, this opera was the first full-length one
in English; and in this form, at least, Congreve must be given
some credit for innovation. But these slight pieces, indicative
of the kind of writing he was to do for the rest of his life, are
hardly compensation for the loss of Congreve the dramatist.

In 1703, Congreve may have met the true love of his mature
life in Henrietta, Duchess of Marlborough. In that year he wrote
The Tears of Amaryllis for Amyntas, a pastoral elegy on the
death of the only son of the Duke of Marlborough with a dedication to Henrietta's father-in-law, Sidney Godolphin; and in
1706 he addressed an ode directly to Godolphin, the Lord
Treasurer. Congreve was soon on friendly terms with Henrietta,
as her formidable mother, Sarah, Duchess of Marlborough,
remarked when she saw them together. It was also Sarah who
remarked on the inscription that Henrietta put on Congreve's
tomb—"She remembers the happiness and Honour she enjoyed
in the Sincere Friendship of so worthy and Honest a Man"—
"I know not what 'pleasure' she might have had in his company,
but I am sure it was no 'honour'." For the remainder of his life
Congreve lived much in the company of the Duchess (her husband, Francis Godolphin, apparently ignored the entire matter);
he traveled to Bath in 1722 where Henrietta was spending the
season, and he became the father of her child, Mary, in 1723.

At about the time that Congreve was first becoming acquainted
with Henrietta, he joined with his fellow dramatist, John Vanbrugh, in two projects. In March, 1704, they collaborated with
William Walsh on a translation of Molière's *Monsieur de
Pourceaugnac;* and in December they became partners in a
more serious enterprise: the founding of a new theater in the
Haymarket. Queen Anne issued the license with the note that
the theater was for the "better Reforming the Abuses and Immorality of the stage," which must have been a considerable
personal triumph for the two victims of charges of immorality
from Jeremy Collier. In Congreve's epilogue to the opera with
which the theater opened, he promised to give the audience
satirical comedies in the future, but it was obvious that Congreve
was not going to write them. In his *Prologue to the Court on*

the Queen's Birthday he had argued that the way to correct the evils of society was through poetic panegyric on the ideal manners of the court rather than through satire. Congreve's continued disgust for the audience is only too evident in a prologue written in 1707 mocking their inability to appreciate tragedy:

> In vain with Toil the artful Poets strove,
> Your fickle Taste to please, and to improve;
> For to good Plays when e'er WE went astray,
> You warned US of the Errors of that way;
> WE stood corrected by your awful Hiss,
> Conscious too late, that WE had done amiss.[22]

And, indeed, the Haymarket project proved to be a failure. It was so far from the center of town that Cibber suggested that the only nutriment available would be milk from the neighboring pastures; and the acoustics, like those of Dorset Garden, were suitable only for opera. Cibber complained that, though the setting might do well enough for castrati, the voices of actors sounded "like the Gabbling of so many People in the lofty Isles in a Cathedral." Vanbrugh's ingenious architecture proved impractical, and the company had to return to Lincoln's Inn Fields. Congreve, realizing that he had little gift for business, retired from the venture before the end of the year.

The Haymarket Theatre had been financed by the members of the Kit-Kat Club, a literary-political society of Whigs, which included among its members both the great Whig nobility and the best writers of the first decade of the eighteenth century: Addison, Steele, Samuel Garth, Vanbrugh, Walsh, Maynwaring, and the publisher Jacob Tonson, at whose home, Barn Elms, most of the meetings occurred. Through close contact with these men Congreve began to improve his position in life. In 1705 he was made one of five commissioners for wines, the first major government post he held with the exception of brief appointments as manager of the malt lottery and of the customs at Poole in 1697. His new post paid twice the salary of his commissionership for hackney coaches, but it was still small enough to lend some truth to Swift's remark about Congreve's poor stipend. He did not starve in a garret like Samuel Butler, the author of *Hudibras,* but he was never rich. And even this stipend was threatened when the Tories gained power in 1710; only Swift's influence with Harley saved him. With the return of the Whigs, his Kit-Kat friends, Congreve's situation improved

once more. In November, 1714, he was made Searcher of Customs
and a month later secretary of Jamaica, the latter being an appointment for life with a salary of seven hundred pounds a year.

By this time, Congreve's health demanded some kind of income. When he wrote to Joseph Keally in 1706 that he had not
had an attack of the gout for four months, he was apparently
describing what was for him a long period of good health.
Nevertheless, if his truly productive period was finished, he
remained active as a man of letters. In that year he wrote
A Pindarique Ode . . . To which is Prefixed a Discourse on the
Pindarique Ode, a work typical of him in that he wrote it as
an exercise in the form with a preface deploring the awful
poetry which resulted from the incorrect critical theory that
Pindar had written a formless kind of verse. "I hope," he wrote
with somewhat more humility than he had displayed in his
youth, "I shall not be so misunderstood, as to have it thought
that I pretend to give an exact copy of Pindar in this ensuing
Ode; or that I look upon it as a Pattern for his Imitators for the
future: Far from such Thoughts, I have only given an Instance
of what is practicable, and am sensible that I am as distant
from the Force and Elevation of Pindar, as others have hitherto
been from the Harmony and Regularity of his Numbers" (II, 332).
Congreve has, in a sense, come full circle by returning to translations from the Classics with which he began his career.

But illness would have prevented his fulfilling Dryden's prediction that he might be the ideal person to translate all of
Homer. In May, 1708, Congreve was recovering in Bath, and
in October he reported to Keally his return to London and
renewed sickness: "My last day's journey I rode very hard;
which shook me so much, that [it] disturbed the gout which
was in repose. I have been confined a week; but I hope as it
was a forced fit, it will be a short one. I can walk about; and
this is the first letter I write."[23] His illness, however, did not
diminish his vanity; for he comments in the same letter on a
portrait of him painted by Hugh Howard, complaining that it
made him look too fat. Like Pope, Congreve was very conscious
of the way he would appear to posterity; and he was undoubtedly
more pleased by Sir Godfrey Kneller's portrait for the Kit-Kat
series with its romantic feeling and a dramatic gesture toward
a background landscape.

In 1709, Congreve wrote a new prologue to Love for Love,
when Anne Bracegirdle returned to act in it for a benefit per-

formance for Betterton in April; and he continued dabbling
in translation with a version of the third book of Ovid's *Art of
Love*; but, like all the years that lay ahead, this one was full
of illness. "I have been troubled with several light indispositions
and threatenings of the gout from ill weather and easterly winds,"
he wrote to Keally. "But I hope I shall rubb on, tho I have
more frequent colds than ever."[24] To an outsider, like Swift,
these "light indispositions" appeared disastrous; for in his *Journal
to Stella*, between 1710 and 1712, he reported Congreve's in-
creasing blindness, how he was forced to read with a magnifying
glass, "and besides he is never rid of the gout, yet he looks
young and fresh, and is chearful as ever." For all his illnesses,
Congreve remained a good companion; he even presented Swift
with a *Tatler* paper on one of his visits for the continuation of
Addison and Steele's brilliant periodical. Swift summarized the
paper to Stella, " 'Tis about a scoundrel that was grown rich,
and went and bought a Coat of Arms at the Herald's, and a
set of ancestors at Fleet-ditch; 'tis well enough. . . ."

The essay shows how well Congreve had adapted himself
to the age of Queen Anne with its emphasis on the refinement
of manners and morals as expressed in the periodicals of Addison
and Steele. Congreve, in spite of Swift's statement, does not
reveal Foundling, a poor man who has succeeded in the world,
as a scoundrel; his tone is superior, amused, and pitying; and
the tone is very like Congreve in its combination of aloof-
ness, humanity, and scorn of ambition. But the tone is also that
of a new age that has rejected the free, fanciful, and licentious
wit of the 1690's; for people are now to be led to good manners
by mild and humane ridicule. Forceful satire would not do.
Though both Pope and Swift were to write the greatest of all
English satires, they were to raise the form to its height at a
time when the readers were beginning to demand sentiment
and sentimentality. Congreve seems to have entered easily into
this new world, and what did not at all suit the artist may
have thoroughly pleased the man.

For the rest of life, Congreve, now permanently settled in
his apartment off the Strand in Surrey Street to which he had
moved in 1706, contented himself with being more a monument
of literary fame than a productive artist. He prepared a collected
edition of his works in 1710 with the plays arranged according
to the French method of scene structure and with some deletions.
Some lines to which Collier had objected were bowdlerized,

but we must remember that Congreve had been censured by a Middlesex jury for these passages. The changes probably owe more, therefore, to necessity than conviction. And his reputation was additionally solidified by dedications written by the leading writers of the time: Steele's *Poetical Miscellanies* in 1713, Addison's *Drummer* in 1716, and Pope's translation of the *Iliad* in 1720.

In spite of ill-health (he needed Richard Boyle to act as his scribe in 1719 when writing to Pope), Congreve continued some minor literary activity. He corresponded with Lady Mary Wortley Montagu, added what might have been an early translation of the tenth book of Ovid's *Metamorphoses* as a continuation of Tonson's edition of the translation done by Dryden, and wrote an encomiastic introduction to the edition of Dryden's *Dramatic Works* published by Tonson in 1717. The last publication was a long overdue tribute to the great poet who had done so much to establish Congreve's reputation. Three years later he wrote two fables or light comic tales in verse: one a translation from La Fontaine, the other taken from *The Hundred New Novels* of the Queen of Navarre. And, in 1728, just before he died, he wrote his *Letter to Viscount Cobham* with a moral that tells much about Congreve's approach to life:

> For Virtue now is neither more or less,
> And Vice is only varied in the Dress;
> Believe it, Men have ever been the same,
> And all the Golden Age, is but a Dream.
>   (II, 402)

Pope objected that it was "a vile and false moral . . . wherein he differs from all Poets, Philosophers, and Christians that ever writ"; but, unlike Swift and Pope, Congreve obviously did not side with the ancients against the moderns. If he was not optimistic enough to believe that mankind had progressively improved, he did not believe that either humanity or art had regressed.

In his youth Congreve had written a poem to Lord Halifax on the *Birth of the Muse* in which he had argued that the Golden Age might have existed once, but that poetry was invented so that man could conquer time through art. A similar statement appears in his claim that time must inevitably erase the traces of a new Golden Age that William III was bringing to England and that only through art could individual acts of virtue be preserved. Congreve never changed his view. A hero may attempt to restore virtue to the world, but man will remain the same, whether in Augustan Rome or in eighteenth-century England. He preserved his satirical and skeptical view of human possibilities to the end, even though his message was one which Pope did not want to hear and which a theater audience certainly did not wish to be reminded of. Congreve, who lived into an age which was beginning to value the pleasure of tears, valued tenderness but not tears. As a young man his vision of the world inspired him to write the best of Restoration comedies with a vigor and force never seen on the stage before. He died in a different age, a Georgian gentleman and a *philosophe*.

IV *Congreve and His Time*

The explanation of Congreve's art and personality from his few letters, the comments of his friends, and the fragmentary facts of his life, must, at best, be unsatisfactory without some knowledge of his milieu and the set of customs and ideas by which he lived. Over three centuries now separate us from the Restoration of King Charles II to the throne of England—and two and a half of those centuries were antagonistic to Restoration drama. Thomas Thornton's introduction to Otway's *The Atheist* is typical of nineteenth-century attitudes: "The dialogue has more freedom and vivacity than the other comedies and abounds with that species of licentious wit which secured its favourable receptions with the audiences whose minds were corrupted, by habit and example, to a perfect relish of grossness, and contempt of decency. Marriage, and all those decorums which embellish social life, and may be said to hold society most firmly together, are despised and ridiculed; and unbounded freedom, or rather licentiousness, extolled and set up in their stead."[25] In order to understand the milieu of Congreve's plays and Thornton's attack on the morals of Restoration drama, we must understand contemporary attitudes toward three things: libertinism, wit, and marriage.

F. W. Bateson finds much significance in a letter from Congreve to Edward Porter in 1714 requesting that his friend purchase a portrait of Lord Rochester, England's great libertine poet. Whether, as Bateson suggests, Congreve identified himself with Rochester is difficult to say; but it seems likely that he would have admired this combination of libertine, wit, polished gentleman, patron of the arts, and writer of some of the best

satires and lyrics of the Restoration. Rochester was skeptical
about human reason, sometimes viciously realistic and at other
times farcical in his treatment of sex, and the model for the
rake-hero of Restoration comedies. When he died as a young
man in 1680, writers seemed a decade later to assume that
a brilliant age of wit had passed with him.

But the wits were still a faction in the 1690's. Mainly young
men, they followed ideals present in Congreve's expanded
"Imitation" of Horace's ninth ode:

> The present Moment's all our Store:
> The next, should Heav'n allow,
> Then this will be no more:
> So all our Life is but one Instant *Now*.
> Look on each Day you've past
> To be a mighty Treasure won:
> And let each Moment out in haste;
> We're sure to live too fast,
> And cannot live too soon.
>   (II, 238)

Libertinism, hardly an organized philosophy, changed as the
seventeenth century grew older; and the libertine of the 1690's
was a far cry from the disciples of Theophile de Viau, who died
after imprisonment in 1626, or even from Lord Rochester and
his companions. Dale Underwood in his interesting study of
the dramatist, Etheredge, who makes the mistake of regarding
libertinism as a static philosophy, treats it too exclusively as
an English phenomenon and finds too much of Renaissance
humanism in it. By the 1690's many libertine ideas had become
part of the general philosophy of the Enlightenment; and writers
like Congreve, who looked to France for many of his ideals,
might have found in a refined libertinism a way of life that
suited a gentleman of the times.

The first thorough description of libertine beliefs appears in
1623 in the attack of the Jesuit, Le Père Garasse, on the followers
of Theophile de Viau.[26] Garasse accused the libertines of skepticism or antirationalism and of affecting a superiority of wit or
intellect in matters of religion—of arguing that religion was only
for the masses and that all restraints of morality were merely
custom. The libertines might follow their natural instincts and
their senses to achieve the only good attainable in the world.
Garasse depicts such men as determinists, materialists, wor-
shipers of nature, free lovers of wine and women, atheists or
deists, and disbelievers in spirits or the devil.

For all his rhetoric, Garasse was not very far from the truth. In his *Satyre Première* Theophile de Viau pictured man as an animal; his birth is the same as a beast, but a beast has the advantage of not having to fear a hell. If birth is horrible, old age is worse. Happiness is only found in freedom—freedom to follow one's passions. Similar themes are echoed throughout the century in La Mothe Vayer, Des Barreaux, Cyrano de Bergerac, and Saint-Evremond, who especially, must have been enormously influential. Living in England, Saint-Evremond wrote on epicureanism, on a genteel and retired love of pleasure as opposed to the fierce sensual indulgence of the earlier libertines, with a combination of grace and enthusiasm. To philosophers like Pierre Gassendi and Thomas Hobbes, a sense of fear and power might underlie these thoughts; but, by the end of the century, libertinism had become a gentleman's creed. Moderate pleasure, retirement, love of art and gardens; skepticism, and refinement of manners then became the new libertine ideals.

In England, libertinism must have been an exclusive and aristocratic cult; but certain attitudes—distrust of speculative reason, especially in matters of religion; contempt for the puritanical distruct of the senses; belief that government was a power structure surrounded by a myth of divinity—were probably common enough. In his version of the Don Juan myth, *The Libertine* (1675), Thomas Shadwell dramatized in melodramatic, vulgarized form some of the libertine ideals. Don Juan argues that sense should guide the reason and that nothing can be evil that gives pleasure. Following nature, he has committed incest with his two sisters and murdered his father. "My bus'ness is my pleasure, that end I will always compass without scrupling the means; there is no right or wrong, put what conduces to my pleasure," he asserts; and he defends murder as an art, arguing that art justifies all. The audience of 1675 must have shuddered with delight.

Libertinism also appeared in vulgar form in such pornographic works as *The Whores Rhetoric* (1683) in which old bawd Mother Crisswell informs a young disciple that "liberty was the first and greatest benefit of nature" and that the youth is the true "golden Age . . . which ought to be spent in as great variety of pleasure, as Gold is malleable into diversity of forms." But such gross reductions, either to melodrama or to pornography, did not affect the genuine basis and appeal of libertinism. It was through making an art of life that the ideal

of the "honest man," or *honnête homme*, might be attained;
but Dale Underwood in his study of Etherege finds this the
most prevasive irony in the makeup of the libertine: "He too
subscribes to 'civilization' at the same time that he subscribes
to naturalism."

Actually, the answer was quite simple and without paradox
for later libertines, who added the concept of controlling passions to their doctrine. A writer on Christian prudence like
Gracián gave advice on how to succeed in a world governed
by self-interest and deceit. "Be all things to all Men," he advised
in his *Arte de Prudencia*, "a discreet Proteus, learned with the
learned, saintly with the sainted. . . . But this savoir faire calls
for great cleverness. He only will find no difficulty who has a
universal genius in his knowledge and universal ingenuity in his
wit." Lying, as both Congreve and Gracián knew, was the way
of the world. "Know how to play the card of truth," wrote Gracián,
"for when it deals with the destroying of illusion it is the quintessence of bitterness." Honesty is the ideal for the libertine, yet
life is an art—and no hero of Congreve dies of what Gracián calls
"the fool's disease."[27] As we shall see, some of Congreve's heroes
learn through the action of the play that too much honesty is
out of keeping with the prudential policies of the world.

"*Urbanity* and *Civility*," wrote William de Britaine in *Humane
Prudence* (1682), "are a Debt you owe to Mankind." These were
the ideals of the 1690's; and, if a man could not come to terms
with the world—learn the art of manners without compromising
his honesty—he could always withdraw, like Epicurus, to his
garden and have nothing to do with the mass of knaves and
fools that make up the majority of humanity. Congreve's heroes
and heroines make their terms with the world and its masquerade. In Wycherley's *The Gentleman Dancing Master*, Hippolita, the heroine, defends the freedom of the age against her
aunt who attacks the morality of "this masquerading Age."
Hippolita accepts the title for the age and retorts, "By what I've
heard, 'tis a pleasant, well-bred, complaisant, free, frolic, good-
natured, pretty age: and if you do not like it, leave it to us
that do."

Hippolita's response is significant in a number of ways. It
has all the centempt of youth for age, and of the libertine
(female variety) for the moralist. Even more interesting is her
defense of masquerades which were regarded as dangerous
because they disguised the personality and allowed women to
escape from those customs which held her within conventional

morality. The disguise might conceal the prostitute, it might be useful for the machiavel, but it might also be a means by which the libertine could live by the code he enjoyed.

The combination of libertinism, wit, and antimatrimonial attitudes was commonplace in the Restoration—a syndrome assumed by every writer of comedy. In *Country Conversations* (1694), James Wright complained that "some of our Late Comedies have given the greatest Countenance to Libertinism that can be by setting forth the extravagant Debauches of the Age as the True Character of a Gentleman, and only Fools and half Witted Creatures to be Considerate and Sober . . . they have continually Rail'd against Marriage as a Curse and Imposition upon Nature; and at the same time set off Whoring with all the Delicasy of Expression and most obliging Character they could invent." The writer of *A Search after Wit* (1691) raised the question, "Who that has Wit wou'd be ever in love?" And the anonymous author of *Remarques on the Humours and Conversations of the Gallants of the Town* (1673) describes how "those Heroes," the wits, will scorn you if you are not up on the latest prologue or refuse to show contempt for virtue. He speaks of them as individualists, atomists, atheists, and detractors of the past and states that they qualify for the title of "wit" by writing plays, drinking, beating the city guards, and raping women. "I do believe," he continues, "that never in any age was there such a violent and universal thirst after the Fame of being Wits, and yet no Age has possible discharg'd it self with less real applause in those pretences."

Why was wit so important? We may think of it in Freudian terms, as a mere activity of the associative unconscious; but, for the Restoration, wit was an indication of native intelligence ("natural parts")—a sign of the true gentleman or artist as opposed to the fop, the pedant and the fool. Dr. Walter Charleton, in his *Brief Discourse Concerning the Different Wits of Men* (1669), describes it as a combination of three qualities: acumen, or quickness in apprehension; ranging, or the ability to hunt after what one knows; and retention. It brings into play judgment and imagination—the powers of distinguishing differences and perceiving resemblances. The true wit, as David Abercromby pointed out in his *Discourse of Wit* (1686), is a man who is always witty, unlike those who will by chance throw off a witticism; he is cynical about marriage; and he is, more often than not, malicious. The ideal comic hero of the age was the young man who could combine wit with good nature, a rare blend. In describing Beaugard, a witty rake of Thomas Otway's *Soldier's Fortune*, Lady Dunce suggests the difficulty in finding such a paragon: "Surely 'tis impossible to think too well of him, for he has wit enough to call his good nature in question, and yet good nature enough to make his wit suspected." In the world of the wits, Fainalls were more common than Mirabels.

That many comedies turned into mere displays of wit is not surprising considering the importance of it for the age. Nor is it surprising that writers like Thomas Durfey and Thomas Shadwell should have protested. Durfey, who considered himself a master of comic intrigue and plotting, attacked the imaginary future critics in the prologue to *A Fond Husband* (1676):

> But in this Age Design no praise can get:
> You cry it Conversation wants and Wit;
> As if the Obvious Rules of Comedy,
> Were only dull Grimace and Repartee.

And Shadwell praised the comedy of Jonsonian "humours," criticizing "some Women, and some Men of Feminine understandings, who like slight Plays onely, that represent a little Tattle sort of Conversation like their own." But Shadwell, who joined the writers of witty comedy later in his life, made a significant adaptation in *Bury Fair* (1689), where he used the traditional epicurean wit, Wildish, as a foil for the "Stoic" wit, Bellamy, who utters such moral commonplaces as, "He that Debauches private Women, is a Knave, and injuries others: And he that uses publick ones, is a Fool, and hurts himself." Few critics believe that Shadwell was successful in passing off Bellamy as a wit, but there was a growing feeling that debachery was foolish and hardly an adequate means of distinguishing either a wit or a libertine, especially since both the truewit and the libertine were supposed to be men of intelligence, superior to those about them. Two years later, in *The Scourers*, Shadwell delineated the reform of Sir William Rant, a truewit and libertine, on seeing his distorted image in the would-be wit and rake, Whachum. Sir William's reform is completed by a lecture from a kindly father; there are tears, and sentimental comedy is just around the corner.

The attack on the wits was mounting, but they were still a faction—indeed, an organized one—in the 1690's. In *The Pacificator* (1700) Defoe described in mock-heroic terms the battle in the 1690's between the wits and the antiwits. Defoe was mostly concerned with the controversy between the wits of Will's

Coffee House, led by Tom Brown, and by Dr. Richard Blackmore, the author of numerous long and tedious poems; but the larger issues of the time creep in: moralists against immoralists, ancients against moderns, pedants against artists, and scientists against humanists. One point is clear: not only were the wits in disgrace, but that art whose end was pure esthetic delight had fallen into obloquy as well. Blackmore argued in *A Satyr against Wit* that art must be justified by a moral purpose and that the wits should find some "useful" profession:

> Who can produce a Wit and not a Rake
> Wise Magistrates lewd Wit do therefore hate,
> The Bane of Virtue's Treason to the State.
>
> . . . .
>
> A Wit's an idle, wretched Fool of Parts
> That hates all Liberal and Mechanick Arts.[28]

Wit was not respectable, nor did it regain favor until Mr. Spectator promised to temper wit with morality and enliven morality with wit; and the wit of *The Spectator* was of a different species from that of the Restoration.

The rout of the wits (and, with their defeat, the disappearance of something essential to Restoration comedy) was caused by a changing moral climate and its effect on the women in the audience rather than by any immediate depreciation of wit itself. During the 1690's, women were frequently praised for having superior wit to men, and who can say the ladies did not believe it? What the women in the audience detested was the libertine attitude toward love and marriage present in almost all Restoration comedy. When Thomas Thornton criticized in his edition of Otway the "grossness" of Otways' remarks on marriage, he was appealing, in 1813, to an audience which regarded marriage as sacrosanct, the family as inviolable, children as pure angels. If Thornton appears smug to us today, it would be erroneous to think that he does so because of our superior understanding of psychological and social forces, because Freud has informed us of infantile sexuality, or because the rising divorce rate and premarital sexual freedom have let us see what man *really* is. The fact is that marriage can seem beautiful in a work like Tolstoy's *Anna Karenina* because the author confronts life honestly. The trouble with Thornton and all but the most recent critics of Restoration comedy is that they turned away from the truth. Restoration comedy showed

the unhappiness of marriage, violent struggles between father
and son, and girls of fourteen longing for sex. By the end of
the 1690's, the dramatists were telling these truths to audiences
that wanted to be entertained with comfortable myths of love
and marriage.

Antifeminism and antimatrimonial attitudes have deep roots in
the literature and conduct books of the entire seventeenth
century. John Fletcher, whose comedies formed a model for
the Restoration dramatists, created rakes like Mirabel in *The
Wild-Goose Chase* (1621?), who regards women as mere instruments for his pleasure, and Valentine in *Wit without Money*
(1614-1620), who expresses his disgust with women in general,
widows in particular, and the inevitable products of marriage:
the son who wishes his father dead, and the daughter who runs
off with the servant. In a writer like Thomas Killigrew, who
bridges the gap between the Caroline and Restoration stage,
the attitude is even more pronounced. His hero in *Thomaso
the Wanderer* (1663) tells his friends how he has found a
perfect mistress and has none of the pains of marriage: "Our
vows are built upon kindness only, they stand & fall together;
we neither load, nor enslave the mind with Matrimony; no
laws, no tyes, but what good Nature makes, binds us; we are sure
to meet without false wellcome, or dissembling smiles, to hide
the Sallary of a sin, or blinde the Fornication of a *Platonique*
Friendship."[29] Though Thomaso, the hero, finally marries a
rather "Platonique" woman, this novel-length, two-part play is
full of such attacks on marriage, the double standard, and laws
binding sexual freedom. Thomaso's two friends, Edwardo and
Ferdinando, even contemplate going to a savage island where
they can live the life similar to that soon to be depicted in
Henry Nevile's *Isle of Pines* (1666) in which one man abandoned on an island with four women populates his land in the
manner of a biblical, or perhaps a libertine, patriarch.

The comic jesting of the rakes of Restoration comedy takes
on more serious overtones in a tragedy like Otway's *Orphan* in
which the underlying disgust for women seems like the product
of a diseased imagination. But Otway was merely reflecting what
appears in many didactic treatises of the time. Though sup-
pressed as first and almost burned by the public hangman,
Francis Osborne's *Advice to a Son* (1656) reflected ideas which
were close to the hearts of many Restoration writers. "Marriage,"
Osborne wrote, "like a Trap set for Flies, may possibly be ointed
at the Entrance, with a little Voluptuousness, under which is

contained a draught of deadly Wine, more pricking and tedious than the Passions it pretends to cure." Osborne argues that, unlike the happier animals, man is trapped by the "severity of Law" and "Custom." To this state is added his "stupendous Folly" of becoming the victim of that "soft passion" called love, "causing Madness in some, Folly in all; placing, like stupid Idolaters, Divinity in a silly Creature." Marriage is a trick of the government to create a secure unit in the family; the trouble is that is gives "stronger Security to the Commonwealth, than suits with Prudence or Liberty." Behind Osborne's arguments are the libertine's rejection of custom and a philosophy based on a law of diminishing sensual returns. The simile comparing marriage to the tediousness of eating the same dish of meat every day was a brutal but universal image in Restoration comedy and the conduct books. Osborne's final recommendation to those who must marry is to do so for money; marital bliss is exactly proportional to the size of the wife's dowry.

Such ideas are echoed repeatedly in the literature of the Restoration. William Ramesey in *The Gentleman's Companion* (1673) argued that since love was pure "folly" a man should keep two mistresses to avoid it. "W. H." in his poem, "A Just, True, and Honourable Description of Marriage," printed in *London Drollery* (1673), stated that it was better to frequent prostitutes than to marry:

> You kiss and you clip, stay, and do what you please,
> And the worst you can fear is but a Disease;
> And Diseases, you know, may hope to be cur'd,
> But the Torment of Marriage can ne'er be endur'd.

William Seymar in his *Conjugium Conjurgium* (1673) maintained that marriage itself is an incurable disease and no cure for love. The conclusions of all these writers is the same: no marriage can be happy.

By the 1690's, however, this position had been severely attacked both by social philosophers and defenders of the female sex. Philosophers on the Continent like Hugo Grotius and Samuel Pufendorf attempted to find a rational standard of human behavior in the form of a codified natural law. They refused to accept either "laws" based on animal behavior or that of the savage as their basis; for, though customs might become corrupted, men were still the product of human society. In England, Sir Thomas Culpepper acknowledged in *Essayes or Moral Discourses* (1671) that customs might be judged false when they "derogate from that due order, and respect of Nature and humane society"; but he also refused to dismiss all custom as an evil or accept a position of moral relativism. The anonymous author of *Remarques on the Humours and Conversations of the Gallants of the Town* (1673), an attack on the libertine attitude toward marriage, argued that society depends on marriage, that there is something beautiful in motherhood, and that the country has its pleasures—pleasures as great and certainly healthier than those of the town. And in 1676 Richard Cumberland, who attacked Hobbes's lupine concept of man, substituted for it a creature motivated by love and benevolence as well as self-interest and a society based on the family as the social unit. The libertine concept of the "good marriage," summed up in Rochester's famous couplet, "With an Estate, no Wit, and a young Wife:/ The solid Comforts of a Coxcomb's Life", was very much alive in the 1690's, but no intelligent writer of Congreve's time could make the kind of statements that appear in Osborne's *Advice to a Son* without some awareness of the complexity of the issue and the new defense of the family.

The author of the *Remarques* noted a contradiction in the attitude of the wits in that at times they appeared to idealize "Love, Honour, and Friendship," an observation which he may have drawn more from reading contemporary drama than from actual contact with the "Gallants of the Town"; but he was right in seeing an idealization of both the sexually emancipated woman and the platonic heroine. At its worst, the Restoration portrait of the female libertine was merely a pornographic projection of the sexually aggressive woman; at its best, it recognized the absurdity of a double standard and was sympathetic toward the talents and problems of women. In Killigrew's *Thomaso the Wanderer* the hero eventually marries his platonic love, Serulina; but Angellica, his mistress and a female libertine, is allowed to plead her right to enjoy sex as much as a man and to argue the benefit of a constancy that proceeds from freedom. By Congreve's day such arguments had become extraordinarily subtle. The generous, intelligent, independent Miss Lucy of Southerne's *Sir Antony Love* (1691) frees her lover without complaint and proclaims that in all gambling "one side must be the Loser; but Marriage is the only Game, where nobody can be the Winner." She is unquestionably a sympathetic figure; the female libertine who began as an object of humor and curiosity had become a serious pleader for equality among the sexes.

On the other hand, the platonic heroine of both Restoration comedy and tragedy was a static character. Usually drawn from the heroine of a French romance, she was as outrageously unreal in the drama of the court of Charles I as she was in the drama of Congreve's time. In John Bank's *Cyrus the Great* (1695) the heroine, Panthea, has merely to stare at a man to have him fall madly in love at her feet. The *précieuse* dialogue underscores the platonic affect:

> But what is she that shines above the rest,
> As Cynthia does amongst her Starry Train,
> Shedding more precious Essence from her Eyes
> Than Phoebus wantonly each morning draws
> From Beds of Violets, or the Dew of Roses.

Combined with the new admiration for feminine wit and independence, this tendency to platonic idealization resulted in a revised attitude toward women in both society and the theater. The audiences of the 1690's were quite self-conscious about their refinement. They could still laugh at the farce of a Durfey; but, from playwrights who demanded serious consideration, they expected subtle artistry and content.

Congreve is best understood within this milieu. He was a wit, a neo-Epicurean, and a relativist in morals. At times, he treated his women characters like a *précieuse* platonist; and, when he was not idealizing them, he was treating them with respect. He accepted the usual Restoration concept that humaniy was motivated by self-interest, but he also showed men and women as operating contrary to their most selfish interests. He viewed love as folly and a successful marriage as nearly impossible; but his heroes fall in love and marry, with hope but with no illusions. Unlike his heroes, Congreve never married; yet there is evidence for his genuine love of two women. His poetry was about love. Sometimes it was cynical, as in his translation of Ovid; sometimes, tender and pathetic, as in his selections translated from Homer. Congreve shared with Southerne and Vanbrugh a critical moment of balance between an older comedy of wit and a new sentimental comedy, between an age of wit and an age of sentiment; and there is every reason to believe that Congreve, the man as well as the playwright, was a product of his time.

CHAPTER 2

Taking Comedy Seriously

> Sir, by yours and Mr. Collier's leave, the Business
> of the Stage is not so paultry a Concern as he is
> pleas'd to call it: Can that be paultry whose Business
> 'tis to encourage Vertue, and discountenance Vice,
> to shew the uncertainty of Humane Grandeur, to
> expose the Singularities of Pride? etc. Your Party I
> confess is not without their trifling Evasions to pre-
> tend this Book not Answer'd. If the Author be
> Easie, Genteel and Witty, like the *Vindicators of the
> Relapse, etc.* [by Vanbrugh] then 'tis *Banter.* If it
> be mixt with just Repartees, admirable Reflections,
> like the *Amendments* [by Congreve], then 'tis Scur-
> rilous. If like others, the Matter be seriously and
> plainly handl'd with sound Reasoning, then 'tis Dull.
>
> Tom Brown, *The Stage-Beaux
> Toss'd in a Blanket: or Hypocrisie
> Alamode*[1]

CONGREVE never attempted to rival his friend and patron,
John Dryden, as a literary critic. Dryden was the first English writer to leave behind a large body of criticism, and while
it is apparent that Congreve studied Dryden's ideas carefully,
he wrote no elaborate prefaces or formal essays. But Congreve
did leave us two important critical statements, important if
only for the light they shed on the theories underlying his
practices as a writer of comedy. Neither his essay in the form
of a letter to the critic John Dennis, "Concerning Humour in
Comedy," nor his *Amendments of Mr. Collier's False and Imperfect Citations* have that quality of memorable statement
that seemed always available to Dryden, yet they reveal that
Congreve took comedy far more seriously than his master.
Though he is influenced by Dryden's statements on comedy,
Congreve reveals no influence of Dryden's contempt for comedy
as a vulgar form.

I Contemporary Attitudes toward Comedy

Since Dryden has such a formative influence on Congreve's critical attitudes, it might be useful to summarize the older poet's views. Dryden's contempt for comedy was in keeping with the opinion of French critics like Hedelin, who based his judgment on the comedy of his native country. Since French comedy was more farcical than its English counterpart, it is hardly surprising that he felt that the style of comedy was to be "low and mean":

Comedy was the picture of the Actions of the people, in which were generally represented the Debaucheries of young people, with the tricks and acts of Slaves and Courtezans, full of Railleries and Jests, ending in Marriages, or some other pleasant Adventure of common life; and this Poem was so much confin'd to represent a popular life, that the style of it was to be low and mean, the expressions taken out of the mouths of ordinary people; the passions were to be short, and without violence. In a word, all the Intrigues were to be upheld by slight and cunning, and not by the sublime and marvellous part of humane life.[2]

But if Dryden assumed a similar position because of admittedly personal reasons, he also wrote some excellent comedies and made some interesting comments on the nature of comic form. Many of his theories were developed in opposition to Thomas Shadwell and followers of the Jonsonian "humours" school of comedy. Dryden argued that a better type of comedy than Jonson's might be created by mixing the verbal wit of Fletcher with the "humours" of Jonson. In fact, he leaned much more toward a comedy of wit and at one point attacked Jonson's outdated "Mechanique humour":

> Wit's now arriv'd to a more high degree;
> Our native Language more refin'd and free.
> Our Ladies and our men now speak more wit
> In conversation, than those Poets writ.[3]

Dryden developed these ideas most thoroughly in his preface to *An Evening's Love* (1671), where he distinguished between true comedy and farce and argued for a witty, urbane comedy. He suggested that the wit of characters should be shaped to suit their personalities and insisted that "the first end of Comedie is delight, and instruction only the second." These may seem like critical commonplaces, but they were controversial points during the Restoration. Congreve held many of them as articles of faith, and Jeremy Collier would have none of them.

By the 1690's, the achievement of English comedy was obvious
to all; and Dryden's snobbish pose had given way to claims
that comedy was more real and hence perhaps superior to
tragedy itself. In 1692, Peter Motteux wrote in the May issue
of *The Gentleman's Journal* that

Dramatic Poetry indeed aims at a just Representation of Nature, and
that which deviates least from our common apprehensions of Nature's
force, has the greatest Beauties, and certainly takes best with a
judicious Auditory. However, Comedy seems most concern'd in a close
adherence to the Rule, for a thousand various humors are the proper
Subject of it; nothing out to appear forc'd there, for humane Follies
should not be represented beyond their genuine standard.

Motteux proceeded to attack farce as the "Ape of Comedy,"
because it was unnatural and to describe tragedy as an elevated
form of art which was somewhat removed from the passions of
the audience. What Dryden once thought the disadvantage of
comedy as an art form—its resemblance to ordinary life—has now
become for Motteux its chief excellence.

Others argued that comedy might claim the dignity of satire.
Renaissance critics had been careful to separate the two according to their proper ends—laughter for comedy, indignation for
satire—but Charles Gildon, in a letter attached to Durfey's *The
Marriage Hater Matched* (1692), argued that satire had always
been the true end of comedy "since from its very beginning 'twas
design'd to correct Vice and Folly, by exposing them." Wycherley
stood as the great example of the satiric playwright, and at
various times even Dryden and Shadwell dropped their special
theories of comedy to defend their works as satires. The playwrights of the 1690's frequently had to defend themselves against
charges of satiric attacks on individuals by insisting that their
satire was always general. It is not surprising that, writing in
1708, John Downes should have thought that *The Way of the
World* was less successful than everyone expected because it
was "too Keen a Satyr."[4]

II *"Humour," Wit, and Character*

In Congreve's essay "Concerning Humour in Comedy," he was
addressing a critic who would have been familiar with the
debates on the nature and end of comedy. Though Dennis is
sometimes associated with rigid neo-Classical critical views, he
was also an admirer of Shakespeare and Milton; and he was to
become a defender of Restoration comedy in opposition to the

type of sentimental elements that Steele and others introduced into comedy in the eighteenth century. Addressing a professional critic, even a friend like Dennis, must have forced on Congreve a necessity for care and clarity; and, not surprisingly, the final product is more analytical than exploratory. Kames was to object to the rigidity of Congreve's discussion of "humour"; but, at a time when the Royal Society was stressing exactitude in language, it is not surprising that Congreve preferred to narrow his definition.

Congreve is aware of the difficulties confronting him. He points out the shift in the meaning of "humour" from the way Jonson used the word, as the influence of the four "humours"—air, water, fire, earth—on character, to its modern meaning. But Congreve finds the modern meaning somewhat superfluous. A character who makes "humorous" remarks is actually what Dryden called a "Character of *Wit*," but wit itself differs according to each man's character. Congreve argues that "even a Fool may be permitted to stumble" on witty remarks and that part of the art of writing comedy consists in creating wit that is suitable for "humorous" characters: "Tho' I make a Difference betwixt *Wit* and *Humor*"; he writes, "yet I do not think that Humorous Characters exclude Wit: No, but the Manner of *Wit* should be adapted to the *Humour*" (I, 2). Though this addition of wit to "humorous" characters may seem simple, even Alexander Pope wondered if Congreve's fools were "fools indeed" because they occasionally stumbled on a semblance of wit. And, though Dryden suggested the possibility of combining the comedy of wit with the comedy of "humour," Congreve is the first to formulate a comic method for the combination.

Congreve then proceeds to attack playwrights who misuse Jonson's term either by passing off unnatural "Grotesques, Figures, and Farce Fools" or by creating characters with personal defects as characters of "humour." There can be no question but that Congreve has Durfey and, to a lesser extent, Shadwell in mind; for Durfey had proclaimed, "I don't overload my Plays with Wit. Plot and Humour are my Province."[5] His Van Grinn in *The Marriage Hater Matched*, a character who laughs all the time, would fit Congreve's first category; and the half-blind Fumble in *A Fond Husband* is a perfect candidate for the second. Congreve's objections are based on the idea that true comedy does not depend on a process of dehumanization or on a cruel feeling of superiority, though there is a good deal of posturing in this objection to that element of comedy which Henri Bergson was

to describe as the very basis of laughter. Congreve praises
Dennis for disapproving of Jonson's Corbaccio in *Volpone*, but
both Corbaccio and Fumble are reminiscent of *commedia dell'arte*
figures, classic comic types. And Congreve was not above ap-
propriating some elements of low comedy from Durfey, who
always knew how to make his audience laugh. All we should
expect from a writer-critic, however, is that he reflect his personal
bias; Congreve was at least true to himself, for few of Congreve's
comic effects depend on the kind of distortion practiced by
Durfey.

The remainder of the essay is concerned with the distinction
among characters of habit, of affectation, and of "humour." Of
these, "Habit" is the least difficult and the least important. He
defines it as "a Singularity of Manners, Speech, and Behaviour,
peculiar to all, or most of the same Country, Trade, Profession,
or Education." Such characters may be used in the same manner
as farce characters, but they would have satisfied neo-Classical
taste by being natural. Though affectation may become a habit
in time, it differs in being voluntary. Congreve puts the entire
problem in neat, aphorisms:

> *Humour* is from Nature, *Habit* from Custom; and *Affectation* from
> Industry.
> *Humour*, shews us as we are.
> *Habit*, shews us, as we appear, under a forcible Impression.
> *Affectation*, shews what we would be, under a Voluntary Disguise.
> (I, 5)

"Humour" is superior to affectation, according to Congreve's
theory, because it is more natural—because it is a universal
trait which will be understandable in all nations at all times.
It is easy to see how this would suit with neo-Classical theories
of verisimilitude, but the deduction is overly logical for a prac-
ticing playwright; and Congreve handles it cautiously.

As an example of a character of "humour," Congreve chooses
Jonson's Morose, a character who cannot stand any noise. The
"humour" is natural enough, but in Morose it is carried to
absurd lengths. This absurdity raises for Congreve the problem
of verisimilitude, and his answer is important: the stage is not
an exact picture of reality. Morose is larger than life, and it is
"his excess of this Humour, that makes him become Ridiculous,
and qualifies his Character for Comedy." Congreve then asks
what would happen if a similar enlargement were not practiced
in creating witty characters. "I believe," says Congreve, "if a

Poet should steal a Dialogue of any length, from the Extempore discourse of the two Wittiest Men upon Earth, he would find the Scene but coldly receiv'd by the Town" (I,6). There is nothing very radical in this statement. Congreve was probably relying on Hedelin at this point, and Dennis would hardly have raised an eyebrow. Yet eighteenth-century critics complained that Congreve's tendency to a Rabelaisian inflation of even the most witty dialogue of real life was his "chief fault."[6]

The fact is that Congreve was free from that literal acceptance of the "Natural" so common among the contemporaries of Dr. Johnson. For all Congreve's rejection of the mechanical distortion of farce, he always conceived of the play as an abstraction of reality rather than as a mirror image. His reason for putting the character of "humour" above the character of affectation was that the first required more thought and more craft. Like his later admirer, Henry Fielding, Congreve was willing to insist on criteria for the artist that would distinguish his work by its learning and complexity from that of amateurs and hacks. Actually, Congreve says nothing disparaging about the character of affectation, and his examples of such characters are drawn from Plautus and his favorite, Terence. Two curious aspects of the character of affectation, as Congreve conceived of it, are his insistence that the character be aware of his affectation and his statement that all women belong in this category. It is well to think of this when dealing with that artful creation, Millamant.

At the end of his essay, Congreve speaks of his desire to see an English comedy composed entirely of characters representing a "True and Distinct Humour." And who would be a better candidate for writing such a masterpiece than a certain playwright who had just shown his thorough grasp of the entire problem? There was every reason for Congreve to have believed himself equal to the task since he had just created his brilliant "humours" character, Foresight, in *Love for Love*. Yet in his last comedy, he had moved away from the comedy of "humour" to the comedy of affectation. Everything he says in his dedication to *The Way of the World* suggests a movement toward a more complex concept of character than his neat distinctions between the characters of habit, affectation, and "humour" would allow. Perhaps he came to realize how different his practice was from his theory. Ben in *Love for Love*, who is a good example of the breakdown of Congreve's distinctions, would have to be classified as a character of habit, among whom Congreve listed "all Country-Clowns, Sailors, Tradesmen, Jockeys, Gamesters and

such like" (I,7); but Ben is far more complex than a typical
sailor dressed in appropriate clothes and using sea terms. He
has his own wit, which is not exactly the false, affected wit of
Congreve's city fools; and he has a fully delineated personality.
The fact is that, once Congreve allows all his characters a certain
kind of wit—whether true or false, affected or natural—he goes
beyond his own classifications. Nevertheless, "Concerning Humour in Comedy" is a useful exercise in definition. He is writing
on only one aspect of comedy, and even on this subject he feels
he is merely giving a "bare hint" of the problem. Of Congreve's
thoughts on the ridiculous and affectation there is only a sketch,
but, considering his practice as a writer of comedy, there is
reason to believe that these were the subjects that interested
him most and on which he might have written with greater critical insight.

III   Art, Morality and the World of the Play

When Congreve wrote his comments on "humour" to Dennis
on July 10, 1695, he probably never thought that within three
years he would be involved in a bitter defense of his dramatic
career. At the end of April, 1698, Jeremy Collier published his
witty and influential *Short View of the Immorality and Profaneness of the English Stage: Together with the Sense of Antiquity
upon this Argument.* When Collier singled out Congreve for a
large share of abuse, Congreve replied with his *Amendments
of Mr. Collier's False and Imperfect Citations* less than three
months later. Though Collier is often depicted as a fearless
crusader and his opponents as embarrassed pornographers caught
in the act, though the legend is that Congreve was either too
angry or too hurt to reply effectively and that Vanbrugh had
no grounds for a defense, Collier was actually a moral bigot
who was more at home burning books than writing about them,
and a rigid neo-Classical critic without taste or discrimination;
but Congreve, Vanbrugh, Elkanah Settle, Dennis, James Drake,
and the other critics and playwrights who replied to Collier's
attack managed to vindicate their plays on solid, esthetic grounds.
As Joseph Wood Krutch has ably demonstrated in his *Comedy
and Conscience in the Restoration* (1924), Collier's attack was
not the first launched against the stage during the reign of
William and Mary. The court favored, as we have noted, a
general reform; and all the new young writers—Addison, Steele,
Swift, and Defoe—supported some kind of regulation of the
stage. In defending themselves and their plays, the playwrights

were swimming against the current of the times. Dennis, who
has sometimes been praised for his effort to defend the drama
against Collier's attack on moral as well as esthetic grounds,
was actually routed from the field by a nonentity like George
Ridpath.[7] That their contemporaries thought the playwrights
had lost the battle to Collier is not surprising; that modern critics
should still believe that Collier won the battle on critical grounds
is a misreading of history and criticism.[8]

Between Congreve and Collier there could be neither communication nor understanding. Collier insisted that "Things are
in a great measure governed by words," and he steadfastly
refused to consider any word or passage in its context. He was
not opposed to the immorality of the theater but to the institution
itself. To Edward Filmer's suggestion concerning a moral theater,
Collier replied that "the *acting* a religious *Play* upon the modern
Theatre, would be next to a Libertine's preaching in a House
of *Prostitution*."[9] One of his central images is that of disease
and infection: a villain or a fool on the stage, no matter how
thoroughly he might be punished, would merely infect the
audience with villainy and folly. Since he objected to moving
the passions in any way, he objected to the very end of drama.
By 1704, Collier could boast that the actors were being harassed,
that the "*Laws* have been let loose upon them; they have been
disciplin'd at *Westminster-Hall*."[10] Congreve and Vanbrugh might
look into the future to readers who would think him the moralist
and Collier the debauchee; but, at the end of the seventeenth
century, even the playgoing audience seemed to be on Collier's
side.

Farquhar remarked that Collier's adversaries showed "too
little wit for the Character of Poets";[11] and this certainly was
true—if by wit, Farquhar meant that interplay of humor, intelligence, and imagination that was usually understood by the
term. They retained their intelligence and sometimes their
imagination, but, with Collier's attack, their sense of humor departed. Though Congreve attempted a witty tone, he was deadly
serious; his defense of the stage is essentially Aristotelian. Collier
had maintained that "all Imitations tho' never so well Counter-
feited are not for the *stage*. To present Nature under every Appearance would be an odd undertaking. A Midnight *Cart*, or a
Dunghill would be no ornamental *Scene*."[12] Congreve replied to
this attack upon realism in the name of decorum with his own
image taken from painting. Aristotle had maintained that comedy was a species of the "ugly," and Congreve follows him in

maintaining that the task of the comic writer is to depict the real
and ugly as carefully as possible. If, in the process, he creates
"vicious and foolish Characters," he should not be held respon-
sible for their sentiments; for "it were very hard that a Painter
should be believ'd to resemble all the ugly Faces that he draws"
(II, 409). Congreve's defense was that used by realists from
Chaucer to Defoe, and an appeal to Aristotle's theory of appro-
priateness as an inherent element of dialogue.

For his definition of comedy, Congreve turns once more to
Aristotle. Comedy is an imitation of "the worst sort of People,"
not in respect to their rank, as Collier thought, but rather in
regard to their morality.[13] Their vices are "the common Practice
of the looser sort of Livers," and these vices are to be revealed
"after a ridiculous manner: For Men are to be laughed out of
their Vices in Comedy; the business of Comedy is mainly to
delight, though it should instruct as well; And as vicious People
are made asham'd of their Follies or Faults, by seeing them
expos'd in a ridiculous manner, so are good People at once both
warn'd and diverted at their Expense" (II, 408). Like Aristotle
and Dryden, Congreve holds that the primary purpose of art is
delight in defiance of Collier's famous statement that, if "Delight"
was the "Supream Law of Comedy, 'twere well if we had less
on't." Congreve asserts the dignity and seriousness of comedy
as an art with the full realization that Collier's attacks "are rather
Objections against Comedy in general, than against mine, or
any bodies Comedies in particular" (II, 451). To Congreve's
statement that comedy served a moral purpose, Collier would
answer as the Puritan Prynne had sixty-five years before: if you
need instruction, go to a church, not the theater. To Congreve's
plea for realism, he would say that not every kind of reality is
suitable for art. Though Collier pretended to be the judge of
comedy, he was actually trying to be its executioner. Is there
any wonder that Congreve is continually appealing to his readers
to explain objections, which he says he simply cannot understand,
or withdrawing behind a wall of snobbish superiority?

Congreve may have found Collier's style vulgar, but it was in
the best tradition of invective. A sentence like, "This Litter of
Epithets makes the Poem look like a Bitch overstock'd with
Puppies, and sucks the Sence almost to skin and bone," which
Congreve quotes contemptuously, has a vigor which makes Con-
greve's prose seem insipid. But we should not forget that
Congreve's arguments were good, or that he was right and
Collier wrong. Congreve's concept of the play as an intricate

system of relationships—moral, plot, characters, an image of life and manners, and most of all the craft required to combine them to make a great play—and his understanding of the means of achieving the ridiculous through affectation and "humor" reveal him as a competent critic. Collier's criticism is merely a screen for a purely moral attack on art. Since Congreve admitted to a few errors and later expunged some questionable passages from his plays, some critics have thought he was acknowledging his sense of guilt. But the British Museum has a record of the proceedings of the Grand Jury of Middlesex for May, 1698 containing an attack on the plays of Durfey, Vanbrugh, Congreve, as well as on the printers, Tonson and Briscoe, for allowing such works to be published. If certain passages were revised, it was because legal pressures forced the change.[14] In 1762, during that post-Collier era of a reformed stage, Kames questioned how Congreve could sleep at night with those obscene plays on his conscience. Congreve would have given him the same reply he gave Collier: "I do not understand."

CHAPTER 3

Incognita: *The Art of the Novella*

> He aimed at perfection from the very beginning, and
> his design in writing this novel, was to show how
> novels ought to be written. *Biographia Britannica*[1]

CONGREVE'S first published work, the "novel" *Incognita*, has
produced mixed criticism and one witty remark. "It is praised
by the biographers, who quote some part of the preface, that is
indeed, for such a time of life, uncommonly judicious," wrote
Dr. Johnson. "I would rather praise it than read it." On the whole,
however, *Incognita* has been ignored by most critics. Though
H.F.B. Brett-Smith called it "probably the most important as well
as the most deliberate achievement of the English novel between
The Unfortunate Traveller in 1694 and the *Life and Surprising
Adventures of Robinson Crusoe* in 1719,"[2] it receives no attention whatsoever in works with titles like Ian Watt's *Rise of the
Novel*, Francis Stoddard's *Evolution of the Novel*, William Lyon
Phelp's *Advance of the English Novel*, and Wilbur Cross's *Development of the English Novel*. This critical vacuum is not
surprising in books considering the history of English fiction as
an evolutionary progression from a lower literary organism to a
higher form and regarding such a movement as inexorable—as
if fiction operated in a Darwinian literary jungle.

Moreover, those who have commented on *Incognita* have frequently been misleading. Some of the earliest critics attempted
to make it into a *roman à clef*, a true story of a famous incident
that occurred in contemporary London. Charles Wilson insinuated
that he could reveal the mystery, but "as some of the persons
are dead, and others living, yet 'till they are gathered to their
Father, I dare not presume to decypher any one Character,
especially since some Folks more grand in their Talk than their
Power, threaten to prosecute us *to the Extent of their Fortune*."[3]
Others have viewed it as a socio-literary phenomena indicating
a shift in power from the aristocracy (the long romance) to the
bourgeoisie (short fiction of middle-class life). Those who have
considered it from a formal standpoint have reached diverse conclusions; Edward Wagenknecht, for example, calls it "a play in

a novel form," and Walter Allen regards it as a forerunner of the artful novels of Henry Fielding, Jane Austen, William Thackeray, Henry James, and Ivy Compton-Burnett."[4]

The problem with such criticism is that it fails to examine with any care what is genuinely original about *Incognita* and what is traditional—or, for that matter, to inquire in what tradition Congreve was working. Congreve was not writing a "novel" in our sense of the word but what the Augustans called a "novel," and what we, for want of a better term, would call a *novella*. Although Congreve's preface has sometimes been regarded as a revolutionary attack on the long-winded French romances of the seventeenth century with their pseudo-historical characters, Nicolas Boileau's devastating dialogue, "Les Héros de Roman," published in 1688, had already given a death blow to a languishing form.[5] When Peter Monteux's *Gentleman's Journal* made its first appearance in January, 1692, it contained—among poems, puzzles, reviews, and literary gossip—a *novella*. Thereafter, almost every issue contained one or more of these short tales of intrigue. Like the young Shelley when writing his Gothic romances, Congreve was merely working in the most appealing and dominant form of prose fiction of his period.

To certain complaints about the inclusion of *novellas* in his journal, Motteux responded, "As for Novels, I need not Apologize for them otherwise than by saying that the Ladies desire them; besides they are short, and, as often as possible, not only true but Moral."[6] He also noted that having received few new ones from contributors, he had been forced to borrow from the French. Motteux's remarks are significant both concerning the audience and the genre: that women constituted a large part of the audience for fiction had long been known; but, in view of their growing influence among theatrical audiences, their influence upon a journal reflecting sophisticated literary taste such as *The Gentleman's Journal* is important. Equally interesting is Motteux's defense of his *novellas* on grounds of truth and morality, for Congreve's *Incognita* was meant to appeal to an audience already demanding moral conclusions to intrigues; and, as we have already seen, some readers assumed it was a true story in disguise.

Had Congreve looked for an English model for his *novella*, he would have been forced to turn to the writings of Aphra Behn. In her *novellas*, such as *The Fair Jilt* or *The Court of the King of Bantam*, he would have found the typical Restoration *novella*: a story supposed to be drawn from real life (only the names

changed), and a plot that was expected to delight the readers
by chance meetings of characters, sudden "turns" of fortune, and
surprising repetition of events. "I do not pretend to entertain
you with a feigned story, or anything pieced together with romantic accidents," Aphra Behn writes at the start of one of her
tales, "but every circumstance, to a tittle, is truth. To a great
part of the main I myself was an eye-witness; and what I did not
see, I was confirmed of by actors in the intrigue, holy men, of
the order of St. Francis." This insistence on truth, on writing
"without the addition of invention," was intended to assure the
reader that he was not reading some wicked fiction; and, besides,
as Pierre Bayle remarked in his *Dictionaire* in 1697, the reader
who believed a story to be true enjoyed it that much more for
the sense of historical reality. To win conviction for her statements, Behn would use the technique of limited omniscience,
explaining that she did not know some facts because she had forgotten to put them in her "journal-observations."[7]

That Congreve's technique was the reverse of this attempt at
verisimilitude should be obvious to all readers of *Incognita*.
Congreve may have based his plot on a contemporary incident,
and the novel may have had some of the appeal of a *roman à clef*.
Indeed, F. W. Bateson may be right in assuming that *Incognita*
is about London rather than Italy; and we may even go so far as
to imagine Congreve in London near the time of another great
ceremonial event—the coronation of William and Mary with all
the carnival atmosphere that accompanies such a festive occasion.[8]
Yet, despite these attributes, *Incognita* is not a true story; it is
a deliberate work of art which flaunts its untruth at its audience.
In this sense, Walter Allen is right: as a writer of fiction, Congreve is in the tradition of those who, like Fielding, Austen, and
James, conceived of fiction in terms of the reality of art rather
than the reality of life.

But before committing the error of claiming Congreve as the
forerunner of the modern novel, we might well consider the
sources of his techniques. The *novella* reached a height of genius
in Spain where Mateo Alemán's profoundly pessimistic vision of
existence in *Guzmán de Alfarache* and Miguel de Cervantes's
rich and ambiguous view of human nature in the first part of
Don Quixote (1605) and the *Exemplary Novels* (1613) became
more important than surprising turns of plot. Nevertheless, Motteux looked to France for his novels, and so did Congreve. He
named two novels by Paul Scarron in *The Old Batchelor—The
Hypocrites* and *The Innocent Adultery*—and he was probably

aware of Antoine Furetière's *Roman Bourgeois,* a novel in the form of an anti-romance, which appears in the catalogue of Congreve's library under the title of *Scarron's City Romance.*[9] Both Scarron and Furetière employed a self-conscious narrator, mocking his own heroes and their passions, making asides to the reader, and functioning as critics of the very fiction being presented to the reader. Like so many writers of England's Augustan Age, Congreve turned his eyes, therefore, to the polished court of Louis XIV for his literary models.

Some critics have found Congreve's prefixed reminder to his readers of the "pains" which he had taken with the work somewhat naïve, but his statement was far more sophisticated than the usual claims to historic truth. Instead, Congreve was making claims to skillful and artistic construction—to esthetic rather than to moral standards. His major objection to the marcescent romances of his time was that they elevated the reader to a world of imagination which affords a temporary delight but ends in deflation and disappointment, a sensation modern readers must still experience in science fiction, a genre to which the French romances with their fantastic landscape bore some resemblance. "Novels," Congreve argued, "are of a more familiar nature; Come near us, and represent to us intrigues in practice, delight us with Accidents and odd Events, but not such as are wholly unusual or unpresidented, such which not being so distant from our Belief bring also the pleasure nearer us. Romances give more of Wonder, Novels more Delight" (II, 5). This distinction between what we might call the "romance" and the "novel" still prevails, but Congreve's swift transition to a discussion of the relationship between these forms and the drama should warn the critic that he is using his genre terms in a far different sense.

Congreve's homage to the drama is meaningful, since it suggests a hierarchial mimetic theory which establishes that art as the best that comes closest to reality, a theory which had strong roots in contemporary criticism. Though he quotes the famous statement from Horace's *Ars Poetica,* "'Less vividly is the mind stirred by the ears than by what finds entrance through the eyes and what the spectator sees for himself," the context is neo-Classical rather than Classical in its concern with verisimilitude. Congreve lived in an age in which the visual sense had been given both artistic and epistemological priority. It was on the grounds of verisimilitude and avoidance of the marvelous that Georges de Scudéry had defended his own romances, but they had much in common with the sublimity of tragedy; and Congreve seems to have agreed with Corneille that great tragic subjects ran counter to probability.[10] Hence, we have the relationship of the *novella* to comedy, and the grounds for the argument of the esthetic superiority of both forms to romance and tragedy; for the closer a work of art is to our own experience, the more we are able to believe; the more we are able to believe, the greater our pleasure in a work of art.

That Congreve cast his *novella* in the form of a comedy, however, is an oversimplification and certainly far different from what he says himself:

I resolved in another beauty to imitate Dramatick Writing, namely, in the Design, Contexture and Result of the Plot. I have not observed it before in a Novel. Some I have seen begin with an unexpected accident, which has been the only surprising part of the Story, cause enough to make the Sequel look flat, tedious and insipid; for 'tis but reasonable the Reader should expect it not to rise, at least to keep upon a level in the entertainment; for so he may be kept on in hopes that at some time or other it may mend; but the 'tother is such a balk to a Man, 'tis carrying him up stairs to show him the Dining-Room, and after forcing him to make a Meal in the Kitchin. (II, 6)

What Congreve is attempting is to give the *novella* the kind of structure of dramatic plot in which tension builds toward a climax; but, at the same time, he intends to give the *novella* its own integrity, without merging it with dramatic form. He retained the surprise and intrigue of the traditional *novella* but avoided such beginnings as that of Scarron's *Innocent Adultery* in the first paragraph of which a half-naked woman is thrust into the arms of the hero. Congreve followed the advice of François Hedelin's *Whole Art of the Stage* in keeping the main characters continually in action with a technique resembling the *liaisons de scènes* of French classical dama and in creating a plot that prepares the reader for future events.[11] Wagenknecht objected that the "easily anticipated results" were overly simple, but this attainment was precisely Congreve's aim. He admitted that the "design of the Novel is obvious" once the main characters have been introduced, but he saw no fault with this revelation and pointed proudly to the way each incident that seems to impede the action actually contributes and is necessary to it. There is surprise, but it is not the kind that leads the reader to the end by holding him in suspense. Surprise becomes instead a complex arrangement of events according to the rules of art— a technique which was later basic to Fielding's handling of plot.

To this concept of plot, Congreve gave the title, "Unity of Contrivance," a term which has never been adapted by critics of fiction, but one which is unusually precise. Just as Fielding was attempting to give rules for his type of novel as a comic epic in prose, so Congreve attempted to lay down rules for the *novella* —three days, as opposed to twenty-four hours of dramatic representation; a plot which is comic in incident and resolution but which toys with a serious climax and allows for tears and a death; characters whose position in society is below the dignity of those in tragedy and above that of farce; language neither too high nor too low; and appropriate manners. Congreve's excuse of having composed *Incognita* in the "idler hours of a fortnight's time" should not be taken too seriously as either an indication of his disdain of being considered a mere writer or of his carelessness; such a pose was almost obligatory in contemporary prefaces, whether by Dryden or Shadwell; and such a declaration was not exposed for the absurdity it was until Swift's *Tale of a Tub*. No wonder that Congreve thought Swift's work unworthy of a second reading.

The plot of *Incognita* is an amusing confusion of names and identities. Aurelian, the accomplished heir of Don Fabio of Florence, decides to accompany his friend Hippolito from Sienna, where they have been students, as far as his native Florence when Hippolito has been called to return to Spain. Florence is in the midst of celebrations over the marriage of a kinswoman of the Duke when they arrive, and the two friends decide to assume costumes and proceed to the great masquerade. There they immediately encounter the women they are to love and later marry. Aurelian conquers the heart of Incognita ("the lady in disguise"—Juliana's assumed name) by his wit; Hippolito is caught up by Leonora by his having acquired the costume of her cousin, Lorenzo (who lies dying of wounds) and is quickly conquered by her beauty.

Meanwhile, Aurelian, afraid of giving away his name, introduces himself to the lady as Hippolito, chooses to learn of the beauty of his lady rather than her identity, and is left in love with Incognita. We learn from Hippolito's conversation with Leonora that Don Fabio has decided to marry his son to Juliana, the daughter of a Marquess of Viterbo; and that, while Hippolito is disguised as Don Lorenzo, he is in danger of being attacked by the enemies of that nobleman. Thus the intrigue must somehow resolve the problems of a comic plot: Aurelian must somehow marry Incognita, reveal his true identiy to her, and succeed in winning over his father who has already chosen a different wife. Hippolito, who has decided to assume Aurelian's name, must win the love of Leonora and eventually establish his true identity.

The result of these confusions is that the couples fall in love with each other, not because of name or title (Leonora even has to conquer her scruples about loving the man who was supposed to become the husband of her friend), but out of genuine feeling. The resolution of the plot involves many more parallels and turns, some of which are indicative of a thematic rather than a mechanical sense of plot in expanding the concept of confusion of identity. The two friends look alike, and we are told that Aurelian regards Hippolito as his "second self." Their exchange of names and identities leads to one scene in which the two friends mistake each other in a dark room, and Hippolito almost kills his alter ego. At one point Incognita, trying to escape from her marriage to an Aurelian she thinks she has not yet met, disguises herself as a man, and has to be rescued by Aurelian, who hears her cries from an old monastery. Congreve is careful to point out that, at the same time this incident is occurring, Hippolito, searching for Aurelian, enters the Convent of St. Lawrence, where Lorenzo (the man whose costume he has assumed) is dying, proceeds from there into the garden of Leonora's father, Don Mario, and finding her there, swiftly marries her.

The action now switches to the angry guardians, the forces of age and prudence who may destroy all. Don Mario is finally placated by the prospect of having married his daughter to a man whom he and his daughter take to be the wealthy heir of Don Fabio; and Don Fabio and the Marquis of Viterbo, after a dramatic moment of doubt, discover that the true Aurelian has married the true Juliana. She had feared to reveal her identity to the lover she thought to be Hippolito for fear that he would reject the idea of depriving his friend of her. Don Mario is happy enough when he learns his new son-in-law's rank and fortune. Thus, amid all the confusion of names, "love and duty" are "reconciled" in accord with the subtitle of the *novella*, and in a world of deadly duels and confusions, the fairy tale runs its course. In a ritualistic atmosphere of the public marriage celebration involving all of Florence, the lovers find their private happiness. In the end, the plot has affinities to the fairy world of Shakespeare's *A Midsummer Night's Dream*.

Incognita relies heavily on chance, but it would be a mistake to confuse Congreve's purpose with what Furetière called the "wicked Custom that hath been long predominant in Romances, all those Personages are very liable to meet accidentally in remote Countries, how contrary wayes soever they have taken" merely to provide "a Connection to the Piece, which without them could be much dislocated." Instead, Congreve is building a world in which art imposes its own pattern upon the flux of nature. His description of the people at the wedding celebration is an excellent example of this:

A more glorious Troop no occasion ever assembled; all the fair of Florence, with the most accomplished Cavaliers, were present; and however Nature had been partial in bestowing on some better Faces than others, Art was alike indulgent to all, and industriously supplyed those Defects she had left, giveing some Addition also to her greatest Excellencies. Every body appear'd well shap'd, as it is supposed, none who were conscious to themselves of any visible Deformity would presume to come thither. Their Apparel was equally glorious, though each differing in fancy. (II, 14-15)

Just as the natural beauty of the people take on additional coloring through artifice, costume, and disguise, so does Congreve's story benefit from his complex treatment of artifice and disguise in a deceptively easy and natural manner.

In a first conversation together, Aurelian is surprised to find that Incognita does not agree with his contention that clothes indicate the man—that outsides indicate insides. "I should hardly pass my censure upon so slight an indication of wit," she responds; "for there is your brisk fool as well as your brisk man of sense. . . . I confess 'tis possible a fool may reveal himself by his Dress, in wearing something extravagantly singular and ridiculous, or in preposterous suiting of colours; but a decency of Habit (which is all that Men of best sense pretend to) may be acquired by custom and example without putting the Person to a superfluous expence of wit for the contrivance." A Sir Fopling Flutter could reveal himself as a fool on the stage by the absurdity of his costume, but Congreve from the very beginning regarded folly as an inner state. Since Aurelian's costume is dictated by chance rather than choice and since everyone in this world of costume is well dressed, he has to agree with Incognita, compliments her for her modesty, and finds himself confronted with both a serious question of self-knowledge and a rather complicated compliment to his wit. These he chooses to ignore, "there being certainly no greater sign of folly and ill breeding, than to grow serious and concerned at anything spoken in rallery."

This narrative comment should be remembered when we come to the plays; for wit itself is but another form of disguise, a mask

over emotion which one must never remove without expecting
to destroy the game of love itself. Beauty, manners, and wit are
given factors in Congreve's world; and so the mocking narrator
describes the couple's dance but refuses to give details of Incognita's dress for fear of erring "in some material Pin or other, in
the sticking of which may be the whole grace of the Drapery
depended."

The disparity of inside and out, then, takes on a larger sense
in terms of human relationships. Ideally one is to know oneself,
one's feelings and weaknesses; but disguise is a way of life—the
game people play to avoid too many of those rare and important
emotional crises. In *Incognita,* disguise permits a true confrontation. A momentary drop of their masks is all that is necessary to
lend certainty to the lovers' initial feelings; and, once that certainty is established, disguise stands in the way of fulfillment
as the comedy of confused identities takes over. Of necessity, the
two friends transfer some of their love for each other to the
ladies; and Congreve renders this transference symbolically. As
Aurelian enters the dark room in which Hippolito is sleeping,
he arouses his friend, who mistakes him for an assassin. Hippolito thrusts at Aurelian, wounding him under the arm in the area
of the heart. Although Hippolito is shocked at having nearly
committed "the most Execrable Act of Amicide," the friendship
of these young men of eighteen has been dealt the usual wound
that comes when boys grow into men.

But this growth to independence and maturity threatens the
authority of their elders. They even make the mistake of challeng-
ing the public champion who annnounces the relative of the
Duke as the most beautiful of women, though such action was
proscribed by the Duke. By their bravery in the lists, Aurelian
and Hippolito make their presence known and arouse Don
Fabio to act quickly in arranging the marriage contract that is
to bind Aurelian's freedom. Most of the remaining deception and
disguise involves the attempts of the lovers to avoid confrontation
with the threatening elders, though the impending fulmination
of the respective fathers proves to be as much a deception as the
disguises of the lovers. Don Mario threatens to thrust his daughter
out of his family; but, when his daughter faints, he bursts into
tears of fatherly affection. Don Fabio, even at the height of his
disappointment, can manage little more than an ironic intonation. The swift reconciliation with the discovery of the true identity of the lovers is a reconciliaton not merely of duty but of
general love.

Most contemporary *novellas* appealed to readers who liked a dose of suggestive pornography with their fiction. Congreve chose to tell a story which utilized the sentiments of platonic love as seen by a cynical commentator. Though he has been praised for a remarkable maturity of vision, the pose adapted by the narrator of *Incognita* resembles nothing so much as that of Byron's *Don Juan*: it is very much the stance of a man who has recently come to experience some of the realities about the relations of men and women and who strikes a cynical pose to conceal genuine emotions. And, though Sir John Suckling's influence on Congreve does not make its key appearance until *The Way of the World,* the combination of platonism and anti-platonism in that writer seems to have made its impression on him early.

Thus Congreve has the usual platonic laments and the language of eyes and burning hearts. Diction is *précieuse* and indirect with tears rendered as "liquid grief" and with descriptions of the ladies' faces in terms of guardian cupids serving as beauticians. And Aurelian's soliloquy rejecting the paternal bond for love of Incognita is as stilted and charming as in any *précieuse novella* of the time:

and must I lose my Love, the Extract of that Being, the Joy, Light, Life, and Darling of my Soul? No, I'll own my Flame and plead my Title too.—But hold, wretched Aurelian, hold, whither does thy Passion hurry thee? Alas! the cruel fair Incognita Loves thee not! She knows not of thy Love! If she did what Merit hast thou to pretend?— Only Love.—Excess of Love. And all the World has that. All that have seen her. Yet I had only seen her once, and in that once I lov'd above the World; nay, lov'd beyond my self, such vigorous Flame, so strong, so quick she darted at my Breast; it must rebound, and by Reflection warm her self. Ah. welcome thought. . . . (II, 50)

This kind of rhetoric was to vitiate prose fiction throughout the eighteenth century. We find it in full flower in Smollett; there are elements of it in Fielding and Fanny Burney. It was a borrowing from the stage where such effusive soliloquies, though sometimes considered antithetical to verisimilitude, were regarded as vital for producing lyrical and emotional effects. Baneful as such rhetoric was for the novel with its illusion of reality, it is clearly an integral part of the texture of a *novella* like *Incognita*.

It is difficult to say how seriously Congreve expected the reader to take these passages, for he was always undercutting the sentiment if not the rhetoric. Congreve describes Aurelian's posture after he has made his speech as "mute and insensible like an

Alarum Clock, that had spent all its force in one violent Emotion"
(II, 58), a comparison which is deflatingly antiheroic. And,
when Hippolito waits in the garden for the arrival of Leonora
under "an ancient Bay-Tree," Congreve allows himself a more
dircet irony about his second hero after noting the powers of
that tree to inspire poetry: "He was, to tell the Truth, naturally
addicted to *Madrigal*, and we should undoubtedly have had a
small desert of Numbers to have pick'd and Criticiz'd upon,
had he not been interrupted just upon his Delivery; nay, after
the Preliminary Sigh had made Way for his Utterance" (II, 64).
Novellas were frequently larded with poetry at such passages,
and Congreve halts to mock the absurdity of literary convention.

Congreve probably borrowed his mocking description of Hippolito's propensity for madrigal from Scarron's "tender-hearted
whining poet," Don Sancho, who addresses an absurd speech to
a tree; and a comparison between Scarron's and Congreve's
technique is enlightening.[12] Scarron, who has the great advantage
of consistency, allows his characters to become sentimental and
weep; but his position as a detached, ironic observer of the lives
of his characters is always evident. The trouble with Scarron is
that he never informs the reader of any reason for his cynicism:
unlike Fielding, he failed to make the narrator a believable and
sympathetic character within the work. Congreve, like Fielding,
attempted to introduce his personality into fiction; to drop his
cynical stance when his emotions were engaged; and, without
destroying the integrity of his fictional characters and their story,
to participate in their feelings and sensations. His narrator gives
the impression of a man who has observed society, accepts its
codes, and understands all there is to understand about love; but
he believes in romantic love even though he understands just
how silly it is.

Like Fielding, Congreve can be very funnny; and the sighing
contest of the lovers is reminiscent of the ogling operation in
Tom Jones: "There arose another Sigh; a Sympathy seiz'd
Aurelian immediately: (For, by the Way, sighing is as catching
among Lovers, as yawning among the Vulgar.) Beside hearing
the Name of Love, made him fetch such a Sigh that Hippolito's
were but Fly-blows in Comparison, that was answered with all
the Might Hippolito had, *Aurelian* ply'd him close till they were
both out of Breath" (II, 35). When Aurelian has finally found
Incognita, they sigh with "Sympathy"; and Incognita has to
"put all her Sighs into one great Sigh" before she can begin a
narration which, by the way, is not strictly true. For all their

sighing, the fact is that of the four lovers only Leonora shows any addiction for the truth; but she is also guilty of other violations against the *précieuse* code of love and honor.

In discussing this "spirit of Contradiction and of Eve," the tendency of women to lead men into disobedience, Congreve shows a precocious insight into the irrational processes of behavior that underlie a rational exterior. Congreve, who turns to an imaginary critic who may object to Leonora's immediate attachment to Hippolito, argues that "he knows nothing of the Sex, if he does not know that a Woman may be taken with the Character and Description of a Man, when general and extraordinary, that she may be prepossess'd with an agreeable Idea of his Person and Conversation; and though she cannot imagine his real Features, or manner of Wit, yet she has a general Notion of what is call'd a fine Gentleman, and is prepar'd to like such a one who does not disagree with that Character" (II, 42). He then discusses the results of "Expectation," if the man is unable to fulfill the reputation his friends have given him. Will he be rejected at once by the woman? No, because women find out the faults of a man once they have a certain idea of him or, seeing the faults, expect improvement. Since women judge men according to a general type, Leonora's error in mistaking Hippolito for Aurelian was not a serious mistake.

This kind of wit was to make Congreve a brilliant playwright. It cannot be called original or profound, but it has the ring of personal observation and thought. It may not be mature, but it shows remarkable observation for a man of twenty-one. And it was perfect for the antiromantic stance of the narrator of a romantic *novella*. Like Furetière, Congreve directs much of his wit at the dullness of the reader, who is supposed to be expecting the customary narrative clichés of the romance. "Now the reader I suppose to be upon Thorns at this and the like impertinent Digressions," Congreve remarks after a lengthy description of "Madam Night"; "but let him alone and he'll come to himself; at which time I think fit to acquaint him, that when I degress, I am at that time writing to please my self, when I continue the Thread of the Story, I write to please him; supposing him a reasonable Man, I conclude him satisfied to allow me this liberty . . ." (II, 14). Sometimes the author pretends to have forgotten to tell facts to the reader and adds them in a hasty parenthesis; sometimes he suggests that he is working from a variety of conflicting accounts. He delivers a lecture on silence and mockingly states that he intends no reflection on his audience's intelligence. Completely gratuitous events are referred to as the result of a strict scheme of providence. And, in the manner of Sterne in *Tristram Shandy,* Congreve suggests a number of possibilities to explain why a man attempted to attack Incognita, only to conclude that, since the man died in his attempt, there could be no solution. These speculative comments on the narrative have the effect of impeding the progress of the story; narrative time is utilized to frustrate the actual duration of the action.

Such devices should warn us that *Incognita* may be closer in tone to Sterne's *Tristram Shandy* than to Fielding's *Tom Jones* and that, if we are to regard Congreve as a predecessor of Fielding and Austen, it is in part because, like both of these writers, he enjoyed parody. Certainly *Incognita* shares with Austen's *Love and Friendship* the assumption that the reader is completely familiar with the conventions of fiction.

But it would be a mistaken temptation to search for parody everywhere in *Incognita.* Congreve's use of parody was a sign of his wit, not an indication of his contempt for the craft of fiction. Everything indicates that he took the comic art of *Incognita* quite seriously, though it was the kind of art he associated with the *novella,* an art of narrative and plot. Everything shows that he avoided realistic effects that were to be found in the then contemporary novels.[13] This is evident from his use of John Raymond's *An Itinerary Contayning a Voyage Made through Italy* (1648) for what little background he provides about Siena and Florence. Raymond's description of Florence is especially detailed on the statues in the piazza, the churches, and the river Arno that divides the city. From this array of details Congreve merely borrowed the description of Santa Croce and the "faire specious Court" where games and shows were held.[14]

Florence is merely a convenient stage setting. *Incognita* might just as well have taken place in London or Paris without the slightest change in the carefully plotted action. As for a circumstantial concept of reality, Congreve probably shared his contemporaries' disdain for both the realism of the "Dutch" school of painting and for the "low and common" picaresque novel. Even Scarron was attacked for his use of detailed description and farce. In a treatise on fiction written in 1734, *De L'Usage des Romans,* Nicolas Langlet du Fresnoy compared fiction to painting and argued that, just as anyone of taste would prefer Van Dyke to Rembrandt, so would he prefer a refined modern romance or *novella* to the picaresque. This was the correct neo-Classical posture; and, though Congreve admired Scarron and in practice never averse to a bit of farce, he too liked to take the correct stance. He preferred describing the general effect of an object or event on a character to describing the thing itself; and in this aspect he was a child of his age, aware of the disparity between objects and man's perception of them. To describe the *Idea* (this word was always capitalized and italicized) of something in the mind of a character was, in fact, to describe the only way that things might be known.[15] Both neo-Classical attitudes and the intellectual milieu, then, militated against the realistic novel; but Congreve was trying to write a *novella*; and in doing so, as the author of *Biographia Britannica* remarked, "he aimed at perfection from the very beginning."

CHAPTER 4

The Old Batchelor: *From Formula to Art*

> First I must observe, that the Common Parts and
> Characters in our Modern Comedies, are two young
> Debauchees whom the Author calls Men of Wit and
> Pleasure, and sometimes Men of Wit and Sense (but
> that is when they admire the Name of *Lucretius,*
> and seem to have a Judgment above the Common
> Doctrines of Religion) these two Sparks are mightily
> addicted to Whoring and Drinking. The Bottle and
> the Miss (as they Phrase it) twisted together makes
> their *Summum Bonum;* all their Songs and Dis-
> course is on that Subject. But at last, partly for
> Variety of Faces, and partly on Consideration of
> improving their Estates (shatter'd with Keeping)
> they Marry two young Ladies, one of which is as
> wild as possibly can be, so as to scape the Main
> Chance, the other more reserved, but really as
> forward to be Marry'd as her Sister. Another neces-
> sary Ingredient of a Comedy, is a foolish Kt. . . .
> (1694), pp. 4-5
>
> James Wright,
> *Country Conversations*

JAMES Wright's summation of the "Fundamentals of a Modern
Comedy" is drawn mainly from the plays of Etherege and
Shadwell, but it comes uncomfortably close to Congreve's
comedies, particularly his first effort, *The Old Batchelor.* Some
works of art surprise us by their originality; others seem fresh in
spite of partaking in a stylized form. To think that, in reading one
Restoration comedy, one has read them all, is an error equal in
magnitude to believing that, by listening to one Elizabethan song,
one has heard them all. On the other hand it would be a mistake to
ignore those conventions which free the artist and allow him to
concentrate on subtle distinctions where his true individuality and
genius are expressed. Shadwell's answer to critics like Wright, who
attacked him because of his reputation, was that writers of comedies were like cooks "whose Art enables them to dress one

Dish of Meat several ways, and by the Assistance of proper Sauces to give each a different Relish. . . ."[1] But such an answer would not have suited the playwrights of the 1690's, who, operating within the traditional formulas, strove for individual subtlety of statement, tone, and characterization. Though *The Old Batchelor* may be read as a digest of the themes, characters, and techniques of Restoration comedy, it was instantly recognized by audiences and critics alike as the product of a brilliant new talent.

I *The Comic Tradition and a New Talent*

Its excellence was acknowledged by no less than the poet laureate, John Dryden, who (according to Thomas Southerne's account some forty-two years after the event) said that "the stuff was rich indeed, it wanted only the fashionable cutt of the town. To help that Mr. Dryden, Mr. Arthur Manwayring, and Mr. Southern red it with great care, and Mr. Dryden putt it in the order it was play'd."[2] Whatever revision may have been accomplished by Dryden with his thrity years of experience in writing comedy, by Southerne, the master of the new style, and by the witty Maynwaring, the final play was clearly one of the best comedies in years. Poets dedicated poems to Congreve, and J. Marsh described Congreve's soaring like a hawk about his fellow dramatists: "Each Line of yours, like polish'd Steel's so hard, In Beauty safe, it wants no other Guard." And Bevil Higgons noted that, although many writers have followed the rules and created convincing characters, few have had the power of Congreve to generate the wit that makes comedy immortal:

> For that's the Soul, which all the Mass must move,
> And wake our Passions into Grief, or Love.
> But you, too Bounteous, sow your Wit so thick,
> We are surpriz'd, and know not where to pick:
> And while with Clapping, we are just to you,
> Our selves we injure, and lose something new.

The breathless quality of Congreve's wit was as startling to his contemporaries as it has been to modern audiences.

Yet with only slight variation, the formula for the play was the same as that described by Wright. Vainlove, a man who enjoys the hunt for love more than its consolations, is in love with Araminta, who keeps him interested only by her seeming indifference to him. His friend Bellmour, who has a more earthy interest in sex, follows up the conquests that the indifferent

Vainlove throws in his way. Bellmour's true love is the flighty
and witty Belinda, who, like Araminta, feigns indifference to her
lover. The rest of the characters are stock comic types: Heartwell,
an old bachelor who is reluctantly in love with Silvia, the ex-
mistress of both Vainlove and Bellmour; Fondlewife, an old,
impotent, puritan alderman with a young wife in love with
Vainlove, or any other competent male; a cowardly, foolish
night, Sir Joseph Wittal, and his friend Captain Bluffe, a boast-
ing coward; and Sharper, a needy wit who is ready to take advantage of Sir Joseph. We may add to these character types two
clever servants—Setter, who helps both Vainlove, his master, and
Bellmour in their love affairs; and Lucy, who helps Silvia find a
husband—and we have a typical enough cast for a Restoration
comedy.

The plot moves skillfully toward the union of the heroes and
heroines; the rescue of the old bachelor, Heartwell, from a fate
which he himself knows is worse than death; and the marriage of
Silvia and Lucy to Sir Joseph and Captain Bluffe. But it would be
a mistake to think that the excellence of the play depended on
plot. In fact, there is some evidence that Restoration comedy
had reached a stage similar to that of the novel at the end of
the nineteenth century when J. K. Huysmans could argue in
A Rebours that plots were vulgar. Though Charles Gildon and
Thomas Durfey attacked the new comedies as a mere "Bundle
of Dialogues,"[3] many dramatists had apparently come to the
sophisticated conclusion that plot was inseparable from dialogue
and characterization; and, as these became more complex, they
found themselves with too much plot rather than too little.

But Congreve's plots were always dramatic in the sense that
they depended not on changes in character but in events. We
know of Belinda's love for Bellmour from the very start, and it
merely takes her decision to bring about the marriage. The possibility of Vainlove's marriage to Araminta is made more likely
by events which force him to face the possibility of losing her.
And Congreve is at his best in individual scenes when he is
capable of blending subtle characterization and low comedy
into his main plot. Hence the comic force of the return of
Fondlewife to find that Bellmour has visited his wife in the
disguise of Parson Tickletext. Fondlewife's initial anger and final
acceptance of the innocence of his "cocky" is a brilliant psychological study in self-delusion merged with a dramatic action that
is pure farce.

Much of the comedy depends on reversals of situation and

seeming reversals of character. Heartwell, the woman hater, almost marries the faithless and promiscuous Silvia; Vainlove, who detests marriage, seems destined to marry; Belinda, who affects indifference to Bellmour, is forced to acknowledge her love for him. Captain Bluffe is revealed as a coward, and Sir Joseph, who pretends to be a great rake, is exposed as a fool and married to Silvia. The handling of characters of "humour," affectation, and wit shows some originality; but most of Congreve's effects may be found in Shadwell, Durfey, or even Ravenscroft, whom Congreve pillaged along with more esteemed writers like Molière, Dryden, Wycherley, and Jonson. It was mainly Congreve's manner of dialogue that was new.

II *The Mastery of Dialogue*

The opening of *The Old Batchelor* is a good example of Congreve's method. Hodges suggested that the audience would have recognized its brilliance immediately, yet at first glance it appears completely traditional:

Bellmour: Vainlove, and abroad so early! good Morrow; I thought a Contemplative Lover could no more have parted with his Bed in a Morning, than he could have slept in't.

Vain. Bellmour, good Morrow—Why truth on't is, these early Sallies are not usual to me; but Business, as you see, Sir—(Shewing Letters.) And Business must be follow'd, or be lost.

Bell. Business!—And so must Time, my Friend, be close pursued, or lost. Business is the rub of Life, perverts our Aim, casts off the Bias, and leaves us wide and short of the intended Mark.

Vain. Pleasure, I guess you mean.

Bell. Ay, what else has meaning?

Vain. Oh the Wise will tell you—

Bell. More than they believe—Or understand.

Vain. How, how, Ned, a wise Man say more than he understands?

Bell. Ay, ay, Wisdom's nothing but a pretending to know and believe more than we really do. You read of but one wise Man, and all that he knew was, that he knew nothing. Come, come, leave Business to Idlers, and Wisdom to Fools; they have need of them: Wit, be my Faculty, and Pleasure, my Occupation; and let Father Time shake his Glass. Let low and earthly Souls grovel 'till they have work'd themselves six Foot deep into a Grave—Business is not my Element—I rowl in a higher Orb, and dwell—

Vain. In Castles ith' Air of thy own building: That is thy Element, Ned—Well as high a Flyer as you are, I have a Lure may make you stoop. [*Flings a Letter.*]

Bell. I marry Sir, I have a Hawks Eye at a Womans hand—There's more Elegancy in the false Spelling of this Superscription [*Takes up the Letter*] than in all of Cicero—Let me see—How now! Dear perfidious Vainlove. (I, i, 1-38)

The joke about business and pleasure is anything but new; in fact, it was shorthand for identifying the libertine wit. "My bus'ness is my pleasure," says Don John in Shadwell's *Libertine*; and in Southerne's *The Wive's Excuse* (1692), which has many affinities with *The Old Batchelor*, appears the following:

> *Wellvile.* Was not that Wilding left you?
> *Courtall.* He's in his Employments, Sir, very busie.
> *Wellvile.* In pursuit of the Women, I know.[4]

What was there in the play then to cause Bevil Higgons to proclaim, in his poem prefixed to the play, Congreve the new monarch of wit?

First of all, as Higgons suggested, the wit pours out quickly—so quickly that the audience is continually behind the dialogue. The sensation is similar to that experienced in the modern cinematic experiments in time where the audience is forced to complete its associations after the plot has already moved forward. If, as Higgons suggested, the audience also stopped to applaud, the lag between action and understanding must have been extraordinary and the effect of the dialogue breathtaking. Then the wit is not merely quickly paced (Wycherley did something like this as well); it is relatively complex. What does Bellmour mean by a "Contemplative Lover"? That lovers remain sleepless is commonplace enough, and their exhaustion from their torments is only slightly more difficult, but is there not an ironic note in Bellmour's observation? Congreve had already jested about the role-playing of sleepless lovers in *Incognita*.

The next remark on business and pleasure is complicated by an image from bowls, a recreation. Thus the activity of life is compared to a game, the end of which is pleasure, while business becomes the force which makes us turn from pleasure. This image of life as a skillful game functions throughout the play, but here it is quickly succeeded by a personification of time and by metaphors suggesting that all movement on earth is action in time. The libertine conquers time by dwelling above earthly concerns in airy castles or ecstatic spheres of pleasure.

The life of the man of business, on the other hand, partakes of the very element of earth and every action contributes to his digging his grave. Unfortunately the libertine too must find his pleasure on earth, and Bellmour is forced to confess his animal

nature by groveling on the ground to retrieve Vainlove's letter
of assignation. The imagery from hawking does not disguise the
paradoxical resemblance between the libertine and the businessman. More than their rapidity and complexity, it is the ease
with which one metaphor succeeds another that is so startling.
They follow by a process of association which appears so natural
that only after careful thought are we aware that we are in the
presence of that artistry that conceals art.

Even more remarkable than the play of witty imagery is Congreve's ability to create character through dialogue. F. W.
Bateson argued that Congreve resembled Shakespeare in that
the reader could identify each character by his individual voice
even if his name were omitted before his speeches.[5] Certainly
this assertion is true of Bellmour and Belinda. Bellmour is both
a libertine and a skeptic, the latter at a time when the philosopher
David Abercromby could write, "Let us then acknowledge that
there is no true Philosophy in the World but Scepticism; . . . as
the greatest *Wit* of Angels, consists in knowing; the greatest Wit
in Men consists in doubting."[6] He is a man of fancy rather than
reason, as if skepticism had liberated his wit from his judgment.
His cry, "Wit be my Faculty, and Pleasure my Occupation,"
shows a sweep of imagination which is more reminiscent of
Shakespeare's Mercutio than of a Restoration wit. Belinda is also
fanciful, but she is far more than Bellmour's feminine counterpart. She comes to Araminta to complain that she has been
"jolted to a Jelly" in the coach; and, while Belinda stares at
herself in her mirror, Araminta remarks drily that her head is
merely "a little out of order":

> *Belin.* A little! O frightful! What a furious Phys I have! O most
> rueful! Ha, ha, ha: O gad, I hope no body will come this way, 'till
> I have put my self a little in repair—Ah! my Dear—I have seen
> such unhewn Creatures since—Ha, ha, ha, I can't for my Soul help
> thinking that I look just like one of 'em—Good Dear, pin this, and
> I'll tell you—Very well—So, thank you my Dear—But as I was telling
> you—Pish, this is the untoward'st Lock—So, as I was telling you—
> How d'ye like me now? Hideous, ha? Frightful still? or how? (IV,
> viii, 9-20)

Belinda is really concerned about only a few subjects: scandal,
her appearance, and Bellmour. She speaks as she thinks—in short
bursts of energy; and she can hardly keep for more than a few
seconds on any single subject. At one point, she tries to carry
on a literary conversation with Sharper about Abraham Cowley
for whom she has a "great Passion." When Sharper agrees that

Cowley is a great poet, she goes into detail: "Ah so fine! So extremely fine! So everything in the World that I like—O Lord, walk this Way—I see a Couple, I'll give you their History" (IV, xi, 27-29).

Now no one could be further from Cowley with his love of the country and retirement; Belinda is the quintessence of the city and its manners, and is it on the subject of those "unhewn Creatures" from the country that she displays much of her wit. To Belinda, the healthy "Cherry-cheek'd Country Girls" she encounters at Mrs. Snipwel's shop are objects of laughter. When she tells Araminta of her attempt at "the modelling of one of their Fronts, the more modern Structure," Araminta reminds her that she had forgotten what true manners should be and that she might have affronted members of a good family:

Belin. Of a very ancient one, I dare swear, by their Dress— Affront! Pshaw, how you're mistaken! The poor Creature, I warrant, was as full of Curtsies, as if I had been her Godmother: The Truth on't is, I did endeavour to make her look like a Christian—and she was sensible of it; for she thank'd me, and gave me two Apples, piping hot, out of her Under-Petticoat Pocket—Ha, ha, ha: And t'other did so stare and gape—I fansied her like the Front of her Father's Hall; her Eyes were the two Jut Windows, and her Mouth the great Door, most hospitably kept open, for the Entertainment of traveling Flies. (IV, viii, 44-56)

Such attitudes were common even before the Restoration. In William Davenant's *The Wits,* acted in 1633, the life of the country is imagined in terms of dancing in "narrow parlours to a single fiddle,/ That squeaks forth tunes like a departing pig," while London is the "fair metropolis."[7] Only there could the English feel that they could approach the urbanity of France under Louis XIV. Clodpate, the spokesman for the country life in Shadwell's *Epsom Wells* (1672), is comic because everything that he praises represents the opposite of what the Restoration wits regarded as the best in their civilization. Their contempt was similar to that expressed by H. L. Mencken for the inhabitants of America's "Bible belt."

What is new is not Belinda's attitude but her extravagant imagination. She dehumanizes her country girls into "Barn-Door Fowl" and then, to improve on that, into "Friezland Hens." After dehumanizing them, she proceeds to "de-animate" them by comparing them to their father's country house; and she is very witty on remodeling the "more modern Structure," while the other stood with eyes as windows and her gaping mouth as a door.

Yet the absurdity of the image does not prevent the satire from turning in on the speaker. The imaginary father is an ideal squire, practical in his purchases and hospitable to strangers. Araminta's criticism of Belinda leads us to the realization that, in spite of her superior wit, imagination, and manners, Belinda is more absurd and extravagant than those she criticizes. Araminta might have been amused momentarily by the country girls; they would hardly have diverted her. Congreve allows his more conventional lovers to guide his audience's judgment of the attractive, extravagant Bellmour and Belinda.

III   *Character and Wit*

Belinda is affected and a bit foolish, but she is witty; and this quality is important, for, as we have seen, Congreve differed from many of his contemporaries in believing that every character in a comedy might be allowed some appropriate kind of wit, even if it was the false wit of his fools.[8] And Congreve's very attempt to suit wit to the character gives his characters their individuality. In the hands of a lesser playwright, Heartwell the old bachelor who rails at women, argues for lust as truth and love as perversion, and still finds himself drawn inexorably toward Silvia against his will, would have been simply a character of "humour." By allowing him wit, Congreve gives him life. Heartwell's bitter, flailing wit shows his divided nature: his self-knowledge and his passion:

Well, why do you not move? Feet do your Office—not one Inch; no, foregad I'm caught—There stands my North, and thither my Needle points—Now could I curse my self, yet cannot repent. O thou delicious, damn'd, dear, destructive Woman! S'death how the young Fellows will hoot me! I shall be the Jest of the Town: Nay in two Days, I expect to be Chronicled in Ditty, and sung in woeful Ballad, to the Tune of the superannuated Maidens Comfort, or The Batchelors Fall; and upon the third, I shall be hang'd in Effigie, pasted up for the Exemplary Ornament of necessary Houses, and Coblers Stalls—Death, I can't think on't—I'll run into Danger to lose the Apprehension. (III, ii, 17-31)

In order to capture his character so intimately, Congreve resorts to the soliloquy, a device common in beginning playwrights; and in this case, the overheard soliloquy is a stage trick which Congreve in the preface to his next play admitted to be monstrous. Yet the monologue was attractive to the actors and useful to the playwright for creating sympathy and understanding in his audience.[9] Even the clever servant, Setter, is quickly individualized by a Falstaffian soliloquy on reputation and honesty.

Like Shakespeare, Congreve used the soliloquy not only to reveal the intentions of his characters but also to show their inner conflicts. As a rhetorical device, except in such cases where the soliloquizer is a complete villain, an Iago or Maskwell, the soliloquy tends to create sympathy in the audience, even when the object of that sympathy is a foolish cuckold. To the modern sensibility, which tends to regard his plight as pathetic rather than comic, the cuckold is one of the more puzzling comic types of Restoration comedy; but the wits of the Restoration would have agreed with Sir Jolly in Otway's *The Soldier's Fortune* (1680), who states "I never knew a Cuckold in my life, that was not a false Rogue in his heart."[10] He is "false" because he has married a woman to whom he is incapable of giving sexual pleasure.

Sometimes the cuckold is an old rake, who has passed the age of sexual competence, sometimes a middle-class businessman whose capacity for passion is minimal, sometimes simply a fool. In Ravenscroft's *The London Cuckolds* (1682) a variety of the second type—Wiseacres, Doodle, and Dashwell—debate whether it is better to have an innocent, a witty, or a religious wife. All are cuckolded because they forget that, in addition to being husbands, they also have to be men. They outraged the libertines because they were guilty of warping the passions and destroying the full sensual life that their wives deserved. Probably the best indication to the attitudes of the times is contained in the full title of one of Southerne's plays: *The Wive's Excuse: or, Cuckolds Make Themselves.*

Congreve treats his cuckold, Fondlewife, with a certain degree of compassion, or rather, while making him comic, he also makes him human; and to humanize the cuckold is to throw him into the boiling pot of error and passion with the rest of mankind. He belongs to a dissenting religious sect, and his soliloquy shows his addiction to the practice of what Max Weber called "moral bookkeeping" in balancing good against evil. His monologue also reveals his sexual dilemma, rendered partly in the form of double entendres:

I will reason with my self—Tell me *Isaac*, why art thee jealous? Why art thee distrustful of the Wife of thy Bosom?—Because she is young and vigorous, and I am old and impotent—Then why didst thee marry, Isaac?—Because she was beautiful and Tempting, and because I was obstinate and doating; so that my Inclination was (and still is) greater than my Power—And will not that which tempted thee, also tempt others, who will tempt her, Isaac?—I fear it much—But does not thy Wife love thee, nay doat upon thee?—Yes— Why then!—Ay, but to say truth, she's fonder of men, than she has reason to be; and in the way of Trade, we still suspect the smoothest Dealers of the deepest Designs—And she has some Designs deeper than thou canst reach, th'hast experimented, Isaac—But Mum. (IV, iii, 1-18)

Congreve's success in this soliloquy is due to his reliance on an already well-established type. There was the Dissenter, Lump, in Shadwell's *A True Widow* (1676) with his "method," which directs every moment of his behavior, or the religious hypocrite, Testimony, in Crowne's *Sir Courtly Nice* (1685) with his sexual witticisms. Shadwell was content with having observed the way many Puritans conducted their lives; Lump hates the wits, loves business, follows his method, and functions as the kind of card-board "humours" character of the Dissenter which Shadwell found sufficient for his comedy. With Congreve, these observations are just part of the character of the man; they are not offered in place of the whole man.

By following the formula, Congreve could therefore cut corners, assume recognition on the part of the audience, hint a certain character trait, and expect the audience to supply much of the nuance and understanding. He could also suggest a silent dialogue underneath the speeches of his characters, and the ability to understand what the words disguise is often a test for both his characters and his audience. Fondlewife's soliloquy reveals some self-recognition but little self-confrontation. Like Heartwell, he is victimized by his passions, and the rational method of the soliloquy is merely a façade. He upbraids his wife, Laetitia, in the dialogue following the soliloquy, half accusing her of adultery, "a very weighty Sin" that will lie heavily on her; she weeps, just as Silvia weeps when Heartwell threatens to leave; and in both cases the men surrender. Fondlewife is forced to yield to his wife's evocation of their private game of baby talk, one meaningful enough to a man who has returned to a second child-hood in marrying a young wife, and a game of total deception for Laetitia. "I won't be jealous," says the self-deceived Fondlewife, "Poor Cocky, kiss Nykin, kiss Nykin, ee, ee, ee" (IV, iv, 24). Congreve could have found examples for such dialogue in Etherege, Shadwell, and Durfey; but no one before had so successfully mixed a touch of pathos in his comedy.[11] Even such an antisentimentalist as Swift used baby talk with Stella, and we are all guilty of using it at times when we find ordinary language a barrier to expressions of love; but, where it is used to conceal a genuine dislike or impotence, the comedy takes on more serious overtones. Within *The Old Batchelor* the baby talk of Laetitia and Fondlewife is part of the theme of deception that underlies the entire play.

In marrying Laetitia, Fondlewife has involved himself in a self-deception; and he must pay for it. He sees every man as a potential lover for his wife with the exception of the blind Parson Spintext, who is himself a cuckold, his wife, Comfort, having had an affair with Parson Prig. As for Laetitia, she is eager for a gallant to act the part her husband is incapable of performing. When Fondlewife discovers Bellmour in his wife's bedroom, he listens to their lies; and, knowing they are lying, he decides to accept their story. The moral drawn befits an age of skepticism: *"No Husband, by his Wife, can be deceiv'd; She still is vertuous, if she's believ'd"* (IV, xxii, 163-64). If it comes easily enough, self-delusion is one way of solving the problems of life.

But Congreve does not recommend Fondlewife's solution—the solution of a fool in a world of knaves. Cynical about human virtue, the two wits of *The Old Batchelor* have few illusions. They are in love; and, though they understand that theirs is a respectable failing, they also know it is a weakness. Besides, they have not chosen without care: both Araminta and Belinda are rich. When Sharper tries to dissuade Bellmour from marrying Belinda on the grounds that she is "too proud, too inconstant, too affected and too witty, and too handsome for a Wife," Bellmour retorts, "But she can't have too much Money—There's twelve thousand Pound, *Tom.*—'Tis true she is excessively foppish and affected, but in my Conscience I believe the Baggage loves me: For she never speaks well of me her self, nor suffers any Body else to rail at me. Then, as I told you, there's twelve thousand Pound" (I, 30). As for Vainlove, he is fully aware of his tendency to lose interest in women once they yield, and he regards it as a problem in his relationship with Araminta.

Congreve's ideal wit, then, is one who, in the words of John Fletcher, has "travell'd . . . through himself exactly" and come to know himself.[12] Though their situations are vastly different, Congreve sets the same standard of self-awareness for his heroines. Araminta understands that courtship is a game—a serious one which must never become too serious on the surface. When Vainlove starts to profess his love, she puts him off. "Nay come," she says, "I find we are growing serious, and then we are in great Danger of being dull" (II, vii, 43-44). Congreve had already stated in *Incognita* that there was "certainly no greater sign of folly and ill breeding, than to grow serious and concerned at any thing spoken in rallery" (II, 19).

Witty conversation may continue to be the means of communication even at moments of great seriousness, but its usual function is to fill in when there is no necessity for direct emotional confrontation. L. C. Knights suggested that such indirection in the dialogue of Restoration comedy evidenced a failure to deal with human problems, but there are few Restoration comedies without at least one very direct, serious, honest confession, whether in an aside or in conversation. And such statements come with genuine dramatic impact, gaining strength from their distinction from the rest of the dialogue which is understood by the witty characters in the play to function as a deliberate disguise for emotion.[13]

Belinda maintains to the end her affectation of indifference for Bellmour; we know from Araminta that Belinda moans in her sleep longing for Bellmour. That she refuses to confess her feelings does not mean that either she or Bellmour are unaware of them. When Belinda finally consents, she says that she expects from his troublesome courtship that he will make a "more than ordinary quiet Husband" and proceeds to criticize the ardor of men in courtship compared to their performance after marriage. Bellmour denies it: "Courtship to Marriage, is but as the Musick in the Play-House, 'till the Curtain's drawn; but that once up, then opens the Scene of Pleasure." "Oh, foh—no," retorts Belinda, "'Rather Courtship to Marriage, as a very witty Prologue to a very dull Play" (V, x, 37-39). If life after marriage is to be "a very dull Play," no wonder that the heroines torment their lovers so long. After warning men against marriage, Osborne provided a section of warning to the ladies to remind them that after marriage they will be worshipped no longer; their beauty will disappear after they have a few children, and they will become merely the "best of Servants." The truly happy wife was a rarity in Restoration comedy. Congreve merely equips his heroes and heroines with the self-awareness that is a vital ingredient in that miraculous thing—a good marriage.

That Congreve conceives that such a thing is at all possible is a sign of his relative optimism. The strongest arguments against his position are put into the mouth of Heartwell, who, as the title would indicate, is to some extent the central comic figure of the play. In the cast of characters he is listed as "pretending to slight women," which would suggest that he is a character of affection rather than a "humours" character. The real trouble is that his "humour" is so much against the grain of mankind that it leads him to a neurotic contradiction. He has kept from marriage, because he believes, with Osborne, that it is an absurd institution, but he has fallen in love with Silvia in spite of himself. Like Fondlewife, he turns away from the truth because it is painful and yields to his passions while acknowledging his folly. But, unlike Fondlewife, he finds no comfort in evading the consequences of his actions. After Bellmour and Vainlove inform him that he has married a whore, he agonizes over the usual reminders of the evils of matrimony—that Eve caused the fall of man and that, so far from being a "Supplemental Self" to man, a wife is an instrument for torturing him.

Yet when Belinda decides to amuse herself by mocking Heartwell, he becomes an object of pity and, except for our knowledge that his marriage is invalid, almost tragic. He loses his composure so far as to start to draw his sword against Belinda before settling for an effective verbal attack on her morals. Once he has found himself free and Silvia and her maid, Lucy, married to Sir Joseph and Captain Bluffe, Heartwell vows eternal bachelorhood and tries to dissuade Bellmour from marriage. Though Bellmour is not to be convinced that matrimony is without its consolations, Heartwell has the last word on the horrors of marriage:

> What rugged Ways attend the Noon of Life!
> (Our Sun declines,) and with what anxious Strife.
> What Pain we tug that galling Load, a Wife;
> All Coursers the first Heat with Vigour run;
> But 'tis with Whip and Spur the Race is won.
> (V, xii, 103-9)

The Old Batchelor, then, can be viewed as an optimistic play only in the context of the profound pessimism concerning love and marriage that is the hallmark of Restoration comedy. For no sufficient evidence is given to make us expect that the lovers will have greater success in their marriage than those who have gone before. Vainlove may indeed marry Araminta, but everything suggests that he is unable to endure a stable relationship with a woman. Bellmour has a better chance since he is in love and with a woman whose wit resembles his own. But Congreve had not yet developed those ideal couples whose intelligence and sensibility seemed to promise an ideal match. When Vainlove

and Bellmour speak of their love, their language is flat and conventional. Araminta speaks with the voice of the platonic heroine. "If Love be the Feaver which you mean," she says in defense
of that passion, "kind Heav'n avert the Cure; Let me have Oil to
feed the Flame and never let it be extinct, 'till I my self am
Ashes." We are grateful for Belinda's retort, "There was a
Whine!—O Gad I hate your horrid Fancy—This love is the
Devil, and sure to be in Love is to be possess'd" (II, iii, 14-16).

Shadwell and Durfey had begun to introduce sentimental
dialogue into their comedies—appeals to unexamined emotions
of love and patrotism. Congreve avoided the sentimental, but
he did fall into the conventional *précieuse* pattern of platonic-
antiplatonic ideals as a replacement for a realistic rendering of
emotion. Belinda tells Araminta that seeing Vainlove "an absolute
Lover would have concluded the poor Creature to have had Darts,
and Flames, and Altars, and all that in his Breast." Vainlove does
indeed speak of the "Diety" of love and of Araminta as a "Temple
of Love," and the antiplatonic Belinda complains that Bellmour
"has so pester'd me with Flames and Stuff—I think I shan't
endure the sight of a Fire this Twelvemonth." Belinda is very
amusing, but this kind of dialogue is not Congreve at his best.

More interesting is his adaptation of religious imagery to a play
about love. This too was part of the *précieuse* tradition, but Congreve's particular adaptation of the tradition was original enough
to bring the wrath of Collier upon him. Collier objected particularly to Bellmour's questioning Vainlove about his eagerness to
marry Araminta:

Vain. Could you be content to go to Heav'n?
Bell. Hum, not immediately, in my Conscience not heartily? I'd
do a little more good in my Generation first, in order to deserve it.
Vain. Nor I to marry Araminta 'till I merit her. (III, iii, 21-25)

Learning that he is to come to Laetitia in the disguise of a
clergyman, Spintext, Bellmour says, "It adds a Gusto to an
Amour; gives it the greater resemblance of Theft; and among us
lewd Mortals, the deeper the Sin the sweeter" (I, i, 99-101). And
women who take lovers in the image of their husbands are compared to believers who worship the effigies of saints. Congreve
argued that Collier's objections were silly; but, if the clergyman
suspected that religious imagery was being put to the service
of a libertine ethic, he was perfectly right. Some of Congreve's
broadest comic effects are achieved by disguising his rake as a
dissenting parson, and the implication of Bellmour's being caught

by Fondlewife through his having brought along some of Scarron's *novellas* instead of *The Practice of Piety* is that a better disguise of religion would have made his liaison with Laetitia even more successful.

Years before Collier's attack, Henry Higden had christened the play the "Baudy Bachelor" and complained that it showed the "nicest Ladies may be brought . . . to stand the fire of a smutty jest and never flintch."[14] Congreve's play is far from the bawdiest of the many cuckolding comedies of the Restoration, but Higden's response may be a good indication of changing values. Congreve based his very funny comedy on a tried formula; and as a young playwright, he relied on many devices used by Dryden and Wycherley which were no longer considered entirely proper. But the subtlety of the dialogue, especially the conversations between Araminta and Belinda, was very much a part of the comedy of the 1690's. Before *The Old Batchelor,* such dialogue had been the specialty of Thomas Southerne, who may even have contributed something to it when the play was reshaped. In his *New Session of the Poets* (1700), Daniel Kenrick has Apollo dismiss Congreve's claim to precedence among the poets with the reminder that Southerne "writes as well"; but Kenrick was wrong. Even in his first play Congreve had demonstrated that the difference between Congreve and his very accomplished and established rival was that narrow division between talent and genius.

CHAPTER 5

The Double Dealer:
Reality and the World of the Play

> There are but Four Ladies in this Play, and three of
> the biggest of them are Whores.
>
> Jeremy Collier, *A Short View of the
> Immorality and Profaneness of the
> English Stage.*[1]

CONGREVE insisted that Collier's remark about *The Double
Dealer* was based on the false premise that his play constituted a general picture of real life, and he sarcastically rehearsed
what he thought to be his opponent's process of reasoning: "the
Stage is the Image of the World; by the Men and Women represented there, are signified all the Men and Women in the World;
so that if four Women are shewn upon the Stage, and three of
them are vicious, it is as much as to say, that three parts in four of
the whole Sex are stark nought" (II, 412). Congreve uses sarcasm
to avoid answering Collier's argument, and this round was undoubtedly one that his contemporaries thought the playwright
had lost in his battle with the clergyman.[2] Though modern critics
might divide on whether to speak about the "world" of the play
or the play as a reflection of the world, few indeed would con-
tend that a play might be a satire of contemporary life and, at
the same time, a work of art entirely divorced from life; but
Congreve seems to have involved himself in his apparent contradiction.

Part of the explanation lies in Congreve's attempt to write a
correct neo-Classical comedy according to the French model
with strict limitations on the unities of time, place, and action.
He achieved one of the effects that Roland Barthes noted in the
dramas of Jean Racine—a sense of enclosure in space, as if the
characters were trapped within the walls of Lord Touchwood's
house in the same way they are trapped in their passions.[3] And
the house itself has little geographic reality. What it looks like
on the outside, where it is located—these simple questions are

deliberately ignored for a psychological reality of place in which "outside" is merely where Mellefont may be cast if he is disinherited or that distant world of scandal inhabited by "Lady Whiffler, Mr. Sneer and Sir Lawrence Loud, and that Gang" (I, 164).

But the effect of this sense of enclosed space is to suggest a city full of houses in which exactly the same scene is enacted. Collier was right: Congreve suggested a world of knaves and fools, of clever women and foolish cuckolds, of the deceivers and the deceived. Caught in the middle are Mellefont, Cynthia, and Careless: they must use many of the devices of the knaves, yet they must avoid becoming corrupted; and they must never succumb to the temptation of becoming fools, that "sublime and refined Point of Felicity," as Swift was to name it, "called the Possession of being well deceived; the Serene Peaceful State of being a Fool among Knaves." Cynthia contemplates the "'Happiness" of such a state, but she has no choice but to reject it. Like Mellefont and Careless, she has too much moral sense to join the Knaves and too much intelligence for the fools. Lord Rochester expressed dilemma perfectly for his age:

> Mankind's dishonest, if you think it fair,
> Amongst known Cheats, to play upon the square,
> You'le be undone. . . .
> Nor can weak truth, your reputation save,
> The knaves, will all agree to call you Knave.
> Wrong'd shall he live insulted o're, opprest,
> Who dares be less a Villain, than the rest.[4]

Those who represent the ideal in The Double Dealer dare "be less a Villain than the rest." They too play their roles in the comedy, but Cynthia and Mellefont are treated at times with a solemnity that seems to suit more with sentimental comedy than with the witty comedy of the Restoration.

I   An Experiment in Comedy

It is apparent that The Double Dealer was experimental in form and content. The serious tone bears some resemblance to Molière's Tartuffe, and the explanations offered by Molière or one of his disciples in the "Letter on The Imposter" are useful for approaching Congreve's play. The author of the "Letter" argued that ridicule and the ridiculous are the keys to understanding comedy: "Now, as good sense produces in the soul a pleasure mingled with esteem, the ridiculous produces there a pleasure mingled with contempt, because all knowledge which comes to the soul necessarily produces in the judgment a feeling of esteem or of contempt." We judge the ridiculous by a knowledge of "good sense, the default of which it signifies." Through an understanding of decorum and proportion, which are aspects of good sense, we can understand that "incongruity or disproportion," which are the essence of the ridiculous.

Like Tartuffe, Maskwell and Brisk become ridiculous by the distinction between their inner reality and outward appearance: "The reason is that if the ridiculous consists in some incongruity, it follows that all lies, all concealment, deceit, dissimulation, all outward appearance different from reality, all contrariety between actions which stem from a same principle, is essentially ridiculous." And our reaction to such a spectacle on the stage precludes all compassion because ridicule is "the coldest of all the sentiments."[5] We feel contempt, and with it comes the sense of pleasure that has its root in our pride and our complaisance with the ills of others.

Whether Congreve was familiar with the "Letter" or not, he followed a similar pattern. With the exception of Cynthia, Mellefont, and Careless, the rest of the characters seem ridiculous both in their grotesque plotting and passions and in their folly. And Cynthia, more than Mellefont or Careless, is the center of good sense. Mellefont is not a fool, but he is tricked; and, next to Maskwell's, his plots appear naïve. Careless is forced to act a role as a foolish lover; and even his awareness of his situation, his informing the audience that he is barely able to refrain from laughter as he makes love to Lady Plyant, does not protect him from the ridiculous. But Cynthia is never ridiculous. We laugh with her, not at her, as she comments with wit and sensibility on the fools at Lord Touchwood's house; and, when good sense triumphs at the end, it is perhaps even more a triumph for Cynthia than for Mellefont.

The Double Dealer appears to end like a fairy tale. Lord Touchwood joins the hands of the lovers and wishes them "Unwearied Nights, and wishing Days . . . ; mutual Love, lasting Health, and circling Joys" for the rest of their long lives. But the speaker also warns against treachery, and he has been deceived by a vicious wife. He speaks to an audience of cuckolds, seducers, and, to use Collier's term, "Whores." Lord Touchwood and Lord Froth have just discovered their true condition. Cynthia's father, Sir Paul Plyant, remains in supreme ignorance of his wife's activities, but only by what must be an immense effort at self-delusion.

Collier was surely correct in seeing Congreve's play as a commentary on a world full of deceit and evil; and Congreve must take responsibility for his bitter and cynical vision. The marriage of Mellefont and Cynthia may succeed, but the world in which they have to act out their parts affords no comfort whatsoever.

II The Games People Play

At several points in the play the lovers confront the problems they must face, and Cynthia reveals genuine doubts about their future marriage:

> *Cynt.* I'm thinking, tho' Marriage makes Man and Wife one Flesh, it leaves 'em still two Fools; and they become more conspicuous by setting off one another.
> *Mel.* That's only when two Fools meet, and their Follies are oppos'd.
> *Cynt.* Nay, I have known two Wits meet, and by the Opposition of their Wit, render themselves as ridiculous as Fools. 'Tis an odd Game we're going to play at; What think you of drawing Stakes, and giving over in time?
> *Mel.* No, hang't, that's not endeavouring to win, because 'tis possible we may lose; since we have shuffled and cut, let's e'en turn up Trump now.
> *Cynt.* Then I find it's like Cards, if either of us have a good Hand it is an Accident of Fortune.
> *Mel.* No, Marriage is rather like a Game at Bowls, Fortune indeed makes the Match, and the two nearest, sometimes the two farthest are together, but the Game depends entirely upon Judgement.
> *Cynt.* Still it is a Game, and consequently one of us must be a loser.
> *Mel.* Not at all; only a friendly Trial of Skill, and the Winnings to be laid out in an Entertainment. (II, iii, 2-26)

In this "play on words," the two lovers attempt to define love and marriage in terms of various kinds of play. As Johan Huizinga points out in *Homo Ludens,* the decision to engage in play is a rational and voluntary commitment to participate in the irrational. Play can be extremely serious, and it always includes a rigid set of rules, ones which cannot be broken without destroying the entire basis of the game. Cynthia objects to the rules of the game because they are sometimes undignified and because sometimes one of the players refuses to follow the rules. She feels there is not enough allowance for skill and that there must be a loser. Mellefont, who denies that marriage is entirely a game of chance, argues that a true lover returns his winnings. All of this dialogue on games is contained within a contest of wit

which reaffirms their love by revealing their mutual intelligence
and understanding.

Interestingly enough, this exchange is interrupted by the entry
of the musicians to sing a song reminding Cynthia of time and
the intrusion of life on play. Where there is no commitment, there
can be no victory in either games or the real world. And the
song of the musicians also reminds Cynthia that, whether judgment or chance rules the game of love and marriage, the emotional and passionate side of her nature cannot be denied. When
Cynthia later returns to the game image in connection with their
private relations, she compares Mellefont and herself to a team
who become so involved with the other contestants that they
forget the rules of their private game. She cannot see how they
will come together and make a "Match": "My Mind gives me it
won't—because we are both willing; we each of us strive to reach
the Goal, and hinder one another in the Race; I swear it never
does well when the Parties are so agreed—For when People walk
Hand in Hand, there's neither overtaking nor meeting: We Hunt
in Couples where we both pursue the same Game, but forget
one another; and 'tis because we are so near that we don't think
of coming together" (IV, ii, 12-20). But Mellefont, who picks
up the hunting image, insists that the game is in their "Power"
and that, since they are marrying for "Love, Love, down-right
very villainous Love," they may marry no matter what may
happen. Even Cynthia is partly carried away by such a romantic
confession.

But she insists on a trial of Mellefont's wit before she consents
to "die in a Ditch" for pure love. He must demonstrate his ability
to plot; he must prove that the game is indeed one of skill and
that he is an able player. If he loses because of "Chance, or
Destiny, or unlucky Stars, or any thing but the very Devil," she
will refuse to marry him, though she promises not to marry anyone
else. Of course, Cynthia is being witty at the expense of the usual
excuses of lovers; but she is perfectly serious at the moment about
her test of Mellefont's wit. If marriage is truly a game of skill,
he must demonstrate that he has the ability to cope with the tides
of fortune that afflict and destroy most marriages. Her resolution
shows wit and intelligence, but Cynthia is not a heroine to resist
love. She agrees to run off with Mellefont against "Reason it self"
even before that "very Devil," Maskwell, and his fellow villian,
Lady Touchwood, are unmasked as human devils, just as capable
of falling by their own plots and passions as Mellefont.

The ending is somewhat undramatic, but it does make Con-

greve's point. If the honest Mellefont is no match for the knaves
by himself, he has Cynthia and Careless to aid him, while Maskwell, acting without the benefit of friendship or love, plays a
solitary and overly complicated game. The moral is directed
against "*secret Villany,*" a topic appropriate enough for a play so
involved with concealment and mask. In a complicated conversation with Mellefont, Careless maintains that women at a
masquerade use their masks to disguise both their appearance
and inclinations, but his friend disagrees: "'Tis a Mistake, for
Women may most properly be said to be unmask'd when they
wear Visors; for that secures them from Blushing, and being out
of Countenance, and next to being in the Dark, or alone, they
are most truly themselves in a Vizor Mask" (III, iv, 54-59).
Maskwell makes the same observation when he boasts that he
will deceive Mellefont by telling the truth, adding the moral
tag: "*No Mask like open Truth to cover Lies, / As to go Naked is
the best Disguise*" (V, iii, 18-19). Nature itself was a disguise
concealing the dance of atoms or the Cartesian vortex, and it is
significant that Maskwell's plots are discovered when he makes
the mistake of using a parson's gown as a prop in his final
strategem. As long as he relied on the deceit inherent in nature
itself, he was successful.

III   The Fools

Although the intrigues of Maskwell against Mellefont occupy
most of *The Double Dealer,* the characters who give the play
its comic force are the fools. Congreve might have followed
contemporary practice by creating a double plot: one for the
serious characters, and another for the fools; but he preferred to
follow French practice and retain the unity of action. As a
result, the play gives the impression of serious characters moving
through a world of fools. Without making the mistake of attempting to reform her "silly" father, Cynthia laments her lot:

'Tis not so hard to counterfeit Joy in the Depth of Affliction, as to
dissemble Mirth in Company of Fools—Why should I call 'em Fools?
The World thinks better of 'em; for these have Quality and Education,
Wit and fine Conversation, are receiv'd and admir'd by the World—
if not, they like and admire themselves—And Why is not that true
Wisdom, for 'tis Happiness: And for ought I know we have misapply'd
the Name all this while, and mistaken the Thing: Since
    If Happiness in Self-content is plac'd,
   The Wise are Wretched, and Fools only Bless'd.
               (III, xii, 12-13)

The end of the play rejects Cynthia's paradox. True happiness is attainable only by the intelligent and honest; the happiness achieved by the fools at Lord Touchwood's is based on a ridiculous and blinding self-love.

In one of the best scenes of the play, Lord Froth and Lady Froth exchange extravagant compliments and expressions of love. Lady Froth asks her husband to show how wonderful he looked when she once gave him her picture, but lacking a picture, she gives him a mirror. He covers it with kisses, explaining "I saw my self there, and kiss'd it for your sake"; and, after this incredible display of narcissism, he turns to Cynthia and asks:

> *Ld. Froth.* Don't you think us a happy Couple?
> *Cynt.* I vow, my Lord, I think you the happiest Couple in the World, for you're not only happy in one another, and when you are together, but happy in your selves, and by your selves.
> *Ld. Froth.* I hope Mellefont will make a good Husband too.
> *Cynt.* 'Tis my Interest to believe he will my Lord.
> *Ld. Froth.* D'ye think he'll Love you as well as I do my Wife? I'm afraid not.
> *Cynt.* I believe he'll love me better.
> *Ld. Froth.* Heav'ns! that can never be; but why do you think so?
> *Cynt.* Because he has not so much reason to be fond of himself.
> (II, ii, 38-52)

Lady Froth boasts of her affection for her husband in public and sends for her child seven times a day to coo over "little Sappho," who can already sing a song; but even her affair with Brisk is motivated by self-love.

The trouble is that such an extreme self-love makes real love impossible. Lord and Lady Froth and Brisk form a self-admiration circle which feeds on a steady diet of mutual compliments; they have each other to tell how wonderful they are, and who is more to be trusted for a true opinion of one's worth than a circle of one's friends? They all affect wit, though Lord Froth's wit is limited to a pretense at humorlessness while, in fact, he laughs at the silliest remarks. Brisk and Lady Froth play with equal folly at critic and poetess. As Jean Bellegarde remarked at the time, by rendering our faults imperceptible and magnifying our merits, self-love makes us appear ridiculous to others.[6]

But Congreve was not merely presenting a gallery of fools in the manner of Durfey; he was making a statement about folly. Where there is not intelligence enough to govern the passions, Congreve's fools slip into levity and sexual promiscuity. Brisk's wit is reducible to what he calls his "Parts": "Pox on't, why should

I disparage my Parts by thinking what to say? None but dull
Rogues *think;* witty Men, like rich Fellows, are always ready
for all Expences; while your Blockheads, like poor needy Scoun-
drels, are forced to examine their Stock, and forecast the Changes
of the Day" (IV, v, 10-16). Thus self-assured, he reveals his
"violent Passion" for Lady Froth, who, when convinced that
Brisk means it "seriously," confesses her own "violent Passion."
This love making is communicated through a parody of a witty
literary interchange, and Congreve seems to suggest that, although true wit has nothing to do with licentiousness, what passes
for wit is often a back door to promiscuity. Part of the irony of
the conclusion of the play is that Lord Touchwood's blessings
on Mellefont and Cynthia's marriage are heard by Lord Froth,
who has just discovered that the wife, whom he had regarded as
an object to flatter his ego, has been admiring the stars while
lying on her back—and with Brisk as her instructor.

Whereas Lord Froth is bitter against his wife, Sir Paul and
Lady Plyant are a different kind of couple—the gullible and happy
cuckold and his loose wife, who is virtuous only to her husband.
These characters appear in their archetypal state in Etherege's
Sir Oliver and Lady Cockwood in *She Would If She Could*
(1668). Sir Paul is not made to wear a penitential suit by his
spouse, but he is swaddled in blankets, "like a Russian Bear upon
a drift of Snow," so as not to disturb his wife's sleep. Lady Plyant,
who accepted Sir Paul only after a nine-year courtship, has
intercourse with him only when she fears she may be pregnant
by one of her lovers. She has chosen to play the psychological
game which Eric Berne has called "Frigid Woman," a game less
rare than might be supposed.[7] Such a game usually involves
shame and concealment on the part of the husband, but Sir Paul
is so proud of his wife that he tells his sad story to everyone he
meets. That he is capable of believing Lady Plyant a paragon
even when she is obviously flirting with Careless shows how far
his voluntary blindness functions as a protection for his self-love
and sanity.

Because Congreve's art is mimetic rather than farcical and
because, like Fondlewife, Sir Paul is human, we tend to feel some
concern for his plight; but our ridicule chokes off the greater part
of it. His myopia is deliberate, his folly grotesque, and his condition not uncommon; for he conceives himself happy so long
as he knows nothing of his wife's duplicity. "Ay, truly, Mr.
Careless, my Lady is a great Blessing," says Sir Paul, "fine, discreet, well-spoken Woman as you shall see—If it becomes me to

say so; and we live very comfortably together; she is a little hasty sometimes, and so am I; but mine's soon over, and then I'm so sorry—O, Mr. Careless, if it were but for one thing—" (II, vi, 74-80). Sir Paul weeps as he tells his desire to have a son, and in this instance he, who allows his wife to read his mail before himself and to give him a small allowance, might indeed appear sympathetic; but sympathy is impossible in the presence of such folly. We may regard his psychological failure with some pity, yet his boast that the Plyants are "distinguish'd by a languishing Eye" is anything but laughable; for he warns Cynthia the next moment against following Lady Plyant's "rash Resolution" taken on her wedding night to die a maid.

As for Lady Plyant, her aversion to her husband is compensated for by her willingness to accept either Mellefont or Careless as her lover without distinguishing very much between them. As Lord Touchwood replies to his wife's insistence that her sister-in-law's "Honour is very well known," "Yes, I believe I know some that have been familiarly acquainted with it." Lady Plyant is comic because, in her desire to insist on her innocence, she continually slips into double entendres which proclaim her eagerness for a liaison. She too is carried away by self-love, for she is all too willing to believe that Mellefont has an irresistible passion for her and that the whining love speeches of Careless are both sincere and genteel. Acting the part of the indignant wife to the hilt, she plays a larger role in clearing herself from the charge of infidelity than does Laetitia in *The Old Batchelor.* Sir Paul thanks Providence for discovering her liaison with Careless, but Providence will hardly repair his damaged ego; and he is only too happy to thank Providence once more when Careless proclaims that Lady Plyant's "Virtue is impregnable." Indeed her virtue, if she ever had any, might have been.

IV *The Knaves*

If Collier, given his moral outlook, found an immoral basis to this play, surely he had reason. The only Providence that Sir Paul can thank is one which keeps fools ignorant, believing; and, therefore, content. When Sir Paul is informed by his sister, Lady Touchwood, that he is both a cuckold and a fool, he cannot understand what she means. Their confrontation brings together two of the vital elements in the play—the knave and the fool:

L. *Touch.* Hear me; consent to the breaking off this Marriage, and the promoting any other, without consulting me, and I'll renounce all

blood, all Relation and Concern with you for ever,—nay, I'll be your
Enemy, and pursue you to Destruction, I'll tear your Eyes out, and
tread you under my Feet—

Sir Paul. Why, what's the Matter now? Good Lord, what's all this
for? Pooh, here's a Joke indeed—Why, where's my Wife?

L. Touch. With Careless, in the close Arbour; he may want you by
this time, as much as you want her.

Sir Paul. O, if she be with Mr. Careless, 'tis well enough.

L. Touch. Fool, Sot, insensible Ox! But remember what I said to
you, or you had better eat your own Horns, by this Light you had.

Sir Paul. You're a passionate Woman, Gadsbud,—But to say truth,
all our Family are Cholerick; I am the only peaceable Person among
'em. (V, ix, 22-43)

Nothing subjects the ranting Lady Touchwood more to the
ridiculous than her contact with her foolish brother.

Lady Touchwood is not very different in makeup from the
strong, vicious women of contemporary tragedy—Racine's Phèdre
and Roxana in Nathaniel Lee's *The Rival Queens,* Dryden's
Nourmahal in *Aurengzebe*—who attempt to seduce their foster
sons. Women of this type are shown as changing from passionate
love to deadly hatred, which appears psychologically unsound
to a modern audience; but the change was perfectly in keeping
with the then contemporary theory that the two passions were
closely connected. Congreve was not the first to introduce this
type into a comedy—Durfey and Shadwell preceded him—but he
was the first to take her seriously.[8] Lady Touchwood is only one
of the women who dominate the world of *The Double Dealer.*
It is Cynthia who is strong, not Mellefont, who, for all Congreve's protests to the contrary, is too easily gulled; and both
Lady Froth and Lady Plyant dominate their husbands mercilessly.
Neither Brisk nor Careless nor even Maskwell, the only strong
male force in the play, can be regarded as seducers; they are,
instead, somewhat ineffectual instruments of sex-starved women.

Ruled by her passions, Lady Touchwood vents them the only
way she can—verbally. She would exceed the bounds of her
bodily strength and makes the absurd boast to Mellefont, "I'll
hold my Breath and die, but I'll be free" (IV, xviii, 25-26). She
threatens to destroy Sir Paul in five different ways; but, when she
actually picks up a dagger against Maskwell, she quickly and in-
effectually lays it aside. This woman, who longs for power beyond
anything permissible or possible in her environment and who finds
herself limited to menaces and deceit was, as suggested, a stage
type; but she was also Congreve's quintessential woman.[9] In a

tragedy, she can gain the dignity of a terrible death after having destroyed a number of her enemies; in a comedy, she can merely turn on herself and the world in her frustration and desire for revenge. Like Shadwell's Mrs. Termagant, she demands pity because she has been wronged from birth by being a woman.[10] Lady Touchwood regards herself with deadly seriousness; she becomes an object of ridicule because in the comic world of manners her words, unmatched by her actions, appear absurd. As Baudelaire once observed, comedy is not in the subject but in the spectator.[11]

Maskwell is even a more problematic character than Lady Touchwood; but also a type borrowed from tragedies and heroic plays, he is reminiscent of Durfey's comic plotter, Cunnington, in *The Richmond Heiresss* (1693) and of the Machiavellian Ismael in Southerne's *Loyal Brother* (1682). (Betterton, who played the part of Maskwell, had become as famous for such roles as Mrs. Barry was for parts like Mrs. Touchwood.) Maskwell may best be described as an Iago in a comedy; and, like Iago, he must be convincing enough to deceive people who are neither stupid nor unperceptive. Maskwell loses at the end only because he has a weakness—a passion for Cynthia, the one innocent woman in the play. Like Claggart in Melville's *Billy Budd,* Maskwell is attracted by virtue, one which he could only destroy in the possessing. Unfortunately, his soliloquy on his love has the impersonal accent of the stage Machiavel:

Duty to Kings, Piety to Parents, Gratitude to Benefactors and Fidelity to Friends, are different and particular Ties: But the Name of Rivals cuts 'em all asunder, and is a general Acquittance—Rival is equal, and Love like Death an universal Leveller of Mankind. Ha! But is there not such a Thing as Honesty? Yes, and whosoever has it about him, bears an Enemy in his Breast: For your honest Man, as I take it, is that nice scrupulous, conscientious Person, who will cheat no Body but himself; such another Coxcomb, as your wise Man, who is too hard for all the World, and will be made a Fool of by no Body, but himself: Ha, ha, ha. Well for Wisdom and Honesty, give me Cunning and Hypocrisie; oh, 'tis such a Pleasure, to angle for fair fac'd Fools! Then that hungry Gudgeon Credulity, will bite at any thing—Why, let me see, I have the same Face, the same Words and Accents, when I speak what I do not think—the very same—and dear Dissimulation is the only Art, not to be known from Nature. (II, vii, 9-31)

Congreve never displays such banality in his dialogues; Maskwell's soliloquies are artistic failures. Clenches like "cuts . . .

asunder," "universal Leveller," and excessive alliteration such as "fair fac'd Fools" combine with occasional Shakespearean echoes to vitiate an interesting statement. The reason "dear Dissimulation" is indistinguishable from "Nature" is because Maskwell's "Nature" is equivalent to that of the Hobbists—a state of war.

Fortunately, unlike Lady Touchwood, Maskwell is not carried away by his own rhetoric; and his use of words is usually more precise. His analysis of Lady Touchwood's reasons for becoming his mistress is as pointedly accurate as his profession of honest love is subtle. "O Maskwell," says Lady Touchwood, "in vain I do disguise me from thee, thou know'st me, knowest the very inmost Windings and Recesses of my Soul" (I, vi, 110-12). Because he understands her love-hate relation with Mellefont and the sensuality that controls her passions, Maskwell is capable of handling his violent mistress. Whereas Lady Touchwood rants and blusters, Maskwell revels in a vivid and subtle language of deception; and he convinces her that he is doing everything for her sake. "I that had wanton'd in the rich Circle of your World of Love," he asks rhetorically, "cou'd be confin'd within the puny Province of a Girl? No" (V, xviii, 61-63). The tactile image comparing intercourse with a woman and a girl, subtle and distinct as it is, has in it the power to appeal to what Lady Touchwood must still believe to be her fatal charms.

At the end, Maskwell goes off without even Iago's renunciation of speech. When exposed, evil collapses into absurdity; and the fabric of plot and deceit created by Maskwell dissolves into nothing. For Maskwell is but a servant, and his advancement to the position of heir to Lord Touchwood and possible husband to Cynthia depends entirely on Lord Touchwood's admiration for a man who seems to put principle before friendship. Because Maskwell's downfall might arouse pity, Congreve makes the final scene of his disgrace anticlimatic by putting it after the entry of the two comic cuckolds, Lord Froth and Sir Paul, followed by the entire company. Lord Froth has just had an awakening to his wife's infidelity, which comes as he listens to the idiotic ramblings of Sir Paul and sees his wife enter with Brisk. The dialogue reverts to the nonsense of compliment and flattery, and the spirit of comedy once more dominates the spirit of intrigue. Lord Touchwood, who delivers the final speech, is no fool; but he too is a cuckold. If horns must be worn by wise and foolish alike, then what chance have Mellefont and Cynthia? Congreve ends with a wish and a moral: the moral that "*secret Villany*" will not succeed may be deduced from the play, but the wish that the lovers will find ideal happiness in marriage finds little support in the world of *The Double Dealer*.

V   *The Rules and Satire*

Congreve's play might have been better off with a bitter, satiric ending; but the real difficulty was that Congreve was trying to encompass too much. In addition to creating a comedy of the ridiculous which contrasted fools and knaves, he also attempted a correct neo-Classical comedy and a witty satire. The results pleased the *cognoscenti* but disappointed the general audience. In the anonymous *A Comparison between the Two Stages* (1702), Critick argues that *The Double Dealer* is Congreve's most regular, correct, and best play, but Sullen tells him that such a judgment is "against the Opinion of all the Town."[12] Congreve himself was outspoken in his defense of the play; in his dedication to Charles Montague he refers to it as "a true and regular Comedy" and quotes Horace on the work of art which is inimitable: "My aim shall be poetry so moulded from the familiar that anybody may hope for the same success, may sweat much and yet toil in vain when attempting the same.[13] Although Congreve confesses that the play is not *entirely* successful, such self-depreciation, as Dr. Johnson remarked of Swift, is actually a profession of achievement.

What Congreve meant by a "regular" comedy went far beyond any adherence to the unities of time, place, and action; for the "rules" allowed considerable latitude. He adopted the French practice of having one scene smoothly slide into another without ever leaving the stage empty. D'Aubignac had exalted this "union of presence" to the position of a fourth unity; instead of taking the allowable twenty-four hours, Congreve followed D'Aubignac's suggestion that three hours was more in keeping with verisimilitude. The argument was that, since art was imitation, it was best when it most resembled life; therefore, as little as possible was to be done to "deceive the imagination." There was to be no compression or expansion of time on the stage, and the playwright's ability to maneuver time was considered an excellence in itself. The theory seems to depend mainly on a concept of the importance of compression in a work of art, but there is some suggestion of an esthetic of difficulty; for the craft of the artist is shown in his capacity to shape the action of the play within a narrow time scheme without doing violence to probability. Though Congreve states that this kind of "Me-

chanical" excellence is merely equivalent to following the rules
laid down for building a house on a model or for arranging
flowers for a gardener, the comparisons to skilled craftsmen are
hardly derogatory.[14]

Congreve also defends his artistry on the questions of the moral
and his use of soliloquies, both along rigid neo-Classical lines. The
moral, he argues, was conceived first and then the fable was
constructed around it. This process is recommended by the French
critic, Le Bossu, whom Brisk mentions with seeming familiarity
but with obvious ignorance. Unfortunately, the true moral of *The
Double Dealer* is not at all clear; and the tag moral, that secret
treachery will always out—like such a moral in one of Berthold
Brecht's plays—presents more problems than it solves. Many
contemporaries felt that Le Bossu's theory was silly, since arguing
that the *Iliad* had the same moral as one of Aesop's fables said
nothing about Homer's masterpiece; Congreve's critical franco-
philia did him a disservice at this point.[15]

Far more sensible is Congreve's defense of the soliloquy on
grounds of artistic pragmatism. The soliloquy is the only way in
which the playwright can transmit the inner thoughts of a
man who is unable to communicate his secrets to another
character; "and to that end [he] is forc'd to make use of the
Expedient of Speech, no other better way being yet invented
for the Communication of Thought" (I, 115). Una Ellis-Fermor
has argued that the comic art of the Restoration differed from
that of other theaters in finding its signifiance in a world of
words rather than one of silences, gestures, and action.[16] Though
this observation is not always true of Congreve, it is of *The
Double Dealer*. Had not D'Aubignac insisted that there could
be no inarticulate expression on the stage even when the subject
matter involved the inarticulate?[17] In this most correct of Congreve's plays, he relies on language: characters create themselves
as they speak; action is cut to a minimum; confined space governs
movement. Congreve did not impose French critical rules on his
play; the play is inseparable from the rules.[18]

Congreve said that his comedy was not only "regular" but
also "true," but what he meant by "true" is more difficult to dis-
cern. For example, Congreve departed from French criticism in
allowing Lady Touchwood to handle a dagger and threaten
suicide. D'Aubignac had agreed with Julius Scaliger's criticism
of Plautus for just such an action "because that is an undertaking too generous for the *Comick* Theatre."[19] But the English
critics leaned toward a more serious attitude toward comedy

than the French, who regarded it as a debased form. In his *Gentleman's Journal,* Motteux praised comedy as a more realistic form than tragedy and hence more of "a just Representation of Nature," which was the very end of the drama.[20] And a few years later in a preface to a translation of Terence, Laurence Echard praised the Roman playwright for his seriousness and recommended that modern writers emulate him. He also compared modern English comedies with those of the ancients, remarking that "Our *Comedies* excel his in some Delicasies of Conversation; particularly in the Refinedness of our Railery and Satyr, and above all in Repartee."[21] Certainly there is some of Terence's subdued tone in *The Double Dealer,* and the addition of a quotation from Terence's *Self-Tormentor* on the title page of the 1710 edition is significant—not so much of an influence as of the fact that Congreve took his comedy seriously.[22]

For this reason, Congreve's defense of "the Satire of this *Comedy*" in his mocking address to the female audience is important:

They are concerned that I have represented some Women Vicious and Affected: How can I help it? It is the Business of a Comick Poet to paint the Vices and Follies of Human-kind; and there are but two Sexes, Male, and Female, *Men,* and *Women,* which have a Title to humanity: And if I leave one half of them out, the Work will be imperfect. I should be very glad of an Opportunity to make my Compliment to those Ladies who are offended: But they can no more expect it in a Comedy, than to be Tickled by a Surgeon, when he's letting 'em Blood. (I, 116-17)

That the writer of comedy served as a satirist was, of course, one of the common justifications of the form; and Congreve inherited from Shadwell a tradition of realistic satire which he shared with even so undistinguished a playwright as Thomas Durfey. The ladies were offended, but Congreve was fair in saying they are treated no worse than the men. And the foolish men and women, who are so severely satirized, can be satiric themselves. All join in the scandalous conversation about Lady Toothless who is "always ready to laugh when Sneer offers to speak . . . with her Gums bare, and her Mouth open," or about the lady whose beard bristles through her makeup. Cynthia may lament the conversation, but she does not deny its vividness. Even a fool may be amusing on some subjects; and, if Congreve denies these people true wit, he does give them a sense of the grotesque.

In this "true" satiric comedy, then, Congreve creates three worlds: a verbal world of grotesque realism, one of high comedy and wit, and another of genuine evil suggested by chthonic imagery. The play was, as F. W. Bateson argues, an exciting "experiment"; but this statement is merely another way of saying that the result was an exciting failure. Never again would Congreve create such sparkling fools as the Plyants and the Froths, and never again would he write such brilliant satire; but he never quite succeeded in bringing all the disparate elements in the play together. After *The Double Dealer,* he mitigated his satire and reduced the proportions of those characters representing the forces of evil—reduced them enough, at least, to fit them more successfully into his comic world.

CHAPTER 6

Love For Love: *The Lunatic and the Lover*

> Valentine in Love for Love is (if I may so call him)
> the Hero of the Play; this Spark the Poet would pass
> for a Person of Virtue, but he speaks too late. 'Tis
> true, he was hearty in his Affection to Angelica. Now
> without Question, to be in Love with a fine Lady
> of Thirty Thousand Pounds is a great Virtue! But
> then abating this single Commendation, Valentine is
> altogether compounded of Vice. He is a prodigal
> Debauchee, Unnatural and Profane, Obscene, Sawcy,
> and Undutiful; and yet this Libertine is crown'd for
> the Man of Merit, has his Wishes thrown in his Lap,
> and makes the Happy *Exit*. I perceive we should
> have a rare Set of Virtues if these Poets had the
> making of them! . . . To sum up the Evidence. A
> fine Gentleman, is a fine Whoring, Swearing, Smutty,
> Atheistical Man.
>
> Jeremy Collier, A *Short View of the
> Immorality and Profaneness of the
> English Stage*.[1]

A typical opening for a Restoration comedy reveals the rake-
hero reading a volume of Lucretius or Epicurus and
expounding on Libertine themes. "Thou great Lucretius! Thou
profound Oracle of Wit and Sence!" exclaims Bruce at the start
of Shadwell's *Virtuoso*. Shadwell eventually reforms his libertine,
and, except for this apostrophe to Lucretius, it would be difficult
on the basis of his actions in the play to detect that he was
either a wit or a debauchee. Congreve's opening to *Love for Love*
is a notable reversal of the convention; Valentine, who has been
reading the stoic philosopher Epictetus, preaches a mocking anti-
Epicurean sermon to his servant, Jeremy: "Read, read, Sirrah, and
refine your Appetite; learn to live upon Instruction; feast your
Mind, and mortifie your Flesh." Jeremy's reply is pragmatic and
practical: none of the stoics or cynics, or even Plato, will help
Valentine pay his debts. Valentine, however, insists that his
poverty will not prevent his loving Angelica even more than when

107

he was wealthy enough to compete with the rich fops surrounding
her. "So shall my Poverty be a Mortification to her Pride," he
continues," and perhaps, make her compassionate the Love, which
has principally reduc'd me to this Lowness of Fortune." The
combination is curious—philosophy, wit, and passion. But to Congreve these were the qualities of an ideal comic hero, however
immoral and unchristian Jeremy Collier may have thought him.

I   Romantic and Satiric Themes

The outlines of Congreve's play Love for Love bear some
resemblance to the famous story from Boccaccio's Decameron
in which the hero impoverishes himself for love of a wealthy
lady; has to withdraw to a farm without even the slightest
acknowledgment that she is aware of his existence; sacrifices his
last possession, a falcon, to feed her when she comes to ask a
favor; and finally is rewarded by her love.[2] So Valentine ruins
himself for love of Angelica, gives up all as a final gesture of
despair over losing her, and gains her in the end. The details
are very different, but the substance, with its emphasis on true
gentility, is the same; the resemblance suggests the romance foun-
dation on which Congreve is constructing his satire. We are
most aware of it at the end, when Angelica matches Valentine's
moving confession of love with her own praise of Valentine's
generosity, but we are always aware that Valentine is capable
of intense passion and of acting upon it. He was a libertine,
remains a wit, and is capable of true love. Like Mellefont, he is
also capable of being victimized and deceived, but in Congreve's scheme of things, this vulnerability is a minor drawback.

That Congreve should have stressed the satiric elements in
his most romantic play may appear curious, but in the prologue
he begins by speaking of Love for Love in terms of a varied
comic feast with "Humour" and "Plot," but of the chief ingredient
as satire:

> We've something too, to gratifie ill Nature,
> (If there be any here) and that is Satire.
> Tho' Satire scarce dares grin, 'tis grown so mild
> Or shews its Teeth, as if it smil'd
> As Asses Thistles, Poets mumble Wit,
> And dare not bite, for fear of being bit.

Congreve proceeds to lament the demise of satire since Wycherley's Manly in The Plain Dealer lashed the age, and he clearly
conceives of satire in terms of direct invective, such as that

delivered by a constantly satiric spokesman—a misanthrope like Manly or personified figures like Folly or Truth. Congreve's very imagery refers to the hieroglyph of satire with its smiling face, ass's ears, and lash. Although it seems fair enough to allow Congreve some knowledge of his intention, the question of what the satire is all about remains.

When *Love for Love* was revived in 1965 by the National Theatre of England, many critics felt that heavy sociological overtones had been added to the play and regretted the passing of the stylized production in the 1940's with John Gielgud, which had taken Lamb's concept of the artificiality of Restoration comedy as a starting point for a vision of a world which had existed only in the elaborate imagination of those playwrights. Confronted with a realistic interpretation and with sets determinedly placing the play in the late seventeenth century, the critics of the 1960's discovered that it was far more materialistic than they had supposed. Penelope Gilliat, who thought it should be renamed "Love for Loot," probably was unaware that, seven years before Congreve's play was produced at Lincoln's Inn Fields Theatre, Durfey had already written a play called *Love for Money* (1689) and that Congreve may have been echoing Durfey's title.[3]

A comparison of the two plays is enlightening. Whereas Durfey presents a situation involving a general chase after an heiress of fifty thousand pounds—a girl who is still in a boarding school among her fellow "Romps," girls just entering puberty—Congreve reduces the fortune of his heiress, gives her maturity and intelligence, and reserves the adolescent role for Miss Prue. Moreover, Durfey's play has a burlesque quality and a wryness not found in Congreve. As absurd as Congreve's Miss Prue is, she is not so off-color as Durfey's Molly and Jenny, who at thirteen and a half have just discovered sex and cannot tell whether or not it is as interesting as cheesecakes and custard. At one point in Durfey's play there is a dialogue of sensibility between the hero, Young Meriton, and the heiress, Mirtilla, over the question of love without money. She is ignorant of her fortune, though he is not; and, when he mendaciously urges her to marry him and live in poverty, she exclaims:

'Tis not for my own sake that I deny, but Sir for yours; if we were married, perhaps I should love ye, nay love ye dearly; perhaps have children too, some half a dozen pretty smiling Blessings to cling around and help Life's tedious Journey with the dear nonsense of their prating Stories. But should the freezing hand of Want afflict us, what should we do, but sit by our small fire, Tears in our Eyes and throbbing Griefs at Heart, to see our little Flock of unfledg'd *Cupids*, shivering with Cold as wanting necessaries, who looking wishly on us seem to say, why would you marry thus to make us miserable.[4]

Though he may have agreed with the idea behind it, Congreve wisely chose to avoid such appeals to sentimentality. Yet Durfey's play is actually far more bitter: the two schoolgirls, Molly and Jenny, are dragged away by their seducers (one of the girls symbolically drops her doll), while Young Meriton deceives Mirtilla to get her fortune. For all its farcical comedy, Durfey's play is about the rape of innocence, but Congreve's is about what the title suggests: love for the sake of love. That some men might marry strictly for money was the immediate context of his play; that Valentine should act unwisely and still find his reward is the beautiful, satisfying fairy tale which Congreve serves as a delightful feast.

The satire, then, is not concerned with the problem of love for money, but with the entire context of social action; and, for this purpose, Congreve creates a cast of satiric figures. Valentine's friend, Scandal, is actually a "plain dealer," who is cynical about all human motivation, particularly that of women. Valentine's servant, Jeremy Fetch, regards the social world of his master with much the same skepticism and pragmatism with which Henry Straker considers the actions of Jack Tanner in G. B. Shaw's *Man and Superman*. Even the "fools" are capable of satiric invective. Ben is brought in from the sea to present an unworldly but not unperceptive insight into London life, while Prue comes from the country to learn the art of lying and deceit—the art of being a woman in society. Even Tattle has moments of vision, if not of himself, at least of the world around him; and the absurd old men, Sir Sampson and old Foresight, occasionally offer a corrective to the lives of those around them. More than any of Congreve's plays, then, *Love for Love* involves debate and points of view. It would be doing violence to Congreve's art to suggest that it was a play of ideas, but it is one of contrasts and paradoxes.

Some of the ambiguity of *Love for Love* may be due to Congreve's borrowings from Molière's *Don Juan* (1665). In addition to adapting the entire scene involving the attempted gulling of the scrivener, Trapland, Congreve seems to have taken some major hints from that play. What if Don Juan were to reform through true love? What if he were to be seen as a victim rather than as a vicious seducer of everyone in sight? Molière has his hero assume the garb of a hypocrite to fool his enemies and win over his father; Congreve has his hero assume the role of a madman who believes he is Truth. Molière's hero, like Valentine, has almost ruined his father through his debts; but suppose the father were cruel and lacking in understanding? And what if Don Juan had to face a woman like Angelica, witty, sophisticated, and intelligent? Could this experience not save him and reform his life? Need he be led by the Commandant down to hell? Though Don Juan usually acts more like a villain than a hero, more a Maskwell than a Mellefont, Don Juan, like Valentine, serves a satiric function in his attacks on the hypocrisy of the world.

II *Wits and Fools*

But it would be a mistake to regard *Love for Love* in the light of any single influence. The relation between Valentine and Angelica is very much like that between Captain Darewell and Berenice in Durfey's *The Marriage Hater Match'd* (1692); the mad scenes as well as the character of Tattle owe something to Durfey's *The Richmond Heiress* (1693); and the general sophistication of the discussions of sex and seduction are indebted to Southerne's *The Wive's Excuse* (1692). *Love for Love* is almost as derivative as *The Old Batchelor*, but never was a play more Congreve's own.[5] The unique combination of character, language, and plot—all are his. Most of all the wit is pure Congreve, for, while Vanbrugh was often more insightful and Southerne more subtle, no other writer of the time had so much fancy.

Valentine's opening dialogue with Jeremy allows Congreve to display his own and his characters' powers of fancy as his hero suggests that he resolves to rail at the world and to take revenge upon the wits by writing a play, a suggestion which brings forth Jeremy's offer to resign and his brilliant attack on the authors at Will's Coffee House:

I never see it, but the Spirit of Famine appears to me, sometimes like a decay'd Porter, worn out with Pimping, and carrying *Billet doux* and Songs; not like other Porters for Hire, but for the Jests sake. Now like a thin Chairman, melted down to half his Proportion with carrying a Poet upon Tick, to visit some great Fortune; and his Fare to be paid like the Wages of Sin, either at the Day of Marriage, or the Day of Death. . . . Sometimes like a bilk'd Bookseller, with a meagre terrify'd Countenance, that looks as if he had written for himself. . . . And lastly, in the Form of a worn-out Punk, with Verses in her Hand, which her Vanity had preferr'd to Settlements . . . as if she were carrying her Linnen to the Paper-Mill, to be converted into Folio Books

of Warning to all young Maids, not to prefer Poetry to good sense;
or lying in the Arms of a needy Wit, before the Embraces of a wealthy
Fool. (I, i, 108-32)

When Scandal enters a few minutes later to be informed of
Valentine's desire to rail like a satirist in his writings, his
response is in a different style:

Rail? At whom? the whole World? Impotent and vain. Who would die
a Martyr to Sense in a Country where the Religion is Folly? You may
stand at Bay for a while; but when the full Cry is against you, you
shan't have fair play for your Life. If you can't be fairly run down by
the Hounds, you will be treacherously shot by the Huntsmen.—No,
turn Pimp, Flatterer, Quack, Lawyer, Parson, be Chaplain to an
Atheist, or Stallion to an old Woman, any thing but Poet; a Modern
Poet is worse, more servile, timorous, and fawning, than any I have
nam'd: Without you could retrieve the Ancient Honours of the Name,
recall the Stage of Athens, and be allow'd the Force of open honest
Satire. (I, ii, 25-39)

In these passages we have a good example of Bateson's point
concerning Congreve's ability to render each character distinct
with the individual's own words. Jeremy, Rabelaisian and expansive in his satire, begins with a personification of the spirit of
famine, which haunts the world of poetry and wit around Will's;
and he then builds a pattern of related similes, though the porter
and the old prostitute are connected to poetry only through a
fanciful process of association. But this seemingly illogical
process (John Locke called it in his *Essay concerning Human
Understanding* a kind of "madness") allows Jeremy to deliver his
wry warning to Valentine all the more effectively. Jeremy's
wit is both less sharp and more expansive than that of his
betters. Scandal is almost a satirist by profession; in his diatribes
he joins together pimps, quacks, lawyers, parsons, and poets,
implying, by a device that Pope was to use so brilliantly a few
years later, that they are all the same. Scandal's longing to "recall
the Stage of Athens" and with it the strong, personal satire of
Aristophanes is significant; he is all for direct attack and abuse.
Valentine's responses to his servant and friend are pithy and
tend toward understatement. When the crowd of duns is announced below, he merely remarks on the resemblance between
the debtor and the great man who is courted by those seeking
favors. It is left to Scandal to take up the suggestion and to
moralize and apply it to the ways of the world. When in his
pretended madness, he assumes the paradoxical role of Truth,

Valentine also becomes a railer and a satirist; but, as Congreve remarked, by assuming another persona Valentine functions almost as a new character.

Though Jeremy, Valentine, and Scandal are clearly the satirists within the play, the norm from which they satirize the world is not always too clear. Since Valentine has been indiscreet; Jeremy, foolish in remaining with an improverished master; and Scandal, unwise in railing against the evils of the world, their standard can hardly be good sense. Some of the basis for their satirical stance appears in their treatment of Trapland. He is a fool, or at least he is made to seem one; yet he has come, like the other creditors, to collect what is his due. When he finally demands payment, Scandal threatens to make him regurgitate the wine he has drunk at their invitation. To Trapland's protest that he never asked for the wine, Scandal retorts, "And how do you expect to have your Mony again, when a Gentleman has spent it" (I, 228). If the analogy bears little logical connection to the situation, it does convey the contempt of a gentleman for a merchant, a wit for a fool, and a young man for an old one. The standpoint is that of the libertine ethic which regards age as ridiculous and which places a high premium on freedom of spirit and the play of passions. Valentine may be in the process of changing his philosophical position from Epicurus to Epictetus, but there is little sign of it in the play; and he has certainly lost none of his wit in the process. He has few of the conventional virtues of Mellefont. His disgust with Margery, the nurse of his illegitimate boy, for failing to smother him in bed may be part of his witty pose, but it is hardly endearing. If he is rewarded at the end, it is for his generosity and *noblesse*. In short, *Love for Love* uses an aristocratic standard of behavior to belabor its gallery of fools.

But Congreve's gift is to make the world of the fools a very human world. When Tattle enters and is informed that Scandal will never speak well of him, he exclaims with some justification, "How Inhuman!" For, if Tattle is silly with his elaborate pretense at secrecy about his affairs with women, while revealing all, at least his gallery of paintings is composed of portraits of the women he has seduced. Scandal's gallery, on the other hand, has mainly caricatures and what he calls "Hieroglyphics," symbolic representations of the vices, passions, and professions. Scandal and the satirists deal in a non-human world of grotesques; Tattle is a fool, but his folly is human.

The same may be said of Foresight, who is so foolish and

indeed so helpless in his folly as to be a character at whom we laugh without the slightest disapproval, for he transcends moral judgment. He is Congreve's finest "humours" character, for his superstition dominates his entire life, whether as an astrologer or a cuckold. His old nurse treats him like a child as does his wife, whose sleep he has never disturbed in all their years of marriage. Angelica teases him about his cuckolded state, but his anger flares only when he thinks she is insulting the "Celestial Science." Her remarks to her uncle are a good example of the way so much of the play involves a series of extended images on the subject of astrology and (after Ben's entrance) the sea. "I have a mind to go abroad," says Angelica, "and if you won't lend me your Coach, I'll take a Hackney, or a Chair, and leave you to erect a Scheme, and find who's in Conjunction with your Wife. Why don't you keep her at home, if you're jealous of her when she's abroad? You know my Aunt is a little Retrograde (as you call it) in her Nature. Uncle, I'm afraid you are not Lord of the Ascendant, ha, ha, ha" (I, 242). When Foresight becomes angry enough to attempt a witticism on the lack of virgins among the signs of the zodiac, he is so ineffectual that he merely provokes Angelica to genuine laughter.

They are interrupted by the threatening but equally foolish figure of Sir Sampson Legend who, in the extravagant language of a traveler, addresses old Foresight as Nostradamus, Fircu, Albumazar, Haly, and any other astrologer of contemporary books of fortune that pops into his mind. Like old Foresight, Sir Sampson is a "humours" character, reminiscent of Sir Epicure Mammon in Jonson's *Alchemist* in the way ideas seem to grow in his mind and in the way he convinces himself of mad ideas through his own language. He enters with a Hobbesian theory that a child owes his parents a debt for having been conceived by them, rather than owing them obedience because of gratitude —the more customary attitude of the times.[6] Sir Sampson is an egoist; and, as George Meredith suggested, egoism inevitably brings down the imps of laughter. He boasts of his travels, tries to force his sons to actions they find odious, convinces himself that Angelica can find him an attractive man, and boasts of his sexual powers. He is capable of the most servile flattery of Foresight to get him to marry his daughter Prue to Ben, and of deceiving his son with false affection when he thinks him mad. In other words, he is the ideal comic villain—threatening enough to endanger the future of the lovers but foolish enough to make us doubt the possibility of his succeeding.

Suspended somewhere between the wits and the fools is Ben, that "veriest Wag in Nature; an absolute Sea-Wit," as Angelica calls him mockingly. Certainly Ben is not a thorough fool. Though he may be innocent enough to be tricked by Mrs. Frail, even she knows that he will not be overly surprised if he is rejected by her. The fact is that life at sea has completely separated Ben from the other characters socially, morally, and linguistically. His values are relatively simple: "We're merry Folks, we Sailors, we han't much to care for. Thus we live at Sea; eat Bisket, and drink Flip; put on a clean Shirt once a Quarter—Come home, and lye with our Landladies once a Year, get rid of a little Mony; and then put off with the next fair Wind" (III, xv, 89-94). When he attempts to be witty, he speaks entirely in nautical similes and metaphors; and most of our laughter is directed at the absurdity of these remarks, not at their cleverness. But Ben wins our respect because he is entirely his own man. He is willing to obey his father only to the extent of proposing to Miss Prue; and, when Scandal suggests that Ben might be lying, he tells him, "Look you, Friend, it's nothing to me, whether you believe it or no. What I say is true; d'ye see. . . ." Angelica may mock him, but she cannot destroy the integrity of his world any more than he can impinge upon hers.

Ben has something of the quality of Voltaire's Huron in *L'Ingénu*. Both are noble savages let loose on society, and both make social manners seem a bit stiff and hypocritical. Instead of a delicate or subtle song of love, Ben and his shipmates bawl out a bawdy ballad. With little knowledge of gallantry in love, Ben can still give good advice about women to both his father and Tattle. Ben is not the first sailor to appear on the Restoration stage. Wycherley's Manly in *The Plain Dealer* (1677) was a ship captain, and Captains Porpus and Wilding in Durfey's *Sir Barnaby Whigg* (1681) are both sea wits. There is even a captain named Sea Wit in William Davenant's *News from Plymouth* (1635). And even the nautical language was fairly commonplace, for something like Ben's accent appears in Porpus's remarks to his wife on finding two men in her room: he sees her "in danger to prove a Fire ship—forc'd to a surrender by a thorough-shot betwixt Wind and Water, and then to be Mann'd by the Enemy in the Fore-Castle and Poop—with a Pox t'ee."[7] But Ben, a far cry from Durfey's licentious cuckold, remains at the end unchanged and uncontaminated by society. He has been rejected by two women and disinherited by his father, but he still has the sea and other lands to sail to, and, for him, that is the important thing.

His feminine counterpart, Miss Prue, is another matter. Where Ben's world, in which "it's but a Folly to lie," has its own very real values, hers is merely the reverse of that of the adult and the city: she has yet to grow up and lose her country ways. For Congreve, the country can only mean ignorance and barbarity; and childhood, the lack of that maturity which constitutes a complete human being. The Restoration understood very literally those laws that exempted children, along with the insane, from a role in society. Even in the next century, biographers and novelists avoided lengthy discussions of their subjects' childhood, because they regarded such material as trivial or "low." Miss Prue is only at the threshold of life—adult life. Old enough to be seduced, she is ready to run off with Robin, the butler, when Foresight refuses to let her have Tattle. She represents that paradox that so much delighted the libertines—animal sensuality slightly veiled by an innocent education. What she must learn before she can be considered socially acceptable is to control her sex drive or, better yet, to disguise it; and Mr. Tattle willingly begins her education in deceit.

It should be pointed out that the art of lying and of disguise is as much a part of Angelica's life as it is of Mrs. Foresight's and Mrs. Frail's, for it is little more than the art of being a woman in society. Angelica hides her feelings toward Valentine until the very end; but we know just how strong her feelings are from her concern at his madness, from her asides when she feels she is being tricked, and from her final confession that she may seem as fond in the future as she appeared indifferent before. When Valentine, dropping his mask of insanity, asks for some answer to his proposal of love, she pretends to think him mad: "Wou'd any thing, but a Madman, complain of Uncertainty? Uncertainty and Expectation are the Joys of Life. Security is an insipid thing, and the overtaking and possessing of a Wish, discovers the folly of the Chase. Never let us know one another better; for the Pleasure of a Masquerade is done, when we come to show our Faces; but I'll tell you two things before I leave you; I am not the Fool you take me for; and you are mad, and don't know it" (I, 310-11). The speech bears some resemblances to those of Belinda and Cynthia in the earlier plays, but Angelica's defense of disguise is itself defensive. She is sure of her affection for Valentine, but she is not at all certain how disinterested he is. She is, after all, an heiress; and, if she is not surrounded by a train of fops like Millamant, she is pursued by Tattle and Sir Sampson. We also know that Valentine wasted his four thousand pounds in vying with the crowd of suitors about her. Thus, she lies and affects an uncharacteristic coldness and self-interest to protect her tender emotions as well as her fortune.

What gives Angelica the self-control that all the other women in the play lack? When Mr. Tattle gives Prue her lesson in lying at the instigation of Prue's step-mother and her sister, his central lesson is that women must give a clue to their real feelings while giving a surface impression that is exactly opposite. "O Lord," exclaims Prue, "I swear this is pure,—I like it better than our old-fashion'd Country way of speaking one's Mind" (II, xi, 49-51). To test his pupil, Tattle asks Prue to kiss him. She refuses and quickly kisses him; Tattle leads his "apt Scholar" to the bedroom a few minutes later. Only the entrance of the Nurse prevents the final act of seduction. Prue learns nearly everything but discretion, a quality rarely found in a young girl; but in this instance she is not very different from Mrs. Foresight and her sister. Mrs. Foresight sleeps with Scandal after sending her husband off to bed and then denies everything the next morning. As for Mrs. Frail, in the words of Scandal, "we all know her." Only an education in the ways of the world separates Prue from the other women, but their actions may vary according to their condition. Mrs. Foresight has to look elsewhere than to her husband for sexual satisfaction, and her sister has not had the good fortune to find a husband until Tattle is tricked into matrimony. Now Angelica has two substitutes for sexual relations denied to the other ladies. She is genuinely in love with Valentine with a love that looks forward to marriage, and she spends a large part of her time torturing him by pretending complete indifference. The sexual aggression that goes into such behavior can sustain women on the coldest nights.

In creating the character of Angelica, Congreve drew on a common contemporary stage type which found its archetype in Beaumont and Fletcher's *The Scornful Lady* (1616), a play which Congreve obviously knew thoroughly. The Scornful Lady punishes Loveless, her admirer, with commands and indifference. She confesses in an excellent soliloquy that she does not understand her motivation for humiliating her admirer but admits, "I had rather die sometimes than not disgrace in public him whom people think I love, and do't with oaths, and am in earnest then." Only when Loveless provokes her jealously does she yield. A similar type is Berenice in Durfey's *The Marriage Hater Match'd*

(1692), who rants against "that hellish vice called Love," and
says, after she surrenders to it, that her lover will find her actually
as soft and kind as "a plain dull silly House-dove."[8]

III *Madness and True Love*

The pleasure these women find is partly in revenge, the obverse
passion of love, and partly in the power which their sex gives
them over men. As Congreve observed throughout his writings
and particularly in his love poems and songs, the lover craves
favors of his mistress; and every favor she gives is a gain for the
man.[9] The woman's sovereignty ends with marriage; until that
time, the man is the suitor, obeying his mistress's whims unques-
tioningly. For the woman, marriage involves obedience to the
will of the man, and Congreve's women are reluctant to surrender
what power they have. Marriage is a goal received, and the
achievement is always less satisfying than the pursuit. As Congreve's Semele sings:

> I love and am lov'd, yet more I desire;
> Ah, how foolish a Thing is Fruition!
> As one Passion cools, some other takes Fire,
> And I'm still in a longing Condition.
>
> (III, ii, 1-4)

Thus, while she still has power over her lover, Angelica makes
him suffer by her scorn, by her indifference, and, finally, by the
greatest affront she can offer him—a prospective marriage to his
cruel father, Sir Sampson.

But, instead of using Valentine's forfeiture of his right to his
inheritance to increase her personal estate, Angelica tears up the
deed and addresses her "Generous Valentine" in words of deep
affection: "Had I the World to give you, it cou'd not make me
worthy of so generous and faithful a Passion: Here's my Hand,
my Heart was always yours, and struggl'd very hard to make this
utmost Trial of your Vertue" (V, xii, 71-75). Her confession shows
no reversal of character comparable to Durfey's transformation of
Berenice into a "silly House-dove." Angelica has revealed her
feelings clearly enough to the audience when she tells Tattle,
who has found in Valentine's feigned madness an excuse to angle
for Angelica, "O fie for shame, hold your Tongue, A passionate
Lover, and five Senses in perfection! when you are as mad as
Valentine, I'll believe you love me, and the maddest shall take
me" (IV, xvi, 24-27). This statement is a key one, for the mad-

ness, or at least the irrationality, of love is the central theme of the play.

With Valentine, the madness of love has caused the ruin of his estate, but it eventually results in his gaining Angelica; for, if the alternative to true love is a life spent in the pursuit of self-interest or in the folly of self-love, what choice have Valentine and Angelica but to plunge into madness? And, if Valentine is mad to ruin himself for love and Angelica for marrying him in his poverty, what are we to think of the other characters—Foresight, for example, who, coming to hear Valentine prophesy, finds in the ravings of Truth things "Mysterious and Hieroglyphical"? Actually, Valentine's statements after he assumes the disguise of Truth are merely realistic, satirical descriptions of everyday life, perhaps the least mad parts of the play:

Oh, Prayers will be said in empty Churches, at the usual Hours. Yet you will see such zealous Faces behind Counters, as if Religion were to be sold in every Shop. Oh things will go methodically in the City, the Clocks will strike twelve at Noon, and the horn'd Herd Buz in the Exchange at Two. Wives and Husbands will drive distinct Trades, and Care and Pleasure separately occupy the Family. Coffee-Houses will be full of Smoak and Strategem. And the cropt Prentice, that sweeps his Master's Shop in the Morning, may ten to one dirty his Sheets before Night. But there are two things that you will see very strange; which are wanton Wives, with their Legs at Liberty, and tame Cuckolds, with Chains about their Necks. But hold, I must examine you before I go further; you look suspiciously. Are you a Husband? (IV, xv, 22-39)

Had Foresight even the perception of a Polonius, he might have found a method in Valentine's ravings. And is not Ben right in thinking that his father has gone mad in planning to marry Angelica at his age?

The maddest joke of all comes near the end as Tattle and Mrs. Frail sneak off disguised as friar and nun, respectively; the one thinks to marry Angelica; the other, Valentine. Their costumes represent a direct reversal of roles for "Turk Tattle" and the promiscuous Mrs. Frail, and their marriage provides the properly absurd contrast with the union of the hero and heroine. Congreve has frequently been accused of bad taste in resorting to the hackneyed, improbable device of a marriage in disguise. Gellert Alleman, in his *Matrimonial Law and the Materials of Restoration Comedy,* has shown that in Restoration England marriages in masks did occur on rare occasions, but that a marriage involving some mistake in the parties participating in the ceremony could

be renounced.[10] To search for a justification for Congreve's device on historical grounds, however, would be a mistake. It
belongs to the absurd dramatic world of *Love for Love,* and that
world has only the most tangential relation to reality; it is a final
mad trick in which the two most self-seeking characters find
their match in a marriage which will be as bad as that of Valentine and Angelica will be ideal.

Valentine points out the moral to Tattle: "Tattle, I thank you,
you would have interposed between me and Heav'n; but Providence laid Purgatory in your way—You have but Justice." "I
never lik'd any Body less in my Life," says Tattle of his new
wife; and Mrs. Frail tells her sister, "Nothing but his being my
Husband could have made me like him less" (V, xi, 37-38).
Valentine, on the other hand, has attained what is the only
"Heav'n" on earth: a good marriage. There is another moral—
this one delivered by Angelica to Scandal—a femininist moral.
Angelica argues that the fault in courtship usually lies with
the men, not with the women. If there were more lovers like
Valentine to persevere in their love "even to Martyrdom," there
would be more women to reward them. The language in this
section is obviously religious, and its significance did not escape
Collier's notice. The fact is that Congreve is placing his "Heav'n"
in the present life rather than in the one to come. *Love for Love*
is a moving play, but not if we are oriented to thinking of life
as a vale of tears and as a stopping place on the way to a better
life. Congreve distributes his rewards and punishments on earth.

In actuality, only Sir Sampson and Tattle are severely punished; and this fact says something about the nature of the play.
Congreve has presented a plot; but, with the exception of the
marriage in disguise, there is little mechanical plotting. Our
interest is sustained mainly by the characters; and, in this sense,
Love for Love is as original as *The Double Dealer.* The characters
are drawn so clearly, so individually, that they seem to exist
outside the action of the play and, like Pirandello's family in *Six
Characters,* to continue their lives after the curtain falls: Old
Foresight will continue being cuckolded by his wife; Ben, go back
to the sea and his dreamy life; Scandal, continue his materialistic,
satirical approach to the world; and Prue, grow up. As her ignorance is replaced by sophistication, lies will come more naturally
to her.

Love for Love is the height of Congreve's mimetic art. Because
it is so artful, it seems entirely self-contained; because it is so real,
it seems to burst its borders in time and space. Congreve encloses

his action in twenty-four hours, but he has taken it out of the suggested confinement of time and space which we find in *The Double Dealer*. Ben is pulled in from the sea, Prue from the country; Foresight is a wanderer among the stars; Sir Sampson has "made a Cuckold of a King, and the present Majesty of *Bantam*" is his illegitimate child; and the place of assignation for both Mrs. Foresight and Mrs. Frail is that house of ill fame, The World's-End. This expansiveness is also represented by a wider spectrum of characters from different social strata.

Congreve also makes a distinct technical advance in *Love for Love*. There is his usual deliberate building up of characters before they appear on the stage, but Congreve now handles this method in a way that appears perfectly natural. The dialogue is as witty as that in *The Old Batchelor*, but the association of ideas—the process which Congreve imitated in his witty dialogue —operates without strain and with the quality of ordinary conversation. The first exchange between Foresight and Sir Sampson, in which each becomes progressively more irritated, is something Congreve would have been incapable of a few years before. And most of all, Congreve has found his mode—lyricism, romanticism, and optimism superimposed upon that world of cynical libertines and imbecile cuckolds which was the tableaux of Restoration comedy. This play was his gayest and in many ways his best comedy. It is hardly surprising that, after this triumph, he should have turned to *The Mourning Bride* and tragedy as a new field to conquer.

CHAPTER 7

The Mourning Bride: *Success and Failure*

> This Play had the greatest Success, not only of all
> Mr. Congreve's; but indeed of all the Plays that ever
> I can remember on the English Stage—even more
> than the incomparable Otway's.
>
> > Charles Gildon, ed., *The Lives and
> > Characters of the English Drama-
> > tick Poets,* by Gerard Langbaine.[1]

> These Figures [of speech] are some of them as stiff
> as Statues, and put me in mind of *Sylvester's
> Dubartas.*
>
> > Jeremy Collier, *A Short View of the
> > Immorality and Profaneness of the
> > English Stage.*[2]

THE contrast between Collier's slap at Congreve's rants and imagery and the unquestionable stage success of *The Mourning Bride,* which Gildon recorded accurately, though reluctantly, suggests a gap between critical acclaim and popular applause. In an often quoted passage, Sir Richard Blackmore praised it extravagantly for its masterful "Fable," its "Noble" diction, and its artful delineation of character and the passions. But, by the end of the eighteenth century, it was attacked as a mere pantomime; and, if both Lord Kames and Dr. Johnson had some kind things to say about the play, they too criticized it—Kames for the violation of unity of place and Johnson because "we are rather amused with noise, and preplexed with stratagem, than entertained with a true delineation of natural characters." Even Blackmore's praise may be set aside as an overly enthusiastic approval of Congreve's stated moral purpose rather than as a strictly critical judgment. Gildon, who, was adamant in asserting the superiority of Dryden, Thomas Otway, and Nathaniel Lee to the upstart tragedian, lamented that Congreve had "done his Endeavour to please the Town and so notoriously obtain'd his end."[3]

I *Formulas for Successful Tragedy*

Perhaps Gildon was not so far wrong in accusing Congreve of opportunism. The numerous soliloquies and rants in the play gave special advantages to Mrs. Barry, Mrs. Bracegirdle, and Betterton in the same way that many ballets or operas, of little intrinsic worth as dance or music, are retained in the repertory because they enable the *prime donne* to display their talents. These soliloquies were intended to delineate the passions, but presenting passions was to contemporary playwrights delineating ideal and frequently completely unindividualized emotions. In the biography of Thomas Betterton (sometimes ascribed to Gildon), Betterton describes the method of depicting these passions with as much stylization of gesture as we would expect in a ballet.[4] In fact, the tragedy of Congreve and his contemporaries was probably closer to dance and opera than we would suppose. Diction and language had a value of their own, one separate from the action of the drama. As in the tragedy of Racine, the aim of the play was to move from a logical verbal structure to a logical enactment of it, from logos to praxis on the stage, with the thought always in mind that a tragedy was an artistic structure composed of a rhythmic pattern of language.

Congreve may also be regarded as opportunistic on other grounds. *The Mourning Bride* dwells heavily on scenes of blood, horror, torture, and murder, always popular with the English audience; but, as Congreve well knew, such on-stage actions were disparaged by neo-Classical critics who demanded that violence occur off-stage. Even more of an appeal to the audience was the attempt to create a political myth based on the triumph of William III and Mary over the tyrannical James II. In Congreve's preface, dedicated to Princess Anne, he maintained that tragedy might serve for "Use and Information" by enabling those who would have no opportunity to view her to "behold some small Sketches and Imagings of the Virtues of Your Mind, abstracted, and represented on the Theatre."

Congreve is not exactly saying that Almeria may be identified with Anne or her sister Queen Mary, but surely the viewers of *The Mourning Bride* would have had little difficulty identifying this pious daughter of a tyrant with the Queen or the Princess. Congreve's two great predecessors in tragedy, Dryden and Otway, had devoted themselves to perpetrating a conservative myth of divine monarchy in their dramas. Admittedly there had also been tragedies with a Whiggish bias during the reigns of Charles II and James II, and the political tone of both tragedy and comedy became noticably Whiggish after the Glorious Revolution of 1688; but Congreve was the first to capture the proper spirit of an England which had just been rescued from tyranny and Catholic bigotry by the heroic enemy of Louis XIV and defender of Europe's freedom—an England throwing off its mourning to experience a rebirth.

There is little doubt that Congreve wanted to have a popular success. He was hardly unusual in desiring applause and money, and the surprising thing is that he succeeded so well. *The Mourning Bride* is a limited artistic success mostly because of Congreve's slender talent as a writer of dramatic verse, not because he compromised his artistic principles. There is no lack of effective characterization, a vividly somber mood, dramatic plotting, and rich image clusters to convey the themes of passion and time, death and rebirth, love and revenge; but the imaginative spark, one that served Congreve so well in the witty dialogue of his comedies, abandoned him in *The Mourning Bride*. Perhaps he relied too much on rhythm and intonation—that arialike quality that works so well in French classical tragedy—which, in the acting of Mrs. Barry and Mrs. Bracegirdle, may have seemed the heights of poetry but which, in the hands of lesser actresses, may have sounded like the "noise" of which Dr. Johnson complained. But *The Mourning Bride* is not a bad tragedy; many of its faults may be attributed to the theory and practice of tragedy at the end of the Restoration.

In remarking indignantly that *The Mourning Bride* had been more successful than even Otway's plays, Gildon was comparing Congreve with the playwright who had the highest reputation as a writer of tragedy. Dryden, Lee, and Southerne were still names to conjure by; Shakespeare was regarded as an inimitable force of nature rather than art; and Corneille and Racine were considered as playwrights of greater art than "Nature." Otway had begun his career as a writer of rhymed heroic plays in which their superhuman heroes and heroines asserted their will, and he had changed to blank-verse plays like *The Orphan* (1680) in which the dominant tone is pathetic. This development may be viewed in terms of a change from the influence of Corneille's tragedies of will to Racine's tragedies of passion and fate (Otway translated Racine's *Bérénice*), but it seems to be as much attributable to a general *Weltanschauung* as anything else, since Dryden, among others, underwent a similar development. Otway was even more skillful than Dryden or Lee in creating a sense of mood and atmosphere, and he avoided the mixture of comic scenes—that separate, double plot which mars most of Dryden's plays and appears so awkwardly out of place in Southerne's *Oroonoko* (1695). With *The Fatal Marriage* (1694), however, Southerne had shown that the pathos of Otway could be carried even further in the direction of a tenderness bordering on the sentimental.

Congreve was to follow the formulas of his predecessors with the same eclecticism he displayed in writing his comedies. Though the heroic plays had been ridiculed in Buckingham's *Rehearsal* (1671), they continued to be popular; and Congreve drew from them his eriny heroine, Zara, and his tyrant, Manuel. Osmyn and Almeria resemble the tender lovers of Dryden's later plays, and the mood of horror is reminiscent of Dryden and Lee's *Oedipus* as well as Shakespeare's ghost and graveyard scenes in *Hamlet,* the prison scene of *Measure for Measure,* and the sense of impending death and murder in *Macbeth.* From the French, Congreve took his single plot, his avoidance of mixing comedy and tragedy, his structural use of *confidents,* and his general adherence to the unities, though Kames rightly objected to a shift of scene in the last act as a violation of unity of place within an act. And, from Otway and Southerne, he drew his rendering of passions, particularly the tenderness of love.[5] Probably the most original aspect of the play is the tenacity with which Congreve holds on to his poetry of night, his settings of tombs and prisons with their echo of death and desolation. It was an effort to compete with Dryden in an area where he was held supreme— in poetry which evoked a sublime effect through the use of terror.[6] To Congreve's credit, many critics, among them Johnson, thought that in some passages he had won that contest.

II *Passion and Time*

That *The Mourning Bride* begins by evoking music is not surprising for a play with such operatic effects:

> Musick has Charms to sooth a savage Breast,
> To soften Rocks, or bend a knotted Oak.
> I've read, that things inanimate have mov'd,
> By Magick Numbers and persuasive Sound.
>   (I, i, 1-5)

The appeal is to the tragic myth of Orpheus with its dark overtones of a voyage through hell and darkness. Almeria is dressed in black, as are all her attendants, and this visual effect is soon set against the martial music and splendor of Manuel's victory procession. Almeria plunges at once into her tale of woe; and, although music may move rocks and tree, her grief is beyond the power of music to cure. King Anselmo of Valentia has just died in her father's prison, and his son and her husband, Alphonso, drowned immediately after their marriage.

Almeria is in every sense a "mouring bride." Her marriage was never consummated; and, instead of the man she loved, she married death. Hence, she vows to remain a living monument to him, more his tomb than the ocean in which he drowned, and to devour her grief "Glutton-like," just as the seas devoured her husband. She vows to live, to conquer both time and the invasion of sense perceptions in order to keep him forever alive in her memory; yet her entire drift is toward death. The first speech evokes the "silent Tomb"; thereafter, the language of darkness, despair, prisons, and destruction, and the awful figure of the tyrannical father throw a pall over every action.

In the first scene, Congreve succeeds in conveying the major oppositions of his tragedy. Perhaps the most fascinating of these is the conflict between passion and time, which is expanded into the larger theme of the ability of either the passions or reason to change experience and alter sense impressions. When Leonora prays that time will ameliorate Almeria's grief, Almeria replies:

> O no! Time gives Encrease to my Afflictions.
> The circling Hours, that gather all the Woes,
> Which are diffus'd thro' the revolving Year,
> Come heavy-laden with the 'oppressing Weight,
> To me; with me, successively, they leave
> The Sighs, the Tears, the Groans, the restless Cares,
> And all the Damps of Grief, that did retard their Flight.
>
> (I, i, 144-50)

If, as Georges Poulet has so convincingly argued, the age tended to believe in passion as a timeless state, Almeria's rejection of time in the name of her "Grief of Heart" is an assertion of the supremacy of individual feeling over the mechanical movement of physical nature.[7] Her attitude prepares the way for the entrance of Manuel whose lust and will to power aim at controlling every person about him, down to the shackled slave—the direct opposite of Almeria's attempt to control external nature through inner indulgence of her "Misery Eternal."

Manuel's arrival is prepared for by Gonsalez's narration describing how, overwhelmed by their senses, the subjects of the tyrant watched the triumphant procession: "As if they were all Eyes, and every Limb / Would feed its faculty of Admiration"

(I, iii, 22-23). His actual entry followed by that of Zara and Osmyn in chains utilizes the grand spectacle as shamelessly as Dryden does in *The Conquest of Granada* during the heyday of the rhymed heroic play; and, like the superhuman hero-villain of those plays, Manuel is egocentric, jealous, and suspicious—he suffers from the customary paranoia that accompanies absolute power. He quickly establishes his presence by demanding that Almeria marry Garcia, by announcing his passion for Zara, and by ordering Gonsalez to observe any signs of love that pass between Osmyn and Zara. In short, he is a detestable villain—a tragic version of that comic tyrant, Sir Sampson Legend.

In a somewhat overenthusiastic psychoanalytic reading of Racine, Barthes claimed that the fathers of seventeenth-century tragedy could be identified with the primal father of Freud's brother hoard, who is eventually murdered and then deified by his sons.[8] To call this speculative would be an understatement, but this much is true: the age was intrigued by Oedipal themes; and the power-mad, lustful monarch, rival in love to his son or son-in-law, was a stock figure in Restoration drama. This characteristic might owe much to Aristotle's high opinion of Sophocles's *Oedipus,* but it may also be associated with the age's fascination for regicide. An audience which tended to think of a king, or at least his office, as divine, and of rebellion as parricide, must have experienced a shudder of horror, not unmixed with some delight, at seeing a murdered monarch's body on the stage. For the audience of 1697, still happy to have rid itself of a tyrant, there must have been an added pleasure in seeing Manuel as a "type" of James II.

The second act is the best in the play, both dramatically and from the standpoint of Congreve's handling of blank verse. Here his tendency to dead metaphor and tedious, somewhat meaningless alliteration is fully compensated for by the extraordinary evocation of the gloomy, Gothic atmosphere of the tomb. And in this second act, he brings together Almeria and Alphonso, who has survived the wreck of his ship, taken the name of Osmyn, and fought bravely for Zara. Their meeting and Zara's anguish at Osmyn's rejection of her advances provide the material for most of the play; and, in spite of highly dramatic effects, Congreve has some difficulty in sustaining his action beyond the tender and moving meeting of the bride and her husband.

The opening scenes inform us that Osmyn is brooding in the tomb of Anselmo below the aisle of the temple. Congreve suggests the supernatural (ghosts were common enough in contem-

porary drama and almost a specialty for Dryden), but he pre-
fers to avoid a real ghost in favor of the power of suggestion.
As his friend Heli (really Antonio) describes him, Osmyn is a
cross between Hamlet and Dryden's Aurengzebe—a great warrior,
but a man of sensibility. The reason for his melancholy
is kept a mystery, and Congreve resorts to some deliberate trickery
to imply that he is in love with Zara, as Manuel suspects. Raising
doubts and mysteries are not necessarily a sign of bad plotting;
and, to Congreve's credit, he does not leave the audience in
doubt very long. Osmyn's identity is quickly established as soon
as he confronts Almeria.

III *The Poetry of Night*

This confrontation is preceded by the most controversial passage in the play—controversial because Dr. Johnson praised it so
highly. Though he qualified his praise under attack, he never
withdrew it.[9] Almeria and Leonora are startled by a sound like
a human voice as they move toward the tomb, but Almeria tries
to assure her friend it was the wind!

> *Leo.* Hark!
> *Alm.* No, all is hush'd, and still as Death—'Tis dreadful!
> How reverend is the Face of this tall Pile,
> Whose ancient Pillars rear their Marble Heads,
> To bear aloft its arch'd and pond'rous Roof,
> By its own Weight made stedfast and immoveable,
> Looking Tranquility. It strikes an Awe
> And Terror on my aking Sight; the Tombs
> And Monumental Caves of Death look cold,
> And shoot a Chilness to my trembling Heart.
> Give my thy Hand, and let me hear thy Voice;
> Nay, quickly speak to me, and let me hear
> Thy Voice—my own affrights me with its Echo's
> .... shew me Anselmo's Tomb,
> Lead me o'er Bones and Skuls and mould'ring Earth
> Of Human Bodies; for I'll mix with them,
> Or wind me in the Shroud of some pale Coarse
> Yet green in Earth, rather than be the Bride
> Of Garcia's more detested Bed.
>
> (II, iii, 6-26)

This passage is highly imitative in its effects, and it seems clear
that Congreve was thinking of Dryden's wonderful description
in his *Oedipus* (1678).

The comparison is worth making in detail. Dryden's Creon

is speaking to Eurydice, who detests him; and, instead of the sense of companionship in terror between Almeria and Leonora, which we have in *The Mourning Bride*, in *Oedipus* there is a deliberate attempt on Creon's part to raise terror in the listener:

> The thought of death to one near death is dreadful:
> O 'tis a fearful thing to be no more.
> Or if to be, to wander after death;
> To walk, as spirits do, in Brakes all day;
> And when the darkness comes, to glide in paths
> That lead to Graves; and in the silent Vault,
> Where lies your own pale shroud, to hover o'er it,
> Striving to enter your forbidden Corp;
> And often, often, vainly breathe your Ghost
> Into your lifeless lips:
> Then, like a lone benighted Travellour,
> Shut out from lodging, shall your groans be answer'd
> By whistling winds, whose every blast will shake
> Your tender Form to atoms.
>   *Eur.* Must I be this thin Being? and thus wander!
> No quiet after death!
>   *Cre.* None: you must leave
> This beauteous body; and all this youth and freshness
> Must be no more the object of desire,
> But a lump of Clay.[10]

Both poets evoke a mood of sublime horror, death, and rotting flesh; but, whereas Dryden attempts a vivid and concrete picture of the supernatural, Congreve attempts to internalize the experience by concentrating on Almeria's inner fears. Dryden comes off as the better poet, but Congreve as the superior dramatist. Creon's description of life after death is a set speech, objective and general. Almeria is speaking about her own sensations; and, by using synesthesia, Congreve gets the feeling of having all the senses in play. He also achieves a psychological sense of place, the terror of the "vast," and a feeling of immense silence —effects that Dryden is not at all concerned with; and the repetition of "let me hear thy Voice" is at once moving dramatic poetry and good psychology. It was this kind of poetic moment that Congreve meant when, in his prologue, he spoke of writing a play according to "Nature" which would "affect the Heart." If, as one critic suggested, *The Mourning Bride* made its audience's hair stand on end, it was partly through the kind of suggestiveness that one finds in Henry James's ghostly tales rather than through the concrete effects of which Dryden was so fond.

Though, as we have noted, no real ghost appears, Osmyn is an effective substitute, when, at Almeria's cry for Alphonso, he climbs from the depths of the tomb. It is a good dramatic moment. Almeria has been speaking of her eagerness for death, picturing him as a lover who will take her in his arms and press her to his breast. Instead of death, she sees the form of Alphonso, her husband, who catches her as she faints. She awakes to genuine "Tenderness and Love"; and Congreve, who is such a master of understatement in comedy, cannot resist a lengthy scene of idealized love, interrupted only by the coming of Zara, whom Osmyn describes as the "Reverse" of Almeria. In addition to discovering the wife, whom he thought dead, Osmyn finds that his friend Heli is still alive; and such miraculous discoveries lead Osmyn to contemplate his condition.

IV   Sight and Insight

Osmyn's soliloquy is reminiscent of Almeria's belief that she can hold back forgetfulness by the power of her grief. Osmyn also argues for man's capacity to control his experience in spite of his senses, particularly his sense of sight:

> O impotence of Sight! Mechanick Sense,
> Which to exterior Objects ow'st thy Faculty
> Not seeing of Election, but Necessity.
> Thus do our Eyes, as do all common Mirrours,
> Successively reflect succeeding Images;
> Not what they would, but must; a Star, or Toad:
> Just as the Hand of Chance administers.
> Not so the Mind, whose undetermin'd view
> Resolves, and to the present adds the past:
> Essaying further to Futurity;
> But that in vain. I have Almeria here
> At once, as I before have seen her often.
>
> (II, viii, 4-15)

Congreve may have taken his hint from Nathaniel Lee's portion of *Oedipus* in which the hero points out that loss of vision does not change the sight into the soul;[11] but, as in Racine's *Bajazet*, vision and insight are part of the thematic structure of *The Mourning Bride*. In his attitudes, Congreve is a true child of the philosophy of his age, particularly Descartes and Locke. The dualism, the separation of the free mind from the "Mechanick Sense" of the determined body, is Cartesian; but the particular dilemma of sensation over which we have no control, which

we absorb whether we want to or not, shows the influence of
Locke. What Osmyn expresses is that active "secondary perception" by which the mind may create its own world. "The mind,"
wrote Locke, "very often sets itself on work in search of some
hidden idea, and turns as it were the eye of the soul upon it.[12]
Osmyn takes consolation in that inner "eye of the soul" rather
than in an external act of will.

In their tendency to introspection, the hero and heroine, are
both the "Reverse" of Zara, who is interested in taking power,
riches, or love from the world as "Means to gratifie the Will" (II,
ix, 82). Zara's voice is that of the vitiated, feminine will as it
appears archetypically in Corneille's Cleopatre: a woman who
attempts to murder her two sons—admirable, but terrible. Like
Lady Touchwood, her love is of the possessive kind and quickly
turns to hatred when Osmyn rejects her advances. At her urging,
Manuel orders Osmyn imprisoned, though she relents sufficiently
to ask that he be unharmed. In Manuel's final words in the act,
we have words full of sensual import and of the theory that,
only by living in a state of continual love is a man able to ease
the burden of time; but Manuel's love is actually lust, a transfer
of his desire for conquest to the realm of sex.

In prison, Osmyn discovers a letter full of unselfish love for his
son from his dead father, Anselmo. Anselmo at the moment of
death prayed "Not for myself, but him"; and his note sharpens
the contrast between those capable of true love and those dominated by their will and passions. But Osmyn, noticing that the
final word of the note, which should have been "Heav'n," has been
torn away, takes this as a sign of God's indifference, loses the
optimism of his first soliloquy, and falls into skepticism. If
"Thought Precedes the Will to think," and reason itself is merely
"the Power to guess at Right and Wrong" (III, i, 30-33), he *must*
think and question the justice of Heaven. Congreve has Osmyn
reject the fideistic conclusions of Dryden and others on grounds
that Locke would have approved: human reason may be a limited
faculty, and judgments may be made before consideration; but
these are not adequate excuses for abandoning critical thought,
even in matters of religion. Osmyn questions the ways of God,
but his continual appeals to Heaven and his subsequent rejection
of skepticism are adequate credentials for his piety.

Osmyn's revolt against the inevitable gives *The Mourning
Bride* some of the same qualities of Racine's *Bajazet,* in which
the hero is imprisoned in the seraglio under the control of a
powerful woman whom he cannot love.[13] Like Bajazet, Osmyn

is deprived of significant action for most of the play, and he
compares his state to the passivity of the leaves carried by the
winds to rot in some corner. Though Congreve informs us of his
military prowess, he seems more like a victim than a leader of
men. When Heli tells Osmyn of a revolution against Manuel, he
throws off his apathy momentarily only to realize the futility of
his position. As soon as Zara enters and becomes furious to think
Osmyn mistook her for another woman, he is forced once more
into the role of the victim placating his tormentor.

After Zara leaves, Osmyn expresses his admiration for this
woman of "God-like Mould"; but he sees in her wild passions a
force that may "make all fatal," a prediction which sets the stage
for the final scene of slaughter. Almeria, played by the tender
Mrs. Bracegridle, now enters—a vivid contrast to Mrs. Barry's
furious Zara. Almeria, who has returned to the mood of her
first speeches, speaks to Zara of devouring their grief and drinking
their tears in one cup. There is also a return to the imagery
of the tomb scene amplified by metaphors associated with prisons,
dungeons, and torture. At the thought of Almeria's marriage to
Garcia, Osmyn threatens to hurl himself against the walls, to
tear at the pavement and dig into the earth, and to bury himself
alive. Reminded of her initial despair, Almeria joins almost joy-
ously in this consummation of their marriage in death:

> O, let us not support,
> But sink each other, deeper yet, down, down,
> Where levell'd low, no more we'll lift our Eyes,
> But prone, and dumb, rot the firm Face of Earth
> With Rivers of incessant scalding Rain.
>   (III, vi, 124-28)

Congreve's fourth act, the weakest part of the play, contains
too much intrigue, too many characters pursuing different plots.
Manuel learns from Gonsalez about Heli's effort to foment
rebellion in the district of Valentia by announcing Alphonso
alive and in arms; and, having learned from Zara that Osmyn
was plotting against him, Manuel begins to suspect that Almeria
and Zara are involved in a general conspiracy. Zara regrets
having demanded Osmyn's death; and, at the suggestion of her
advisor, Selim, she convinces Manuel that her mutes, trained
in murder, should kill Osmyn. And Gonsalez, learning from the
ravings of Almeria that Osmyn is Alphonso and her husband,
decides to make certain that Osmyn is murdered to ensure his
son's marriage to Almeria. How the machinery creaks!

The only good scene is that between Almeria and her father. Manuel, who becomes more involved with his suspicion that his daughter has plotted parricide than with any armed rebellion against his power, soon threatens to kill his own daughter as well as Osmyn. Though the torture he inflicts on Almeria is only verbal, there is a good deal of sadism in the treatment of his daughter. Almeria, on the other hand, momentarily loses control of her reason and reveals most fully that death wish which has dominated her from the start of the play. She asks the earth to adopt her: "Open thy Bowels of Compassion, take / Into thy Womb the last and most forlorn / Of all thy Race (IV, vii, 33-35). "Drag me," she begs, "harrow the Earth with my bare bosom"; and, as her reason slips entirely, she sees herself assuming the very identity of death:

> Let me go, let me fall, sink deep—I'll dig
> I'll dig a Grave, and tear up Death; I will;
> I'll scrape 'till I collect his rotten Bones,
> And cloath their Nakedness with my own Flesh;
> Yes, I will strip of Life, and we will change:
> I will be Death; then tho' you kill my Husband
> He shall be mine, still for ever mine.
>
> (IV, viii, 95-101)

Congreve eventually overextends his effects when he has Almeria imagine bells tolling for death, see a bloody head and hand, and hear Anselmo's voice calling to her from the tomb. But there are characteristics in these scenes which bridge the gap between the horrors of Jacobean tragedy and metaphysical poets of the early seventeenth century, like Herbert of Cherbury, and the popular "graveyard school" of poetry in the eighteenth century.

The closing act of the play works toward a happy conclusion by making Manuel and Zara the tragic surrogates for Almeria and Osmyn. Manuel has ordered Perez, the captain of the guards, to bind Osmyn with double chains, "supine on Earth"; and the force of the play seems to be driving toward uniting the mourning bride with her husband in the tomb, in death. But Osmyn's soliloquy has already prepared us for seeing Zara as a *pharmakos;* and Manuel, whose love for Zara has turned to hatred at discovering her love for Osmyn (now revealed as Alphonso), seems to seal his fate by striking Perez and by planning to substitute himself for Osmyn in the dark cell to surprise Zara. By deciding to "amuse the Sight" of Zara, Manuel tampers with that very sense of vision which dominates the imagery of *The Mourning Bride* and, according to Locke, causes us to act before reason intervenes.

The slaughter begins early as Alonzo announces to the King that one of Zara's mutes had killed himself after Alonzo had wrested from him Zara's note to Osmyn. Gonsalez, unaware of Manuel's plans to substitute himself for Osmyn, goes toward the cell with a dagger in his hand; his "I would 'Twere done" echoes Macbeth. Finding that Gonsalez has murdered the King by mistake, Alonzo tries to aid his master by cutting off the head and concealing it. Zara comes on the trunkless body; assumes it is Osmyn; stabs her advisor, Selim; and drinks the poison she had intended for Osmyn and herself. Gonsalez and Alonzo are later reported to have died fighting to aid his son against the rebels. Only Zara dies on stage, but the suggestion of violence hovers over the entire scene, and the cell with the headless body of Manuel provides a backdrop as bloody as anything in Jacobean tragedy.

Congreve manages to sustain his themes and image patterns through this miscellaneous carnage. Zara enters the prison with a speech reminiscent of Almeria's evocation of the horror of silence before Anselmo's tomb:

> Silence and Solitude are ev'ry where!
> Thro' all the Gloomy Ways and Iron Doors
> That hither lead, nor Human Face nor Voice
> Is seen or heard. A dreadful Din was wont
> To grate the Sense, when enter'd here. . . .
> Yet more this Stillness terrifies my Soul,
> Than did that Scene of complicated Horrors.
>   (V, viii, 1-12)

Like Almeria, Zara finds that reality, even the horror of the torture chamber, is less terrifying than what the imagination supplies. The most moving scenes occur at these moments of stillness—a stillness suggestive of suspended force and action. And in this silence, surrounded by her silent ministers of death, the mutes, Zara drinks the poison and marries Manuel in death. Her final speech should be a moment of effective dramatic irony, for she dies without knowing that the headless corpse is not Osmyn. But Congreve seems less concerned with a tragic, cathartic effect of pity and terror than with what would have been called "admiration."[14] He saves most of his pathos for Almeria.

If Manuel is destroyed by tampering with sight, Almeria is saved by it. Seeing what she believes to be the headless body of Osmyn, Leonora warns her mistress not to look "For there's a

Dagger/ Ready to stab the Sight, and make your Eyes/ Rain Blood" (V, xi, 14-16). Half expecting to find Osmyn dead, Almeria does not look carefully at the body but prepares to make the sacrifice she has been preparing for throughout the play. She picks up the yet remaining cup of poison; approaches the body to kiss Osmyn for the last time; and, finding no head, drops the poison and almost faints: "Horror! a headless Trunk! nor Lips nor Face,/ But spouting Veins, and mangled Flesh! O, oh!—" Almeria is saved by her sight—perhaps her first sight of death in all its horror; and she is terrified, shocked, even disgusted by what she sees. No one could blame her surely, but there is a feeling that her posturing is over—that, by dropping the cup, she acknowledges her incapacity for that grand gesture she has been threatening throughout the play.

When Osmyn rushes in to sustain her once more and to "wake her into Gladness," Almeria is reborn. Her old life was dedicated to death; Osmyn, now transformed into the husband, Alphonso, offers her the opportunity to throw off her mourning, to change from a bride to a loving wife. She awakes like Sleeping Beauty from her enchantment, and Congreve cannot resist a fairy-tale end demonstrating the power of love to dispel evil. Osmyn offers to "pour the soft trickling Balm Of Cordial Sights" into her lips, and Almeria experiences a new vision as the presence of Alphonso removes her dark idea of the world from her sight; and she comes to trust in her perception:

> Giv'n me again from Death! O all ye Pow'rs
> Confirm this Miracle! Can I believe
> My Sight, against my Sight? And shall I trust
> That Sense, which in one Instant shews him dead
> And living? Yes, I will; I've been abus'd
> This is my Lord, my Life, my only Husband;
> I have him now, and we no more will part.
> (V, xii, 16-23)

She also has learned to trust in God's purpose in the world, and the play ends on a pious note: those who have died were evil, and those who inherit the world of *The Mourning Bride* have survived through their "Innocence" and through the distributive justice of God.

That *The Mourning Bride* was a continuing success for the next century is not surprising. It has a mythic, highly satisfying plot, vivid characters, suggestive and unified imagery,[15] and some superbly evocative speeches. But one of its major faults is indicated in the epilogue with its closing appeal to the feminine audience: "Your tender Hearts to Mercy are inclin'd,/ With whom, he hopes this Play will Favour find,/ Which was an Off'ring to the Sex design'd." By chaining the hero to the earth in a circle of death created by the two women who love him, Congreve allowed little scope for Osmyn to act until the very end, and the play lacks a certain masculine force. But more damaging is the *précieuse* language of many of the speeches. Instead of saying something like "perhaps the King may awake though it is late," Zara tells Osmyn:

> Now 'tis late; and yet
> Some News few Minutes past arriv'd which seem'd
> To shake the Temper of the King—who knows
> What racking Cares disease a Monarch's Bed?
> Or Love, that late at Night still lights his Lamp,
> And strikes his Rays thro' dusk, and folded Lids,
> Forbidding Rest, may stretch his Eyes awake,
> And force their Balls abroad at this dead Hour.
>   (III, iv, 54-61)

This speech is probably the worst example of Congreve's poetry in the play, but it is useful for examination. Congreve cleverly sustains his imagery of torture and pain in relation to sight, but the passage is verbose and the metaphors are reminiscent of Cleveland, or perhaps Richard Crashaw and Abraham Cowley at their worst. The artifice is there all right; but the artificial mode is wrong. And, even when he avoids aureate and *précieuse* diction, with the exception of a few lines and speeches, Congreve, as a dramatic poet, seldom rises above mediocrity.

Congreve tried his hand at what he could do well, but somehow not quite so well as comedy. This failure is best explained by understanding that Congreve's talent was fundamentally imitative. He had been able to mould the formula of Restoration comedy to his own purposes, giving his comedies a highly personal flavor; but he was working with a dramatic mode that had already produced the brilliant plays of Etherege and Wycherley. Restoration tragedy, on the other hand, had not been entirely successful. After Dryden's initial enthusiasm over the rhymed heroic play, even he was willing to admit partial failure. If Dryden and Otway produced a few excellent plays, it may be said that they succeeded because of their magnificent poetry and despite the taste of their times rather than because of it. Congreve's tragedy was intended to please and succeeded in pleasing the taste of his audience, but he was incapable of rising above its taste. That he should have returned to comedy with his next play, *The Way of the World,* in spite of the immense success of his one and only tragedy, may be some indication that he understood where his talents lay.

CHAPTER 8

The Way of the World: *Art as Civilization*

> His characters are commonly fictitious and artificial,
> with very little of nature, and not much of life. He
> formed a peculiar idea of comick excellence, which
> he supposed to consist in gay remarks and unex-
> pected answers; but that which he endeavoured, he
> seldom failed of performing. His scenes exhibit not
> much of humour, imagery, or passion: his personages
> are a kind of intellectual gladiators. . . . His
> comedies have therefore, in some degree the opera-
> tion of tragedies; they surprise rather than divert,
> and raise admiration oftener than merriment.
>
> Samuel Johnson, *Lives of the
> English Poets*[1]

THE *Way of the World,* Congreve's masterpiece, was neither
a popular nor a critical success, but it was hardly the failure
some have supposed. On March 12, 1700, a few days after the
first performance, Dryden wrote to a friend that "Congreve's
New Play has had but moderate success; though it deserves
much better." More severe was the anonymous author of *A Comparison between the Two Stages* (1702), who has one of his
characters dismiss the claim that Congreve worked on the play
for two years with the quip, "I have known better writ in a
month." Most people complained of the lack of plot, and this
same assumption lies behind Johnson's remarks in *The Lives of
the Poets* about Congreve quoted above. Congreve, himself,
confessed that he was surprised that *The Way of the World*
had any success at all, "for but little of it was prepar'd for that
general Taste which seems now to be predominant in the Pallats
of our Audience" (I, 336). And he mockingly begs the "Reform'd"
audience to hiss him if they do not like this play on which he
has lavished so much care: "Damn him the more; have no
Commiseration/ For Dulness on mature Deliberation." That
Congreve has his tongue in his cheek is perfectly obvious, for
The Way of the World is Congreve's final and most effective
answer to Jeremy Collier; and the dedication and prologue are
138

his judgment of an audience that had received with applause
Collier's Procrustean assault on the English stage.

Congreve was answering Collier both in the form and in the
content of his play. In the prologue, Congreve merely says there
was "some plot," but he states in the dedication that he has
modeled himself on Terence in "the artful Solution of the Fable."
The critics who found fault with Congreve's brilliant plot were
the same as those who could not tell the wits from the fools;
they were "hasty judges" accustomed to seeing plays but un-
accustomed to thinking about them. Congreve's best answer to
Collier's attack on comedy was an artistic structure, subtle and
intricate enough so that it would contain its own defense of
art and the civilization that produced it. But Congreve went
further by making the very substance of the play not only an
attack on the Puritan morality that had produced Lady Wishfort
and had warped the life of Mrs. Fainall, but also a defense of the
civilization of England in 1700—a civilization which could prepare its ideal members, Mirabell and Millamant, to confront
the ways of the world with bawdy songs and with plays rather
than with sexual immorality, with wit and games rather than
with painful confrontations.

I Plot and Plots

The Way of the World opens with a card game at a chocolate
house. Mirabell has lost this game, but the real contest has yet
to begin. The dialogue is reminiscent of Henry James's later
novels; what is said is less important than the intention behind
each remark. And these intentions are observable only in the
retorts and in the deliberate attempts to change the conversation
or to shift the grounds of the discussion. Fainall makes a witticism
which changes the subject from cards to love: "I'd no more play
with a Man that slighted his ill Fortune, than I'd make Love
to a Woman who undervalu'd the Loss of her Reputation."
Fainall has actually hinted that, though Mirabell might be indifferent to cards, he is hardly a man to slight a matter of love.
Mirabell, who avoids the suggestion, merely remarks, "You have
a Taste extremely delicate and are for refining on your Pleasures"
—a statement that quickly classifies Fainall as a Libertine and,
at the same time, mocks his pretensions.

The contest is reminiscent of that between Cunnington and
Quickwit in Durfey's *The Richmond Heiress*—a contest of men
and wit. To win, Mirabell must show himself more imaginative

and intelligent than his adversary, Fainall; but at the beginning, they are merely sparring. Fainall scores lightly when he blames Mirabell's ill-humor on Millamant's surrounding herself with fools, but Fainall cannot obtain any admission from his opponent that he is attempting to win over Lady Wishfort in order to avoid losing half of Millamant's fortune. For a short time, Mirabell and Fainall agree to criticize the cabal at Lady Wishfort's and the two false wits, Witwoud and Petulant, who are taken into the group when the ladies need one man to lend them an aura of respectability. Mirabell is particularly witty about Lady Wishfort, who "publishes her Detestation of Mankind; and full of the Vigour of Fifty five, declares for a Friend and Ratafia; and let Posterity shift for itself, she'll breed no more" (I, i, 68-71).

Fainall argues that Mirabell mockingly tells how he "proceeded to the very last Act of Flattery with her"; how he wrote a song for her, had rumors spread that she was having an affair, and informed her that gossip said she was pregnant. "The Devil's in't, if an old Woman is to be flatter'd further, unless a Man shou'd endeavour downright personally to debauch her; and that my Vertue forbad me. But for the Discovery of this Amour, I am indebted to your Friend, or your Wife's Friend, Mrs. Marwood" (I, i, 89-92). Though Mirabell's idea of what would flatter an old woman may appear cynical enough, he is perfectly serious in insisting upon his "Vertue"; for Mirabell's virtue partly consists in that code which regarded young widows as fair game and old women—in spite of the omnivorous taste of that archetypal libertine, Don Juan—as completely unacceptable. Mirabell is unwilling to grant that a complete code of self-interest would have been possible for him, but the conversation leaves no question that Fainall lacks Mirabell's scruples.

At the end of his speech, Mirabell turns the contest against Fainall by insinuating that Mrs. Marwood, who betrayed him to Lady Wishfort, is actually Fainall's mistress; but Fainall avoids that insinuation to inquire whether Mirabell had not rejected Marwood's advances and provoked her hatred. Fainall is obviously curious and makes a weak move, which Mirabell sidesteps by saying that he does not confuse civility with sexual overtures. This provokes Fainall's mocking comment on Mirabell's virtue. "You are a gallant Man, Mirabell," says Fainall, "and tho' you may have Cruelty enough, not to satisfy a Lady's longing; you have too much Generosity not to be tender of her Honour. Yet you speak with an Indifference which seems to be affected; and confesses you are conscious of a Negligence" (I, i,

102-7). Seeing how much Fainall had perceived in his remark, Mirabell decides to counterattack: "You pursue the Argument with a Distrust that seems to be unaffected, and confesses you are Conscious of a Concern for which the Lady is more indebted to you than is your Wife" (I, i, 107-11). The thrust goes home, and Fainall decides to change the subject of this conversation with his "Friend."

The way Congreve moves the action forward while, at the same time, giving information about the characters and the situation is probably unmatched in English comedy. The relationship between Mirabell and Fainall is obviously unpleasant, and it is not surprising that Mirabell was Mrs. Fainall's lover even before she married. (Contempt, as Kenneth Tynan has remarked, often breeds familiarity.) The tension between these men, the cuckold and his wife's lover, cannot be reduced to an exchange of wit nor their dialogue to exposition: it is plot in the truest sense of the word. When Congreve introduces some mechanical plotting in the next scene with the commencement of Mirabell's intrigue to marry off his servant, Waitwell, disguised as Mirabell's uncle, Sir Rowland, to Lady Wishfort, the plot seems gross and awkward. It is only fitting that this "Plot" against Lady Wishfort should come to nothing and that the real resolution should come about through a relationship between characters—the absolute trust placed in Mirabell by Mrs. Fainall.

With the entry of the fools, those half-men and half-wits Witwoud and Petulant, the play assumes some of the dimensions of low comedy. Fainall allows Witwoud some wit, but Mirabell denies it. "He is one whose Conversation can never be approv'd," says Mirabell grudgingly, "yet it is now and then to be endur'd." Witwoud's effort at wit is merely a meaningless stream of borrowed similes, an act of memory rather than of intellect or imagination. Though both Witwoud and Mirabell balance their sentences and speak in aphorisms, one is a wit, the other is not. To Mirabell's query concerning Petulant's sincerity, Witwoud says: "'Tis no matter for that, his Wit will excuse that: A Wit shou'd no more be sincere, than a Woman constant; one argues a Decay of Parts, a t'other of Beauty" (I, vi, 93-95). If we compare this remark to Mirabell's answer to Fainall's commendation of Millamant's wit, the difference is clear enough. "She has Beauty enough to make any Man think so," says the enamored Mirabell, "and Complaisance enough not to contradict him who shall tell her so" (I, iv, 23-25).

Both statements seem clever, but what about Witwoud's? Do

we require wits to be insincere? Is this not, in fact, Witwoud's mistaken idea of wit—a clever remark no matter what the context might be? And is there really a correlation between inconstancy and beauty in women? Mirabell's reply, on the other hand, is a commentary both on Millamant and his own feelings. Specific and pointed, not an unexamined, worn-out maxim, it is passionately alive rather than moribund and fit for Swift's collection of *Polite Conversations*.

At this point, Witwoud announces the arrival from the country of his half-brother Sir Wilfull Witwoud; and Petulant reveals that Mirabell's uncle and enemy, Sir Rowland, is coming to offer marriage to Millamant as a method of disinheriting Mirabell. The first act ends on what seems to be a threat to the happiness of the hero, but we know that Mirabell has some kind of plot brewing; and his careless attitude concerning his uncle is reassuring. The danger to Mirabell's successful campaign to win Millamant, and her money too, seems to come mainly from Fainall. The fools surrounding her are sufficiently irritating to cause Mirabell to threaten cutting Petulant's throat, but they are hardly a match for him. And the same may be said for those parental figures—the keepers of the wealth—Sir Rowland and Lady Wishfort: the first is too shadowy and the second too absurd to represent a genuine threat. But Fainall has proven a close match to Mirabell in wit and has been established as a man of questionable morals.

II *Husbands and Lovers*

The second act begins in St. James' Park with a conversation between Mrs. Fainall and Mrs. Marwood, which parallels in many ways the opening conversation between the two wits. It might be expected that a dialogue between Fainall's neglected wife and present mistress would concern the man they share in common, but both are actually more interested in Mirabell. Mrs. Fainall begins by arguing that women should try to be self-sufficient, the position of Lady Wishfort's cabal and the *bas-bleus* of the 1690's. When Marwood fails to draw a confession from her by stating that she had lied about her aversion for men, Marwood acts as if she had merely been testing Mrs. Fainall; and that lady, who returns the compliment by some ill-concealed irony, calls Marwood "an Amazon, a Penthesilea." Then with apparent indifference, she suggests that, if Marwood really wants to marry a man in order to torture him, she should choose Mirabell. At this Marwood changes color, but she soon forces Mrs. Fainall to do so by suggesting that Mrs. Fainall, for all her pretense to hate Mirabell, is "one of his favourable Enemies." Mrs. Fainall excuses herself by explaining that the sight of her husband accompanied by Mirabell had made her sick, but both women understand each other's affection for Mirabell.

What follows is a scene between Fainall and his wife in which politeness is merely a cover for obvious dislike. He calls her "My Dear," and she, "My Soul"; but, if these terms of affection ever indicated feelings of the slightest passion, they have long since become passwords of mutual hatred. Fainall's seeming concern for his wife's ill health is actually a way of letting her know that he does not like her appearance, and Mrs. Fainall is unquestionably correct in assuming that her husband would not want to be seen with her and that she would be doing both him and Marwood a favor by going away. As she leaves with Mirabell, Fainall wittily comments on how unhappy he would be to lose his wife because, like Alexander, he might weep for having no more worlds to conquer. The line, "Excellent Creature!" seems to echo Othello; and Fainall's thoughts probably dwell at least on the fringe of murder.

Fainall's confrontation with Marwood is one of the most brilliant scenes in the play, for they are lovers like Laclos's Valmont and Merteuil in *Liaisons Dangereuses* or James's Osmond and Merle in *Portrait of a Lady;* it suggests a near tragic vision of love among the hateful. Their interview says everything that can be said about those who have wit without morals, who have passion without the capacity for love, and who are evil without losing our admiration. Marwood urges Fainall to follow his wife, pretending that she is interested in upholding his honor; but he accuses her of being jealous of seeing his wife with Mirabell and confesses that he deliberately allowed his wife to make advances to his friend so he might enjoy Marwood securely. As evidence of Marwood's jealous love for Mirabell, he offers her berayal of Mirabell's plots to Lady Wishfort; when Marwood argues that she did it for the sake of friendship, he laughs at the friendships of women.

But, at this point, Fainall makes a slip; he accuses her of betraying his wife, her supposed "Friend," and puts himself in the position of upbraiding Marwood for her fidelity to him. Provoked, Marwood says that she will not forgive his scorn and threatens to reveal all to his wife and the world—how he ruined her, wasted her fortune, and destroyed her honor. Somewhat shaken by this threat, Fainall reminds her that, by preventing Mirabell from carrying off Millamant, she lost him half of Millamant's fortune, which would have gone to his wife. "And wherefore did I marry," says Fainall, "but to make lawful Prize of a rich Widow's Wealth, and squander it on Love and you?" By this act he has suffered much, he argues; for he has had the humiliation of abandoning his libertine code by marrying—worst of all, by marrying a widow who hates him enough to wish him dead.

The reconciliation of Fainall and Marwood is a masterpiece of Congreve's mimetic art. Fainall holds Marwood's hands as she struggles to run off:

Fain. You know I love you.
Mrs. Mar. Poor dissembling!—O that—Well, it is not yet—
Fain. What? What is it not? What is it not yet? It is not yet too late—
Mrs. Mar. No, it is not yet too late—I have that Comfort.
Fain. It is, to love another.
Mrs. Mar. But not to loath, detest, abhor Mankind, my self and the whole treacherous World.
Fain. Nay, this is Extravagance—Come, I ask your Pardon—No Tears—I was to blame, I cou'd not love you and be easie in my Doubts—Pray forbear—I believe you; I'm convinc'd I've done you wrong; and any way, ev'ry way will make amends;—I'll hate my Wife yet more, Damn her, I'll part with her, rob her of all she's worth, and we'll retire somewhere, any where, to another World, I'll marry thee— Be pacify'd—'Sdeath they come, hide your Face, your Tears—You have a Mask, wear it a moment. This way, this way, be persuaded. (II, iii, 146-66)

The sudden depression into which Mrs. Marwood falls was conventional enough for the time and particularly common in roles written with Mrs. Barry in mind, but what is so moving in this scene is the way Congreve humanizes the emotions of his villains. Fainall's resolution to rob his wife of all she has rises at least partly from a desperate longing to appease his mistress. And his final solution—to retire to another world where they may marry—is curious in view of the title of the play. In his daydreams, Fainall conceives a solution to his life that lies outside the world of manners and morals with which he must deal successfully if he is to gain his ends.

The re-entrance of Mrs. Fainall and Mirabell brings with it an explanation of their relationship. Mrs. Fainall has loved

Mirabell with "Indiscretion" and hates her husband without prudence. Mirabell selected Fainall as an ideal husband to conceal his affair with her—a man of some wit and reputation and yet "a Man lavish of his Morals, an interested and professing Friend, a false and designing Lover." Mirabell regarded him as bad enough to feel no compunction for passing off an illegitimate child upon him if Mrs. Fainall (then Mrs. Languish) had indeed proved pregnant: "A better Man ought not to have been sacrific'd to the Occasion; a worse had not answer'd to the purpose. When you are weary of him, you know your Remedy" (II, [iv], 29-32). Mirabell has indulged in some selective moral judgment: he has regarded himself above marriage to a widow, and he has inflicted upon Mrs. Fainall what must inevitably have proved a bad marriage because he would not choose to deceive a good man by passing off upon him the child that Mrs. Fainall thought she was going to have. There can be no question that Congreve expects us to approve of Mirabell's circumspection; it is also true that Mirabell has brought many of his troubles upon himself. But Mirabell does suggest that they always have a "Remedy" against Fainall if he becomes too troublesome. Like the icon of Saint Thomas, Mirabell holds the devil by a leash.

Mirabell also clarifies the Sir Rowland gambit; Sir Rowland is actually his servant, Waitwell, in disguise. Sir Rowland is to marry Lady Wishfort (not Millamant, as Witwoud thought) and then, after he has revealed his status, Mirabell is to rescue Lady Wishfort by revealing Waitwell's previous marriage to her own servant, Foible. The grateful Lady Wishfort is then to accept Mirabell's marriage to Millamant. The plot is clever—too clever to succeed. It fails to take into account the malice of Fainall and Marwood.

In addition, there is no assurance that Millamant will accept Mirabell even if he wins over Lady Wishfort, though everything suggests that Mirabell is irresistible. Millament enters to tease him with her wit, laugh at his seriousness, and depart like a "Whirlwind." Mirabell is left to brood about his state of love and about the impossibility of telling what a woman will do next. "To know this," he soliloquizes, "and yet continue to be in Love, is to be made wise from the Dictates of Reason, and yet persevere to play the Fool by the force of Instinct" (II, [vii], 11-14). Mirabell likes to be in complete control of situations, but his love for Millamant forces him into the cardinal sin of responding seriously to her raillery.[2] Mirabell will have to win her on the level of witty love play, of "enigma" and game, that is the key

to her affection. With the introduction of the newly married
Waitwell and Foible, the second act ends on a note of relief
from the sometimes tense and always indirect confrontations
of the world of manners. They are not lacking in wit, but their
concerns are economic and material: sex, tips, a farm as a reward
if all goes well. Though Waitwell jests about his future inability
to live with himself after playing the role of Sir Rowland, he
knows well enough that folly has little to do with social rank
and that the only real change in his life is the very real marriage
he has contracted with Foible.

III   *The Way of Women*

The third act opens with a complete contrast to the practical
concerns of the servants with Lady Wishfort's sitting at her
toilet waiting for Foible to help reverse the effects of age by
using cosmetics. The scene is similar to one in Southerne's *The
Maid's Last Prayer* (1693), and a comparison is instructive for
showing what Congreve avoids. Southerne's Lady Wishwell
rejects the thought of using a wash: "I use the Wash! a Woman
turn'd of fifty was ne'er design'd to be lookt upon: I may Wash,
and Patch, and please my self; cheat my Hopes with the daily
expence of Plaister and Repairs; no Body will take the Tenement
off my Hands." Because Lady Wishwell finds consolation in
misdirecting the affairs of a younger woman and because she
has some self-awareness, she forgoes our sympathies; but Congreve's Lady Wishfort is always comic, always ridiculous. Re-
fusing to accept the influence of time, she believes she can
construct, through paint and powder, a convincing new façade
to an antique building. Her life is filled with such contradictions:
she has established a cabal of women to oppose a world ruled by
men, yet she is longing for a husband; she sets herself up as a
woman of exemplary morality and has a library of Puritan
writers, including Collier's *Short View* and William Prynne's
earlier attack on the stage, *Historio-Mastix* (1633), to prove it,
but her hatred for Mirabell arises from thwarted desire. "What's
Integrity to an Opportunity," she says in seeming to speak of
Mirabell's possible seduction of Foible; but she is actually speaking for herself.

After Foible has outraged Lady Wishfort by reporting Mirabell's nasty remarks about her, Lady Wishfort is eager for the
marriage with Sir Rowland. But Mirabell's plot runs into inevitable disaster when Marwood, hidden in a side room, overhears
all, including Foible's conversation with Mrs. Fainall praising

her "Generosity" in helping her lover in his attempt to win Millamant. If Marwood's bitterness over Mirabell's refusal to acknowledge her advances had previously aroused her anger, she is now furious at hearing from the mouth of a servant her sexual attraction for him and his detestation for her. After Foible and Mrs. Fainall have left, she broods over what she has heard, repeating the terrible words, "Madam Marwood has a Month's Mind, but he can't abide her." She sees Mrs. Fainall's "Generosity" as the product of a surfeit of sexual pleasure; Mr. Fainall, as a man who has been deceived; and Mirabell, as a man against whom she must revenge herself.

But, just as Fainall does not appear competent enough to challenge Mirabell, Marwood is no match for Millamant. After Millamant enters, having broken her fan in vexation at Petulant, Marwood urges her to rid herself of such fools by acknowledging her love for Mirabell. She couches her advice in insultingly realistic similes comparing Millamant's effort to keep her love a secret to a pregnant woman's attempting to bind in her "great Belly" or to a fat woman who cannot manage to conceal her face behind a mask. Millamant's response is more subtle. "I'll take my Death, Marwood," says Millamant striking a catty, feminine note; "you are more Censorious than a decay'd Beauty, or a discarded Toast." The implication, of course, is that Marwood is both. Marwood still has the upper hand as she warns Millamant not to tear another fan, but Millamant has what Marwood would like most of all—Mirabell's love. By the end, Marwood's rout is complete:

> *Mrs. Mar.* Mr. Mirabell and you both may think it a Thing impossible, when I shall tell him by telling you—
> *Milla.* O dear, what? for it is the same thing, if I hear it—Ha, ha, ha.
> *Mrs. Mar.* That I detest him, Madam.
> *Milla.* O Madam, why so do I—And yet the Creature loves me, ha, ha, ha. How can one forbear laughing to think of it—I am a Sybil if I am not amaz'd to think what he can see in me. I'll take my Death, I think you are handsomer—and within a Year or two as young.—If you cou'd but stay for me, I shou'd overtake you—But that cannot be—Well that Thought makes me melancholick—Now I'll be sad. (III, xi, 26-41)

The song that Millamant calls for now underscores her triumph: "If ther's Delight in Love, 'tis when I see/ That Heart which others bleed for, bleed for me" (III, xii, 18-19). For Congreve, the nature of women's love is tied to ambition; Millamant is never so eager to agree to accept Mirabell as when she knows she is triumphing over other women. Marwood threatens future disaster, but our confidence in the capacities of the hero and heroine to deal with Fainall and Marwood is greater than ever.

If Marwood seems destined to destroy the Sir Rowland plot, her scheme to encourage Lady Wishfort in matching Millamant with Sir Wilfull Witwoud becomes patently absurd with the entrance of this last and most congenial of the fools in the play. Like Clodpate in Shadwell's *Epsom Wells*, Sir Wilfull is a lover of the country; but Congreve uses him as he used Ben as a corrective to the city fops and particularly to Witwoud. When Mirabell learns that Sir Wilfull is merely a half-brother of Witwoud, he suggests that he might then be only half a fool; and this observation proves to be true. Perhaps the idea of a man of forty setting out on a grand tour, a voyage of education, appears less amusing to us than to the audience of 1700. It would be a mistake to see it in terms of a plea for adult education; but, if Congreve had thought that a grand tour at forty was slightly grotesque, he would not have objected to Sir Wilfull's quest for an education. Sir Wilfull turns out to have a warm heart and proves helpful to the lovers at the end.

Marwood and Fainall have the last scene in this third act, and a comparison between this and the melodramatic encounters between Maskwell and Lady Touchwood in *The Double Dealer* is a good index to Congreve's growth as a writer of comedy. Fainall has been informed how Mirabell had cuckolded him "in Embrio" before he even married, and his tone is both angry and witty as he comes to see himself as a "Rank Husband . . . all in the Way of the World." Marwood soothes his anger and urges her lover to wrest Mrs. Fainall's fortune and half of Millamant's from Lady Wishfort. Satisfied that they have both been wronged and content with their plans for revenge, Fainall and Marwood change the tone of their dialogue to a self-mocking wit that is their basic mode of communication. They agree that, since marriage is an honorable institution, cuckoldom must be the same; and Fainall guarantees to provide for Marwood in the event that Foible tries to destroy her reputation. As for accepting Marwood's insistence that she hates Mirabell, Fainall is willing to do so as an act of faith; and he renounces jealousy as the condition of husbands, a status which he disavows from this point forward, closing with a moral tag: *"All Husbands must, or Pain, or Shame endure;/ The Wise too jealous are, Fools too secure"* (IV, i, 110-11). Congreve allows his villains wit and, within the milieu of libertine ethics, a kind of honesty that is appealing. There is always something sympathetic about a man who can ease his anguish through wit and humor; Fainall's failure in marriage and his cynicism provide a test and balance for Mirabell's hopes in his marriage to Millamant.

IV   *Ruder than Gothic*

The fourth act opens with the ironic juxtaposition of two courtship scenes. First, Lady Wishfort eagerly prepares to receive her ancient lover, Sir Rowland; second, Millamant keeps Mirabell waiting, but she readies herself by singing Sir John Suckling and other "filthy Verses." The first couplet is innocuous enough, but it is intended to suggest the entire poem—a poem about the fickleness of women that ends with the image of the flower being always ready for the bee. The thought of Sir Wilfull's approaching courtship makes Mirabell's presence more appealing to Millamant, and she decides not to send him away. The next song she touches on is Edmund Waller's "The Story of Phoebe and Daphnis Applied," in which the lover fails to attain his mistress but is inspired as Apollo was in pursuing Daphne. There is a temporary return to Millamant's doubts about marriage, but she is obviously at what most Restoration dramatists and Mrs. Fainall call "the Critical Instant"—a moment of sexual decision. Sir Wilfull enters now instead of Mirabell, and Mrs. Fainall locks him in the room with Millamant to establish a third courtship situation.

Mrs. Fainall's intentions are obvious. She thinks that a short session with Sir Wilfull will ensure Mirabell's chances. The situation is like a more comic contest over Portia and the three caskets in *The Merchant of Venice*. While Sir Wilfull tries to escape, Millamant continues singing, this time a song about Suckling's perennial theme on the falsehood of women but with some mention of the falsity of men and an even greater emphasis on sexual desire than in the first song. After sufficiently confusing Sir Wilfull, who knows nothing of Suckling, Millamant sends him out through another door, as Mirabell enters to complete a verse of Waller that she has started—a significant gesture. Sir Wilfull says he hopes he will understand her "Lingo one of these Days," but he never will. She curls her hair in verse epistles, and is herself that inspiration of art and civilization that inspires both Mirabell and Congreve as Daphne inspired Apollo and provided the Laurel that became the symbol of achievement. "Like Daphne she, as Lovely and as Coy" (IV, v, 1) says Mirabell as he enters, and Millamant is already won.[3]

The famous proviso scene is rightly regarded as Congreve's most masterful stroke and perhaps as also the height of Restoration comedy. Kathleen Lynch has traced this and similar scenes back through Suckling to the French romances,[4] but the important point is that these scenes would have been familiar enough to Millamant and Mirabell for them to play with them, sometimes seriously, sometimes laughingly, as a reference for their wit and sensibility. One which Millamant and Mirabell could be supposed to know was the first of two provisos in Otway's *The Soldier's Fortune* (1680) in which the lovers agree to part:

> *Silvia.* O hideous marriage!
> *Courtine.* Horrid, horrid marriage!
> *Silvia.* Name, name no more of it.
> *Courtine.* At that sad word let's part.
> *Silvia.* Let's wish all men decrepid, dull and silly.
> *Courtine.* And every woman old and ugly.
> *Silvia.* Adieu!
> *Courtine.* Farewell!

Millamant and Mirabell are actually playing the roles of Silvia and Courtine, or any of a dozen similar heroes and heroines.

When, after Millamant makes a series of unreasonable demands, he eventually counters with a cynical reminder to the things she should avoid—corseting while pregnant, drinking, indulging in scandal—Millamant pretends to be shocked:

> *Milla.* O horrid *Proviso's!* filthy strong Waters! I toast Fellows Odious Men! I hate your odious *Proviso's.*
> *Mira.* Then we're agreed. Shall I kiss your Hand upon the Contract? (IV, v, 147-51)

What exactly are they agreed to? Is it not that the provisos are absurd in view of the love between them? In fact, Millamant will have to give up some of her liberty; and, as a married man, Mirabell will not be able to get up as early as he pleases; if he did, he would indeed be an "Idle Creature" of a husband. Mirabell and Millamant would no more violate the natural politeness that springs from understanding and love than they would follow a set of silly agreements. That each so fully comprehends the role each plays in this ritual is an indication of the perfect harmony between them.[5]

Many of their agreements are seriously intended to avoid a marriage like that of the Fainalls. Millamant insists that she will not be called "Names":

Ay, as Wife, Spouse, my Dear, Joy, Jewel, Love, Sweet-heart, and
the rest of that nauseous Cant, in which Men and their Wives are so
fulsomly familiar—I shall never bear that—Good Mirabell don't let
us be familiar or fond, nor kiss before Folks, like my Lady Fadler and
Sir Francis: Nor go to Hide-Park together the first Sunday in a new
Chariot, to provoke Eyes and Whispers; and then Never be seen there
together again; as if we were proud of one another the first Week,
and asham'd of one another ever after. Let us never Visit together,
nor go to a Play together, but let us be very strange and well bred:
Let us be as strange as if we had been marry'd a great while; and
as well bred as if we were not marry'd at all. (IV, v, 51-66)

Though Millamant may seem reticent in her grudging concession
that she might eventually "dwindle into a Wife," their behavior
by the end is such that Sir Wilfull finds it embarrassing. Neither
can escape the depth of love each feels for each other. Fainall
and Marwood have wit enough and passion enough, but they
lack the capacity for true love.

As Millamant is overcoming her reluctance to becoming a
"Wife," the lovers are interrupted by that "very Wife," Mrs.
Fainall. To Mirabell, Millamant will merely concede, "I'll endure
you"; but her thoughts run so deep that she is unable to follow
Mrs. Fainall's remarks about the fools who have become drunk
and quarrelsome. "Well, If Mirabell should not make a good
Husband," Millamant says in response to her inner thoughts,
"I am a lost thing;—for I find I love him volently" (IV, vii, 7-9).
Within the context of *The Way of the World,* such a brief
confession has as much force as pages of D. H. Lawrence.[6] Instead
of reveling in such emotions, Congreve sets it off by ending
the act on scenes of low comedy and burlesque. The drunken
fools enter. Petulant proposes sullenly to Millamant and, un-
disturbed by his being rejected, goes off to sleep with his maid.
Sir Wilfull sings his cavalier songs in praise of the superiority
of wine to women, while Lady Wishfort and Witwoud comment
on his smell and Millament leaves in disgust. The fourth act
closes on the wooing of Lady Wishfort by Waitwell in the guise
of Sir Rowland—a grotesque parallel of the courtship of the lovers.

Lady Wishfort spends most of her effort trying to convince
Sir Rowland that there is no carnality in her thoughts of marriage,
though her eagerness to take revenge against Mirabell is a
transparent excuse for bringing a man to her bed. "O, she is
the Antidote to Desire," laments Waitwell to his wife as Lady
Wishfort leaves momentarily. The act might have ended on this
amusing scene, but Congreve raises dramatic expectation by

introducing a note from Marwood revealing the entire Sir Rowland plot. Waitwell argues that the note is merely another plot
by Mirabell, and Lady Wishfort is so eager to end her sexual
fast that she is ready to believe anything rather than that she
will not be married. The act ends in suspense. Though we know
that Fainall and Marwood will not allow Mirabell to succeed,
Lady Wishfort still believes in the reality of Sir Rowland. Congreve has resolved the affections of his lovers but little else;
and, if the vengeful Fainall is successful, Millamant may lose her
money and, perhaps, even her marriage.

V *The Way of the Widows of the World*

The final and fifth act turns, not on love, but on money and
reputation—unromantic subjects but certainly important ones
for those who wish to follow the way of the world. Mrs. Fainall
has married the impoverished Fainall to protect her reputation,
and he has married her to get her money. It seems only appropriate, then, that this act should be the crux of their conflict.
Fainall has made his disclosures to Lady Wishfort, and he
threatens to expose his wife's affair with Mirabell to the world
unless he be given all of Lady Wishfort's fortune and Millamant's
six thousand pounds. Mrs. Fainall takes some comfort in believing
that her relations with her husband are ended and in knowing
of his affair with Marwood, but Lady Wishfort is horrified at
the thought of her daughter's public humiliation, a terrifying
experience in the tight little society of eighteenth-century England. Even the marriage of Mirabell and Millamant appears to
be in jeopardy, as Millamant's maid, Mincing, brings in the
news that, rather than lose her money, Millamant will marry
Sir Wilfull.

Lady Wishfort enters to accuse her daughter of a vicious life
and to urge Marwood to join her in retiring from the world
to a pastoral existence as "Shepherdesses." But Mrs. Fainall pretends to know nothing of an affair with Mirabell, threatens to
expose Marwood to the world, and defies her enemies to bring
her to a public trial. At this point, Lady Wishfort hesitates over
her daughter's claims to innocence and points out that her
education makes these claims probable. Mrs. Fainall was reared
away from society and without any exposure to men. A chaplain
disguised as a woman lectured her "against Singing and Dancing,
and such Debaucheries; and going to filthy Plays; and prophane
Musick-meetings, where the lewd Trebles squeek nothing but

Bawdy."[7] She was married by her mother to a Mr. Languish, who died soon after. Our sympathy goes out to this victim of a Puritan education—Congreve's reduction of the kind of education Collier might have sanctioned. Millamant, knowledgeable in the filthy verses of Suckling, has the understanding that enables her to live virtuously in a civilized world. Mrs. Fainall, who "would have swoon'd at the Sight or Name of an obscene Play-Book" (V, iv, 27-28), fails to win a good husband and has to satisfy herself with an extramarital affair with Mirabell, which, however pleasurable, is ultimately unsatisfactory.

But whether Mrs. Fainall is innocent or not is less important to Lady Wishfort than the scandal, and it is graphically described by Mrs. Marwood. The Duke of Norfolk's divorce, which lasted from 1687 until 1700, was notorious. The first parliamentary divorce had been granted as recently as 1698, and not until three years later was a commoner given a divorce that allowed re-marriage. Though a modern divorce is relatively quick and simple, the psychological sense of shame and exposure is almost unendurable, no matter how privately the matter is handled. How much worse to undergo a divorce in 1700! Mr. Fainall once remarked that "'tis against all rule of Play, that I should lose to one who has not wherewithal to stake" (III, xviii, 68-70). Fainall, now more certain than ever that he holds all the cards, demands that Lady Wishfort give up all.

The resolution of the play depends entirely on Mirabell's wit, charm, and knowledge of the ways of the world. He comes before Lady Wishfort, purportedly to renounce his contract with Millamant to allow Sir Wilfull to marry her, but actually to win Lady Wishfort to his side. All her hatred for him melts at one glance, and she accepts his offer of help. Mirabell's first act is to expose Marwood's affair with Fainall; but, in spite of her horror at exposure, Fainall is unmoved. "If it must all come out," he says with none of the generosity of a lover, "why let'em know it, 'tis but the *Way of the World*. That shall not urge me to relinquish or abate one Tittle of my Terms, no, I will insist the more" (V, xi, 4-7). But Mirabell now orders Waitwell to appear with the "Black-Box" that he promised to bring when he was playing Sir Rowland. Just as finishing Millamant's quotation was the key for entering the charmed circle of love, so the black box is a magical key for a worldly victory. The deed conveying Mrs. Fainall's entire estate to Mirabell before her marriage to Fainall is a sign of her complete trust in a perfect gentleman.

"Even so, Sir," says Mirabell, "'tis the *Way of the World*, Sir;
of the Widows of the World" (V, xiii, 43-44).

Evil is driven out like a scapegoat, and comedy reasserts
itself. After an unsuccessful attempt on the life of his wife,
Fainall departs; and, after a taunt from Mrs. Fainall, Marwood,
muttering futilely about revenge, follows her lover. Lady Wishfort is transformed from the threatening old witch into the kind
fairy godmother, and Sir Wilfull from a threatening rival into
Mirabell's friend. Only Petulant and Witwoud, the complete
fools, remain unchanged in order to indicate that the world
remains the same. Though Mirabell and Millamant are finally
united, another reconciliation must take place in the future.
Mrs. Fainall must eventually come to terms with her husband
to ensure her respectability; and, as Mirabell suggests, Fainall's
finances are so desperate that he must comply. Although the play
ends on a moral tag commending honesty in marriage, the real
lesson is economic: only by prudently guarding their wealth can
women cope with the ways of the world.

VI *Character and the Movement of the Play*

Yet even this moral is hardly the essence of the play, which
consists mainly in Congreve's ability to take types common to
Restoration comedy and give them a breathing reality without
destroying their qualities as artificial creations. In tracing in
the dedication the kind of comedy he was writing back to Theo-
phrastus and ultimately to Aristotle, Congreve was placing an
unusual emphasis on character—not, perhaps, without some
thought to the prose "character" as it existed as a seventeenth-
century genre by such writers as Joseph Hall and Samuel Butler.
Congreve did not neglect plot for the sake of character, but
that much of the action is absorbed into the extraordinary dialogue is perfectly true.

Perhaps the best example of this is Lady Wishfort, who as a
type, bears some relation to Samuel Butler's prose character,
"The Ancient Amorous Puritan Lady." To view her as a tragic
or even as a sad figure would be an error equal to thinking of
her as a problem in geriatrics. Her only reality is within the
world of the play, and there she is a character of affectation
who is comic partly because her affectations are at once grotesque
and transparent and partly because of her unusual use of
language. When she becomes angry with Foible, she erupts into
a stream of language at once realistic, detailed, and fanciful:

Out of my House, out of my House, thou *Viper,* thou *Serpent,* that
I have foster'd; thou bosom Traitress, that I rais'd from nothing—
Begone, begone, begone, go, go,—That I look from washing of old
Gause and weaving of dead Hair, with a bleak blue Nose, over a
Chafing-dish of starv'd Embers, and Dining behind a Traverse Rag,
in a shop no bigger than a Bird-Cage, go, go, starve again, do, do. . . .
Away, out, out, go set up for your self again—do, drive a Trade. . . .
Go, hang out an old Frisoneer-gorget, with a Yard of Yellow Colber-
teen again; do; an old gnaw'd Mask, two Rows of Pins and a Child's
Fiddle; A Glass Necklace with the Beads broken, and a Quilted Night-
cap with one Ear. Go, go, drive a Trade,—These were your Com-
modities, you treacherous Trull. (V, i, 1-9)

William Mason commented in his *Memoirs* of Thomas Gray that,
although Lady Wishfort was an "unnatural" character because
no one ever combined so much folly with so much fancy, any
attempt to make her more natural would only render her less
entertaining. Mason was aware that the customary test of character for his period could not be applied to Lady Wishfort.[8] She
possesses that larger-than-life quality which belongs to that
successful rendering of reality in an art that has only an oblique
relationship with the reality of life.

The difficulty is that, when she appears, we have the feeling
of action and time being suspended; and this particular effect
accompanies all those characters in the play who create their
own world of words. On the stage such a suspension of forward
movement creates a problem in pacing that is related to the
treatment of time in general. Congreve limits the action to an
afternoon and evening, thereby gaining a sense of compression;
but the play frequently moves backward in time, and sometimes
seems to stand still. Mirabell's and Fainall's plots seem to project
the play forward, as do the longing of Lady Wishfort for Sir
Rowland and Sir Wilfull's plan to travel abroad. Yet much of the
dialogue reverses the flow of time, for we are as much interested
in the past relationships of the characters as in anything tran-
spiring in the present. In fact, as the tag moral suggests, the
play is an investigation of the effect of the past on the present.
Congreve does not abandon present stage action; but, with the
exception of Sir Wilfull's drunken antics, most of the action is
reducible to gesture. *The Way of the World* is a type of theater
that stands in direct opposition to that proposed by Antonin
Artaud which has so many modern disciples—a theater of
language rather than one of cruelty.

VII *Comedy as Civilization*

In his prologue Congreve stated that his play would contain
"some new Thought," but this newness is hardly apparent unless
the title is to be taken seriously. The world is very much at issue
in this play; in fact, it might have been called "The World Well
Found" as a response to the subtitle of Dryden's *All for Love:
or, The World Well Lost*. Congreve sets out to create two lovers
who are as ideal as Anthony and Cleopatra, and he then has
them come to terms with their world and succeed in it. Witwoud
even refers to Millamant as "handsome as Cleopatra"; and, like
Anthony, Mirabell confesses that he is in love in spite of a
rational awareness of his folly. She is so beautiful that she is
always accompanied by a convoy of beaus; he, so handsome
that every woman in the play is in love with him. Unlike Anthony,
Mirabell has learned the ways of the world and is able to outwit
his Octavius, Fainall, at every turn.

The world in which they succeed is that newly sophisticated
eighteenth-century London that Congreve loved. The city produces its Witwouds and Petulants, parasites of the coffee and
chocolate houses, men who are symptomatic of the ego deflation
that comes with impersonal crowds; for they seek some kind
of notoriety to draw attention to themselves to compensate.
Witwoud enters asking whether any messages have come for
him, and Petulant is so desirous of being thought important
that he hires people to call on him or calls upon himself in
disguise. They feel, in short, as we feel when we do not receive
enough mail—as if we are being ignored by our friends and
the world in general. But, if the city has its quota of fools, it
also has its concerts and theaters, its Millamants and Mirabells;
and, outside it, are the kind Sir Wilfulls, but, as Millamant points
out, "Rustick, ruder than *Gothick*."

In Congreve's time, the ideals of a ferocious libertinism were
giving way to a delight in finer pleasures. Saint-Evremond maintained that Petronius was the ideal man: the urbane artist who
wrote a satire on the excesses of luxury rather than upon luxury
itself. When Bernard Mandeville published his *Fable of the
Bees* (1705) just five years after *The Way of the World,* his
defense of luxury merely followed a growing trend of the time.
Mandeville argued that the luxuries of civilization made Western
man superior to the savage; and, as an end in themselves, they
were superior to those Christian values that advocated a return
to primitive simplicity. "As for the Hatred of villainous Actions,"

wrote Saint-Evremond, "it ought to continue so long as the World does, but give leave to Gentlemen of refin'd Palats to call that Pleasure, which gross and ill-bred People call Vice, and don't place your Virtue in old musty Notions which the primitive Mortals derived from their natural Savageness."[9] This assertion might be Congreve's.

In spite of Congreve's refusal to acknowledge the relationship between his plays and the real world, they are very much about a world—one which is here and now. If Christian ideals were inescapable because so deeply imbedded in his age, Congreve does his best, nevertheless, to avoid mentioning them. In this respect, Congreve was little different from most contemporary writers of comedy; but the world of Congreve's comedies is so complete and convincing that Collier's sense of a deliberate exclusion of serious Christian content is understandable. Mirabell operates on the assumption that, within his world, the most important point is love, marriage, and the way he and Millamant can manage to live together as individuals and as a family. She is concerned about her liberty and her tea table, about how they will appear in public, and about how she may avoid associating with fools just because they happen to be her husband's relatives. Swift left his sermons, Addison his prayers, Steele his *Christian Hero;* but, in spite of Congreve's devout education, there is little in his life or writings to indicate a leaning toward religion. And Congreve's art is not only secular in its avoidance of religion. *The Way of the World* establishes a concept of art and civilization, of manners and morals, which finds its fullest expression in the wit, intelligence, and moral values of Congreve's hero and heroine.

CHAPTER 9

Poetry and Minor Writings:
The Artist as Dilettante

> O! Congreve, cou'd I write Verse like thine,
> Then in each Page, in ev'ry charming Line,
> Should Gratitude, and sacred Friendship shine.
> Your Lines run all one easie, even Feet;
> Clear is your sense, and your Expression sweet:
> Rich is your Fancy, and your Numbers go
> Serene and smooth, as Crystal Waters flow
> Smooth as a peaceful Sea which never rolls,
> And soft, as kind consenting Virgin Souls.
>
> Charles Hopkins, "To Mr. Congreve"[1]

I Poetry

IN his own day, Congreve had a considerable reputation as a poet. As Pope was to do with greater success, he set himself up as the heir to Dryden and, unlike Pope, with Dryden's approbation. Edward Howard, who coupled Congreve with Dryden, argued that both were superior to Virgil. "I will here be bold to affirm," he wrote in his *Essay Upon Pastoral* (1695), "that that Great Youngman (Mr. Congreve) has in his Pastoral Alexis upon the Death of the Late Queen, evidenced himself to the World, to have sufficient degree and quantity of unmingled Fire and pure Rapture of the *Poet* . . . to constitute Ten Virgils, nay, and enough to furnish out a Theocritus."[2]

Even one of Congreve's severer critics acknowledged his "large share of Reputation in Pastoral."[3] Though his reputation diminished considerably during the eighteenth century, Steele praised his poem, "Doris"; and his renown as a writer of pastorals is reflected in the remarks of his earliest biographers, Charles Wilson and Giles Jacob.

There can be little question that this reputation was almost entirely the product of Congreve's fame as a dramatist. When, in the middle of the eighteenth century, critics began judging the poetry for its own sake, the demolition began. After an un-

158

flattering comparison between Congreve's and Pope's translations of Homer, William Melmoth concluded that Congreve's verse was "languid," "inelegant," "heavy," "tasteless," and lacking in the "least spark of poetry."[4] Dr. Johnson, who concurred in this judgment, hated not only writers of pastoral but Whigs, and Congreve was both. Johnson wondered that the poet who could compose some remarkable passages in *The Mourning Bride* could write the drivel that appears in his pastorals. *The Birth of the Muse,* he called "a miserable fiction"; the translations from Horace, "feebly paraphrastical"; and the "petty poems . . . seldom worth the cost of criticism." He finds Congreve's thoughts "false and sometimes common," and he notes that the versification is "weakened with expletives and his rhymes are frequently imperfect." At only one point is Dr. Johnson demonstrably wrong: he argued that there was not a quotable line in Congreve's songs, but frequent reprintings of them in music books throughout the eighteenth century indicate considerable popularity. In the twentieth century, F. W. Bateson has argued that, though it "would not be exact to call Congreve a great Poet, . . . he was a good poet."[5] But Bateson's hint that he was surpassed only by Pope cannot be taken seriously.

Neither a sprinkling of modern revaluation nor comparison to the voguish metaphysicals will make Congreve into a good poet, much less a great one. In a sense, his poetry is reminiscent of the productions of many writers who abandon their major form to dabble in another—of Keats's plays or Melville's poems. Congreve's poetry is almost always flawed, frequently interesting, and worth reading if only because it adds in various ways to our understanding of his plays. Between the last years of Dryden's life and the rise of Alexander Pope's star, there was no sign of a truly great poet. Congreve surely never attained the polish of such a good minor poet as Prior, or even the vigor and satiric force of Defoe's lampoons. But, in competition with William Pittis, John Tutchin, Thomas Yalden, and Francis Manning, Congreve seemed a likely prospect to fill Dryden's shoes.

A glance at his most famous poem, *The Mourning Muse of Alexis. A Pastoral Lamenting the Death of Queen Mary,* provides insight into some of his faults as a poet, particularly as an occasional one. The occasion was one of national mourning for a beloved queen, and the author of *Albion's Tears* (1695) called on the poets to mourn in verse:

> You cannot soar too high,
> Within the Limits of Mortality.

> Rack, Rack, each Metaphor
> Your flatt'ring Tribe have heretofore
> Appli'd to Woman-kind.

To Congreve's credit, he put fewer metaphors on the rack than most of the elegists of the time; but what Johnson described as "yelling" out grief is fully evident in the passage he quotes:

> The Fawns forsake the Woods, the Nymphs the Grove,
> And round the Plains in sad Distractions rove;
> In Prickly Brakes their tender Limbs they tear,
> And leave on Thorns their Locks of Golden Hair.
> With their sharp Nails, themselves the Satyrs wound,
> And tug their shaggy Beards, and bite with Grief the Ground,
> Lo Pan himself, beneath a blasted Oak
> Dejected lies, his Pipe in Pieces broke.
> See Pales weeping too, in wild Despair
> And to the piercing Winds her Bosom bare.

(II, 205)

Whatever we may think about Johnson's strictures on the artificiality of pastoral, Congreve's faults extend beyond the failings of the form. His rhymes are awkward, and he is forced to wrench syntax to achieve them. Expletives destroy concision and tension, while the strongest poetic effect is limited to a seemingly compulsory alliteration of two syllables a line. No doubt the age appreciated the evocation of set Classical scenes, but their frozen, statuesque feeling could only be effective in the hands of an Alexander Pope; and even he, as Dr. Johnson remarked, had difficulties with his pastorals.

Much of Congreve's worst poetry can be blamed on the taste of his age, but he was certainly no poet to rise above the popular poetic modes of his day. He had a weakness for *précieuse* clenches; and, in seeking forms which would allow for a full expression of emotion, he frequently wrote irregular "pindaric" odes—that one form that allowed almost complete freedom from the restrictions of neo-Classical restraint. In his poem, *To the King, on the Taking of Namure*, Congreve calls for new powers of fancy: "For Fancy, wild and pathless Ways will chuse,/ Which Judgment, rarely, or with Pain, pursues" (II, 208). But what he achieves is rhetoric, not poetry. He envisions himself carried to the battlefield and wonders at the power of poetry to create vivid images:

> Are these by Fancy wrought!
> Can strong idea's strike so deep the Sense!

O sacred Poesie! O boundless Power!
What wonders dost thou trace, what hidden Worlds explore.
(II, 209)

Prior was to compare writers of such pindarics to a squirrel running in a revolving cage, "Always aspiring, always low"; and, since Prior also indulged in writing pindarics, he ought to have known. In 1706, Congreve contributed to the destruction of the form by describing the regular three-part structure of the genuine pindaric ode and calling the English version "for the most part . . . either Horrid or Ridiculous" (II, 334). But if his *Pindarique Ode, Humbly Offer'd to the Queen* and *To the Right Honourable Earl of Godolphin* are less rhetorical and more restrained than his earlier odes, they are, in fact, duller. Had he written more short lyrics and fewer odes, Congreve might have retained some of his reputation as a poet.

He began his poetic career with some translations of Horace and Homer. The latter were highly praised by Dryden, who remarked that in the "pathetic," Congreve had surpassed Homer. What is interesting about this absurd overpraise of Congreve's performance is that it reveals the kind of reputation in poetry Congreve wanted. Both the choice of subject (the lamentations of the women over the body of Hector) and the rendition indicate that Congreve wanted to be thought a poet of sensibility. His translations of Horace, actually imitations or paraphrases, are more Congreve than Horace; and they are far better poetry than Thomas Creech managed in his translations. But then the story was circulating that Dryden had urged Creech to translate Horace in order to ruin the excellent reputation Creech had gained with his translation of Lucretius.

Congreve was at his best when he was under no pressure to be sublime: writing light love poems, easily conversational epistles, or witty prologues. Even the irregular ode which he published in Gildon's *Miscellany* of 1692 and later renamed "On Mrs. Arabella Hunt, Singing," is far superior to any of the odes that he wrote to curry political favor. It is actually a charming, undisguisedly *précieuse* poem on music. Many of these early poems are reminiscent of Richard Crashaw or Shelley, with some of those poets' virtues and many of their faults. He was capable of such sentimental poems as "Absence," which begins with the romantic expostulation: "Ah! what Pains, what racking Thoughts he proves,/ Who lives remov'd from her he dearest loves!" (II, 241). But Congreve achieved complete success only in those meditations on love and change when he captured

something of the tone that appears in the comedies. The lyric
beginning "False though she be to me and Love" is a good
example:

> In Hours of Bliss we oft have met,
>   They could not always last;
> And though the present I regret,
>   I'm grateful for the past.
>   (II, 241)

F. W. Bateson thought he detected something of the Earl of
Rochester's tone, yet the combination of sentiment and realism—
the recognition of the way love lingers—is pure Congreve.

Less serious and more cynical is Congreve's poem on the infidelity of Cloe:

> Tell me no more I am deceiv'd;
>   That Cloe's false and common:
> I always knew (at least believ'd)
>   She was a Very Woman;
> As such, I lik'd as such caress'd,
> She still was constant when possess'd,
>   She could do more for no Man.

II

> But oh! her Thoughts on others ran,
>   And that, you think a hard thing;
> Perhaps, she fancy'd you the Man,
>   And what care I one Farthing?
> You think she's false, I'm sure she's kind;
> I take her Body, you her Mind,
>   Who has the better bargain?
>   (II, 243)

As the second stanza reveals, the dramatic context involves a
reply to a man with whom Cloe has flirted. The speaker implies
that whatever thoughts of other men she might have, she is
probably true in body to him, if not in spirit; and, if she is not,
why, women are like that. The speaker's response is obviously
intended to remind his listener of his physical intimacy with
Cloe. If she is indeed "common," she certainly "could do more
for no man"; therefore, he has no cause to worry. There is much
of Millamant's favorite poet, "Natural, easie Suckling," in the
mocking antiplatonic pose; and, in this poem at least, Congreve
matched content with form. The syntax is natural and the rhyme
clever and significant if occasionally inexact. The song he con-

tributed to Dryden's *Love Triumphant,* "How Happy's the Husband, whose Wife has been try'd!" and one included in *Orpheus
Britannicus,* "There Ne'er Was So Wretched a Lover as I,"
reveal the same cynicism and wit. Admittedly, these poems are
rather slender productions; but they do show considerable talent
and prevent the critic of Congreve's poetry from living up to
Swift's ironic definition of a critic, "A discoverer and collector
of writer's faults."

Two other poems on love are of considerable interest: "Doris"
and "To Cynthia Weeping and Not Speaking." In its content if
not in its form, "Doris" bears comparison with the characters in
Pope's *Epistle to a Lady.* As Dr. Johnson suggested, "Doris" is
about a woman like Mrs. Frail in *Love for Love.* It has the
delightful quality of shifting between a satiric caricature and a
realistic portrait, between admiration and distaste for this aging,
promiscuous, cold woman. The tone is similar to Prior in his
witty vein, just as Congreve's "To Cynthia" recalls Prior's sentimental tone in "To Cloe Weeping." But "To Cynthia" is clearly
a combination of Classical imitation and personal experience—
of the influence of Propertius's poems to his mistress, Cynthia
(particularly II, 15 and II, 25), and of Congreve's reaction to
a very real woman: "O the dear Hour, in which you did resign!/
When round my Neck your willing Arms did twine,/ And, in a
Kiss, you said your Heart was mine" (II, 282). To his readers,
Cynthia may have seemed like Mrs. Bracegirdle, who played that
role in *The Double Dealer;* but, whoever Congreve had in mind,
the Cynthia of this poem is a flesh-and-blood mistress. "To
Cynthia" is not a good poem, but it is a passionate one in an
age that was coming more and more to think the love lyric a
genre unworthy of serious consideration.

Most of Congreve's other poetical efforts took the form of
epistles and an occasional prologue or epilogue. As a meditative
poet, Congreve lacked sufficient technical gifts to relieve dull
didacticism. The best of this group of poems are his two to
Richard Temple, *Of Pleasing* and *Letter to Viscount Cobham.*
The first, written some time before 1726, is a meditation on
human vanity which is reminiscent of the Earl of Rochester's
Satyr against Mankind in its sweeping cynicism. But, whereas
Rochester anatomized man in his natural state, Congreve is concerned with man in society, particularly with his desire to please,
his strongest drive, after his desire for obtaining "Wealth, or
Pow'r, or Ease." The difficulty is that men usually desire to
please in precisely those areas where they have no ability or a

complete deficiency of talent. An extension of Congreve's theory
of affectation in comedy, it is important for that if for no other
reason. His second epistle to Temple, and a better poem, is his
last composition, which has the subtitle "Of Improving the Present
Time"; and in it Congreve strikes an Epicurean pose: one should
act as if each day is the last and not expect any change in the
human condition. The first moral is taken from Horace's "Epistle
to Albius Tibullus"; but, as Alexander Pope remarked, the second
is Congreve's own. I quoted it in my first chapter as an example
of Congreve's thought, but it is worth reconsidering as a poetic
statement of Congreve's intellectual stance:

> For Virtue now is neither more or less,
> And Vice is only varied in the Dress;
> Believe it, Men have ever been the same,
> And all the Golden Age, is but a Dream.
> (II, 402)

"I have read my friend Congreve's verses to Lord Cobham,"
wrote Pope, "which end with a vile and false moral, and I
remember not in Horace to Tibullus, which he imitates, 'that all
times are equally virtuous and vicious' wherein he differs from
all Poets, Philosophers, and Christians that ever writ."[6] Since
the Scriblerians liked to beat their own age with pejorative comparisons to the Classical past, it is not surprising that their most
active advocate should object to Congreve's skepticism about the
degeneracy of the present. That Pope found the poem unchristian
may say much for Congreve's philosophic position.

As a writer of prologues and epilogues Congreve never ap-
proached the only man who succeeded in raising this form to
an art: John Dryden. Congreve's are witty enough, and he often
used them to make a serious commentary on the theater. For
example, in his prologue to *The Husband His Own Cuckold*
(1698), he took the occasion to attack bad playwrights and plays,
blaming the lack of good theater on those who do not realize
the kind of craft that goes into a good play. He is particularly
severe on the new women playwrights:

> You'll find that Pegasus has Tricks, when try'd,
> Tho' you make nothing on't but up and ride;
> Ladies and all, I'faith, now get astride.
> Contriving Characters, and Scenes, and Plots,
> Is grown as common now, as knitting Knots;
> With the same Ease, and Negligence of Thought,
> The charming Play is writ, and Fringe is wrought.
> (II, 274)

This prologue is far better than the average one, but the tone is not quite right for the form. Dryden's prologues and epilogues could be unbelievably silly at times, but he dared more and achieved more: his wit was coarser than Congreve's, and he was not afraid to carry similies and metaphors beyond the bounds of customary moral and poetic decorum. In Dryden's *An Evening's Love* (1668), the prologue is an extended comparison between the relationship of a dramatist to his audience and a tired husband to his bored and wayward wife; in the epilogue to *Tyrannick Love* (1669), Nell Gwyn, in the role of a lovesick princess, who has committed suicide, refuses to allow herself to be carried off in a manner proper for a tragic figure and insists that she be permitted to deliver an attack on the "damn'd dull Poet, who could prove/ So senseless! to make Nelly dye for Love." Congreve was incapable of taking such risks. However great Congreve's comedies may be, his poetry fell far short of the expectations raised by Dryden when he announced Congreve as his poetic successor.

II *Minor Writings*

The few pieces of prose and drama that Congreve wrote after 1700 suggest the dilettante rather than the aspiring artist. The slight essay he handed to Swift on February 13, 1711, for insertion in the *Tatler* has a narrator tell how a *nouveau riche* named Foundling has become wealthy enough to purchase some portraits to pass off as ancestors, a coat of arms, and a lord who is poor enough to be willing to marry his daughter for her dowry. Congreve, who assumes the role of an established gentleman, is amused by the thought that anyone could believe that he could become a gentleman merely by purchasing a few external symbols. A slight hint of contempt, which is not endearing, suggests that Congreve had perhaps been associating too much with the aristocracy. An even greater disappointment is the slight dedication to Dryden's *Dramatick Works* in 1717. Congreve must have known Dryden well; and, living at a time when the short biographical character was a fine art, Congreve might have better performed the debt that he owed his benefactor; for too much space is wasted in thanking the Duke of Newcastle for erecting a monument to Dryden and in praising the Duke's "Munificence." His description of Dryden's character and his poetry is extremely general: we learn that Dryden was shy and that his poetry would remain poetry even if the rhymes were removed and the words jumbled.

More interesting are the two pieces for music; the masque; *The Judgment of Paris;* and the opera, *Semele;* but it is difficult to judge an opera libretto as poetry or even as literature. In his preface to *Albion and Albianus* (1685), Dryden maintained that words, as they are used in librettos, are intended to gratify the ear rather than the understanding, and that the chief things to remember were to use double rhymes and to order the words and meter for the voice rather than for the page. Congreve seems to have taken this advice seriously, and his first effort in this form, *The Judgment of Paris,* had music written for it by the best composers of the day, who competed for a prize of two hundred guineas for the best score. Those entering included John Eccles, Daniel Purcell, and the winner of the competition, John Weldon. In the same year, 1701, Congreve had his poem *A Hymn to Harmony in Honour of St. Cecilia's Day* set to music by John Eccles. As poetry, it seems to have many of the same faults as Congreve's pindaric odes; and the work suffers by comparison with Dryden's and Pope's great poems on the same subject. Nevertheless, Congreve strikes out one good stanza:

> Thy Voice, O Harmony, with awful Sound
>   Could penetrate th'abyss profound,
>   Explore the Realms of ancient Night,
> And search the living Source of unborn Light.
>   Confusion heard thy Voice and fled,
> And *Chaos* deeper plung'd his vanquish'd Head.
>   Then didst thou, Harmony, give Birth
>   To this fair Form of Heav'n and Earth;
>   Then all those shining Worlds above
>   In Mystick Dance began to move
>   Around the radiant Sphere of Central Fire,
>   A never ceasing, never silent Choir.
>
> (II, 246)

The rest of the poem, like *The Judgment of Paris,* depends on whatever beauties the music may lend it.

Semele, which was apparently never performed in spite of the rumor of rehearsals during 1707, is a far more serious effort; and it has even been considered by some to be the first full opera libretto. Some of the songs have the quality of those in Congreve's plays; and, in the recitatives between Jupiter and Semele, he has the chance to create some semblance of character and dialogue; the seduction of the narcissistic Semele by Juno is charming. Semele is ripe for a fall, for even the love of the chief of the gods cannot satisfy her:

I love and am lov'd, yet more I desire;
Ah, how foolish a Thing is Fruition!
As one Passion cools, some other takes Fire,
And I'm still in a longing Condition.
Whate'er I possess
Soon seems an Excess,
For something untry'd I petition;
Tho' daily I prove
The Pleasures of Love,
I die for the Joys of Ambition.

(III, ii, 1-11)

The opera ends with Apollo's descending in a machine to promise the coming of Bacchus and with him wine, a cure for and protection against love.

Congreve might amuse himself with a *jeu d'esprit* like his collaboration with Vanbrugh and Walsh on a translation of Molière's *Monsieur de Pourceaugnac*, which they called *Squire Trelooby* (1704). Congreve was probably exaggerating only slightly in passing off his share in the translation as the work of two mornings. Though he denied that the printed version was related to the play that was performed, one line, which was definitely in the Congreve version, suggests that the wits took advantage of a contemporary scandal concerning a sadistic magistrate who enjoyed whipping the whores sent to his prison.[7] (He fell into difficulties when he whipped a young lady of rank by mistake.) Congreve refers to the play as a "farce" that made "people laugh"; but, as for true comedy, he had no intention of trying his hand at it again. The greatest comic genius of the time buried his talent for three decades before his death. With the new sentimental comedy, he could have had little sympathy; the spirit of the 1690's died rapidly after the turn of the century. Farquhar continued writing his brilliant if somewhat diluted version of Restoration comedy until his death in 1707. But we may say with Dennis that "Congreve left the stage early, and comedy left it with him."

CHAPTER 10

Conclusion

Boundless thy fame does as thy genius flow,
Which spread thus far, can now no limits know:
This only part was wanting to thy name,
That wit's whole empire thou might justly claim:
On which so many vain attempts were made,
Numbers pretending right their strength assay'd,
But all alike unfit for the command,
Only defac'd and spoil'd the sacred land;
Which thou, as its undoubted native lord,
Has to its ancient beauty this restor'd;
Where with amazement we at once may see
Nature preserv'd pure, unconstrain'd, and free,
And yet throughout, each beauty, every part,
Drest to the strictest form of gracing art.

> Catherine Cockburn (Mrs. Trot-
> ter), "To Mr. Congreve, on his
> Tragedy the Mourning Bride"[1]

IF Mrs. Trotter's praise of Congreve is couched in the conventional compliments of the day, it is, nevertheless, a good
sample of what Congreve's contemporaries thought of him. He
was, like John Donne before him, the monarch of wit, not, like
Donne, because of his strong lines, but because his plays captured the freedom and reality of "nature" in a form that adhered
generally to the rules of neo-Classical criticism. He came at
the end of a great period of English comedy—a comedy based
on a unique combination of verbal wit and cynicism about human
motivation, particularly if that motivation had anything to do
with love. The plays are brilliant, yet everyone, student and
teacher alike, has difficulty remembering the individual plots
and characters of Restoration comedy. This is not because they
are all alike, but because in our rapid courses in the drama everything tends to coalesce; and we blame the plays rather than the
system of education.

It is best to speak of Restoration comedy as a style in the same
way that we speak of a school of painting in which the artists

strive for excellence within an established body of conventions. If the usual product of such schools is a dull imitation of previous models, it is also true that such models often provide the basic formulas for the true genius. Congreve's period prized the "imitation"—a form in which the writer could show his genius by his originality in adapting a satire of Horace and Juvenal to contemporary life without doing violence to the intention of the older poem. Mozart's indebtedness to the music of his contemporaries and Congreve's borrowings from the plays of Dryden, Shadwell, and Wycherley are best understood in this light. To appreciate Congreve fully, we must be prepared to grasp the originality, subtlety, and intelligence within the formula.

In discussing the individual plays of Congreve, I have tried to keep in mind the intellectual, social, and political milieu in which they were written. The reign of William and Mary was based on a revolutionary situation; and, if it inherited much from the past, it was prepared to regard the past in a new light. Recently, Aubrey Williams has suggested a Christian reading of Congreve, arguing that "to the extent that *Incognita* and the plays do reveal God's hand in the most fashionable intrigues, and in the most fashionable settings, these works must be read as being, in their own special ways, so many justifications of the ways of God to man—as being so many drawing-room theodicies of the greatest civility, urbanity, and wit."[2] Insofar as this suggestion attempts to establish an ethical basis for Congreve's plays it is a useful one, but it seems to me a very limited way of viewing the writings of Congreve and his decade. Congreve lived in a Christian world and received a Christian education, but he also lived in the Enlightenment and in a decade of unusual intellectual curiosity. It was the time of John Locke, John Toland, Thomas Burnet, Pierre Bayle, and Wilhelm Leibniz; it was also a time when arguments for the emancipation of women, for Deism, for divorce, and for wild social and economic schemes were listened to with attention and, sometimes, with respect. If Congreve's plays are to be seen as "drawing-room theodicies," the concept of good and evil to be found in them will have to be seen in terms equal to the complexity of the period and the subtlety of the artist and thinker who created them.

In a brief study such as this one, I have been able to suggest only a small portion of the forces at work behind Congreve's plays. Speaking of the inevitable selectivity of historical studies, Levi-Strauss concludes: "History is therefore never history, but history-for. It is partial in the sense of being biased even when it claims not to be, for it inevitably remains partial—that is, incomplete—and this is itself a form of partiality."[3] I must confess to this type of partiality. A full study of Congreve would have to read the social and economic causation underlying the very substance of his character and his action. I have preferred to concentrate on a detailed reading of the plays in relation to the way Congreve's period was mirrored in the writings of his contemporaries on love and marriage and, more particularly, in the plays of the 1690's. That decade of playwrights took the often crude comedies of the time of Charles II and made them artful and sophisticated. In the hands of Congreve and Vanbrugh, Restoration comedy became at once more passionate and explorative (Collier would have said more immoral and profane) on subjects connected with manners and morals. If some of the vigor of Etherege, Wycherley, and Dryden was lost, much was gained. It was the high point of English comedy, and its greatest master was Congreve.

Notes and References

Chapter One

1. Alexander Pope, *Correspondence,* ed. George Sherburn (Oxford, 1956), III, 449.
2. William Congreve, *Letters and Documents,* ed. John C. Hodges (New York, 1964), p. 48.
3. *Ibid.,* p. 188.
4. For most of the facts concerning Congreve's life, I have drawn upon John C. Hodges, *William Congreve the Man* (New York, 1941).
5. For Congreve's education, see Hodges' *Congreve,* pp. 12-29; and Irvin Ehrenpreis, *Swift* (Cambridge, Mass., 1962), I, 34-88.
6. For Congreve's relationship with Keally, see Kathleen Lynch, *A Congreve Gallery* (Cambridge, Mass., 1951), pp. 23-36.
7. *Prologues and Epilogues in the Irish Theatre,* Harvard College Library Ms. English 674F, fol. 21. See also William Clark, *The Early Irish Stage* (Oxford, 1955), p. 95.
8. Peter Motteux, *The Gentleman's Journal,* I (May, 1692), 9; (June, 1692), 15; II (May, 1693), 153; (June, 1693), 222-23; (October, 1693), 325, 335-38.
9. Gilbert Burnet, *An Essay on the Memory of the Late Queen* (London, 1695), p. 80.
10. John Harrington Smith, *The Gay Couple* (Cambridge, Mass., 1948), pp. 108-37.
11. Kathleen Lynch, *The Social Mode of Restoration Comedy* (New York, 1926), pp. 182-217.
12. See Dane Smith, *The Critics in the Audience of the London Theatres from Buckingham to Sheridan* (Albuquerque, 1953), pp. 37-38.
13. *The Poetical Register* (London, 1719), p. 41.
14. *Gentleman's Journal,* II (January, 1693), 61.
15. Egerton Ms. 2623.
16. In William Congreve, *The Mourning Bride, Poems and Miscellanies,* ed. Bonamy Dobrée (London, 1928), p. 245. Subsequent citations to Congreve's works appearing in my text will refer to this volume as volume two of the two volume edition of Congreve edited by Dobrée in the World's Classics series. The first volume, published originally in 1925 with the title *Comedies,* will be cited in the text as volume one. Citations from the plays will be according to act, scene, and line number.
17. *Gentleman's Journal,* II (November, 1693), 374.

18. "Preface," *King Arthur*, quoted in Jacob, *Poetic Register*, p. 43.

19. Ed. Staring Wells (Princeton, 1942), p. 104.

20. *Letters and Documents*, pp. 20-21.

21. P. 84.

22. Quoted in D. Crane Taylor, *William Congreve* (New York, 1963), p. 200.

23. *Letters and Documents*, p. 51.

24. *Ibid.*, p. 54.

25. Thomas Otway, *Works* (London, 1813), III, 99.

26. *Les Libertins au XVIIe Siècle*, ed. Antoine Adam (Paris, 1964), pp. 33-62.

27. Gracián, *The Art of Worldly Wisdom*, trans. Joseph Jacobs (New York, 1943), pp. 123-25.

28. *A Satyr against Wit* (London, 1700), pp. 5, 7.

29. Killigrew, *Comedies and Tragedies* (London, 1664), p. 346.

Chapter Two

1. (London, 1704), p. 25.

2. François Hedelin, D'Aubignac, *The Whole Art of the Stage* (London, 1684), Part II, p. 141.

3. "Epilogue," *The Conquest of Granada*, Part II, in *Dramatic Works*, ed. Montague Summers (London, 1932), III, 164.

4. For a fuller discussion of the question of satire and its relation to Congreve's comedies, see my article, "Congreve, Collier, and the World of the Play," *College English*, XXX (April, 1969), 555-61.

5. *Love for Money* (London, 1691), p. 18.

6. See *Biographia Britannica*, 2nd ed. (London, 1789), IV, 79-80.

7. See Ridpath, *The Stage Condemned* (London, 1698), 189-94.

8. For some suggestions of what still needs to be discussed in connection with the Collier controversy, see Edward Hooker's review of Sister Rose Anthony's *The Jeremy Collier Stage Controversy* (Milwaukee, 1937), in *Modern Language Notes*, LIV (May, 1939), 386-89.

9. *A Farther Vindication of the Short View* (London, 1708), p. 33.

10. *Mr. Collier's Dissuasive from the Play-House* (London, 1704), p. 9. For similar reports of actors arrested, see Arthur Bedford, *The Evil and Danger of Stage-Plays* (London, 1706), pp. 4, 223.

11. *Adventures of Covent-garden*, in *Complete Works*, ed. Charles Stonehill (London, 1930), II, 207.

12. *A Short View of the Immorality and Profaneness of the English Stage*, 4th ed. (London, 1699), p. 204.

13. Renaissance and neo-Classical critics misunderstood Aristotle on the end of comedy and on the kind of characters appropriate to it. As Butcher pointed out, such critics indulged in a "perversion of language" by reading class distinctions into Aristotle's ethical concepts. See S. H. Butcher, *Aristotle's Theory of Poetry and Fine Art*, 4th ed.

(New York, 1957), pp. 229-38; and for a subtler interpretation, Gerald Else, *Aristotle's Poetics* (Cambridge, Mass., 1957), pp. 69-82, 186-90. Voltaire approved of Congreve's treatment of the nobility. "The language," he wrote in his *Letters concerning the English Nation*, "is everywhere that of men of fashion, but their actions are those of Knaves, a proof that he was perfectly well acquainted with human nature and frequented what we call polite company."

14. See Alfred Jackson, "The Stage and the Authorities, 1700-1714 (As Revealed in the Newspapers)," *Review of English Studies*, XIV (January, 1938), 53-62.

Chapter Three

1. 2nd ed. (London, 1789), IV, 69.

2. H. G. B. Brett-Smith, ed., *Incognita*, by William Congreve (Oxford, 1922), p. xii.

3. *Memoirs of the Life, Writings and Amours of William Congreve Esq.* (London, 1730), p. 125.

4. Wagenknecht, *Cavalcade of the the English Novel* (New York, 1943), p. 19; and Allen, *The English Novel* (London, 1960), p. 34.

5. Boileau wrote his dialogue between 1664 and 1665, and his doubts expressed in his preface to this piece in 1710, whether any-one would still be interested in a piece on a form "out of Date and hardly read at all," would have been applicable in 1692. See Nicolas Boileau, *The Posthumous Works* (London, 1713), p. 115.

6. II (February, 1692), 58.

7. *Works*, ed. Montague Summers (London, 1915), V, 277, 369 and Pierre Bayle, *The Dictionary*, trans. Pierre Des Maizeau (London, 1734-38), III, 552.

8. F. W. Bateson, ed., *The Works of Congreve* (London, 1930), p. xxv.

9. John C. Hodges, ed., *The Library of William Congreve* (New York, 1955), p. 97 (item 573).

10. See Scudéry, "Preface to Ibrahim" (1641), and Pierre Corneille, "Discourse," (1660), in *Literary Criticism, Plato to Dryden*, ed. Allan Gilbert (New York, 1940), pp. 576 and 582. See also Madeleine de Scudéry, *Conversations upon Several Subjects*, trans. Ferrand Spence (London, 1683), II, 34-52.

11. (London, 1684), Part I, p. 91. See also Jacques Scherer, *La Dramaturgie Classique en France* (Paris, 1964), pp. 266-84.

12. Paul Scarron, *The Comical Romance and Other Tales*, trans. Tom Brown *et al.* (London, 1892), II, 230. Scarron's *novella, Two Rival Brothers*, has a number of resemblances to *Incognita*, including a character named Don Fabio.

13. An example of a realistic mood and setting may be found at the beginning of the seventh novel included in *Delightful Novels Exemplified in Eight Histories* (London, 1686), p. 137: "The Vast

Number of Candles, that in the Winter Quarter are hung out every Night, and serve as an Ornament to the streets of *London*, began to light those who walk late without Torches, when one of the most Famous Surgeons of that populous City was sent for in great hast. . . ."

14. See E. S. de Beer, "Congreve's *Incognita*: The Source of Its Setting," *Review of English Studies*, VIII (January, 1932), 74-77.

15. For popular discussions of Descartes, Malebranche, and Norris, see *The Gentleman's Journal*, I (February, 1692), 21; I (March, 1692), 23; I (April, 1692), 22; II (August, 1693), 262-64.

Chapter Four

1. *Works*, ed. Montague Summers (London, 1927), IV, 287.

2. British Museum Add. Mss. 4221. f. 341.

3. See Thomas Durfey, *The Marriage-Hater Match'd* (London, 1692), sig. A4.

4. Shadwell, *Works*, III, 28; Southerne, *Works* (London, 1721), I, 310. There may also be an imitation of Rochester's manner in Bellmour's speech, since it is similar to Nemour's imitation of Rosidore (i.e., Rochester) in Nathaniel Lee's *Princess of Cleve* (1680). See Lee, *Works*, ed. Thomas Stroup and Arthur Cooke (New Brunswick), II, 188 (III, i).

5. *Works of Congreve*, (London, 1930), p. xix.

6. David Abercrombie, *A Discourse of Wit* (London, 1686), p. 106.

7. William Davenant, *Works*, ed. W. H. Logan and James Maidment (Edinburgh, 1872-1875), II, 147, 182.

8. "The saying of Humorous Things, does not distinguish Characters; For every person in a Comedy may be allow'd to speak them. . . . Tho I make a Difference betwixt *Wit* and *Humour;* yet I do not think that Humourous Characters exclude Wit: No, but the Manner of *Wit* should be adapted to the Humour." "Concerning Humour in Comedy," *Works*, ed. Dobrée, I, 2.

9. For a discussion of the conflict between the practical demands of the theater and critical principles on the question of soliloquies, see François Hedelin, Abbé D' Aubignac, *The Whole Art of the Stage* (London, 1684), Part II, pp. 57-62; and Jacques Scherer, *La Dramaturgie Classique en France* (Paris, 1964), pp. 245-60.

10. Thomas Otway, *Works*, ed. J. C. Gosh (Oxford, 1932), II, 190.

11. For a sample of baby talk where the parties are insincere, see Durfey, *Love for Money* (1691), p. 9 (I, i).

12. See Lilia-Bianca's description of an ideal man in Fletcher's *The Wild Goose Chase*, ed. A. R. Waller (Cambridge, 1906), IV, 328 (I, iii).

13. See L. C. Knights, "Restoration Comedy: The Reality and the Myth," *Explorations* (London, 1946), pp. 131-54. For the suggestions of the way language may be used to avoid emotional confrontation

and as a form of play, see Eric Berne's *Transactional Analysis in Psychotherapy* (New York, 1961), pp. 83-89; and Johan Huizinga, *Homo Ludens* (Boston, 1962).

14. *Wary Widdow: or, Sir Noisy Parrot* (London, 1693), sig. A3-A3v.

Chapter Five

1. Jeremy Collier, *A Short View of the Immorality and Profaneness of the English Stage*, 4th ed. (London, 1699), p. 12.

2. See for example, *Animadversions on Mr. Congreve's Late Answer to Mr. Collier* (London, 1698), p. 18. Collier clarified his attitude later and showed that Congreve's sarcastic reconstruction was very close to his critical position. See Collier, *A Defense of the Short View* (London, 1699), p. 22.

3. Roland Barthes, *On Racine*, trans. Richard Howard (New York, 1964), pp. 3-8. 97-103.

4. John Wilmot, Earl of Rochester, "A Satire against Mankind," *Poems*, ed. Vivian De Sola Pinto, 2nd ed. (Cambridge, Mass., 1964), p. 122 (II, 161-67).

5. "Letter on the Imposter," in *Theories of Comedy*, ed. Paul Lauter (New York, 1964), pp. 146-47, 150.

6. Jean Bellegarde, *Reflections upon Ridicule*, 3rd ed. (London, 1717), I, 166.

7. Eric Berne, *The Games People Play* (New York, 1964), pp. 98-101.

8. See, for example, Maria's soliloquy in Durfey's *The Fond Husband* (London, 1676), p. 12: "My love refus'd! 'Tis Death to the dull Fool; Death, double Death; Damnation too 'tis likely.—But why did I name it Love? there is no such word; for with this breath I banish it for ever, and in my breast receive obscure revenge, my Hearts delightful Darling! Oh! the pleasure in that slender word Revenge!"

9. Congreve's *Semele* is the best key here. Both Juno and Semele are ruled by passions of love, ambition, and revenge. See especially Semele's song beginning "I love and am lov'd, yet more I desire" (III, ii, 1-11).

10. *The Squire of Alsatia, Works,* IV, 227-28, 240, 278.

11. "De L' Essence du Rire," *Ouvres Complètes*, ed. Y. G. Le Dantec (Paris, 1961), p. 993.

12. Ed. Staring Wells (Princeton, 1937), p. 27.

13. *Ars Poetica*, trans. H. Rushton Fairchild, Loeb Library ed. (London, 1961), p. 470 [11. 240-241].

14. See François Hedelin, Abbé D' Abignac, *The Whole Art of the Stage* (London, 1686), Part I, pp. 22, 34-36, 11-134; Part II, pp. 83, 88. See also Dryden's comparison of the playwrights to builders

in his "To My Dear Friend Mr. Congreve, On His Comedy, Call'd The Double Dealer" (I, 118).

15. Even some French critics questioned Le Bossu's theories. See Jean Le Clerc, *Parhasiana* (London, 1700), pp. 42-48.

16. Una Ellis-Fermor, *The Frontiers of Drama* (London, 1946), p. 97, n.1.

17. *Whole Art of the Stage*, Part II, p. 49.

18. See Daniel Kenrick's backhanded compliment in *A New Session of the Poets* (London, 1700), p. 6: "His *Double Dealer* at a distance stood / At once extremely regular, and lew'd."

19. *Whole Art of the Stage*, Part II, p. 141.

20. I (May, 1692), 18-19.

21. Laurence Echard, trans., *Terence's Comedies* (London, 1694), p. xi.

22. This underscored the quotation from Horace which was retained from the title page of the first edition: "Yet at times even Comedy raises her voice, and an angry Chremes storms in swelling tones." *Ars Poetica*, Loeb Library ed., p. 458 [ll. 93-94]. Montague Summers is correct, however, in denying any important direct influence from Terence. See Summers, ed., *The Complete Works of William Congreve* (London, 1923), II, 3.

Chapter Six

1. Jeremy Collier, *A Short View of the Immorality and Profaneness of the English Stage*, 4th ed. (London, 1699), p. 142.

2. Giovanni Boccaccio, *The Decameron*, 5th day, 9th story.

3. *The Observer Weekend Review*, October 24, 1965, p. 24.

4. Thomas Durfey, *Love for Money* (London, 1689), p. 45.

5. Even in his own day Congreve was regarded as eclectic. The author of *Animadversions on Mr. Congreve's Late Answer to Mr. Collier* (London, 1698), pp. 7, 38, argued that the plays were merely "little Compounds of the Whole Body of Scriblers," and asked, "What has he publish'd that is not stolen?"

6. To have some idea of the moral evil inherent in Sir Sampson's unchristian behavior toward his son, it might be useful to contrast his actions with those of Shadwell's kindly father in *The Scourers*. Mr. Rant advises his son to abandon his life of riot and vice, and after a moving, tearful scene, converts him to a virtuous life. He has sacrificed wealth and a title for his son and loves him as an ideal father should. See Shadwell, *Works*, ed. Montague Summers, V, 138-41.

7. Durfey, *Sir Barnaby Whig* (London, 1681), p. 32. For the possible influence of Ravenscroft's *The Canterbury Guests* on Congreve's sailor, see Edward Norris, "A Possible Source of Congreve's Sailor Ben," *Modern Language Notes*, XLIX (May, 1934), 334-35.

8. Pp. 20, 53.

9. See for example, "Song in Dialogue for Two Women" (II, 242); and "Thus to a ripe, consenting Maid" (II, 369). It was no accident that Congreve translated that section of Ovid's *Art of Love* dealing with this matter.

10. Gellert Alleman, *Matrimonial Law and the Materials of Restoration Comedy* (Wallingford, 1942), pp. 60-79.

Chapter Seven

1. Charles Gildon, ed., *The Lives and Characters of The English Dramatic Poets*, by Gerard Langbaine (London, 1699), p. 23.

2. Jeremy Collier, *A Short View of the Immorality and Profaneness of the English Stage*, 4th ed. (London, 1699), p. 34.

3. Langbaine, p. 24. For a summary of critical opinion, see Emmett Avery, *Congreve's Plays on the Eighteenth Century Stage* (New York, 1951), pp. 19-24. Avery tends to make Kames more severe than he actually is. Though Kames does find fault with the structure, he calls *The Mourning Bride* "one of the most complete pieces England has to boast of." See Henry Home, Lord Kames, *Elements of Criticism*, 4th ed. (Edinburgh, 1769), p. 428.

4. [Charles Gildon?] *The Life of Thomas Betterton* (London, 1710), pp. 40-72, 77-82, 87. Charles Gildon's shrewd observation on the resemblance between La Calprenède's scene in *Cleopatre* involving the meeting of Artaban and Elisa at the tomb of Tiridate and the encounter of Almeria and Alphonso in the temple shows that Congreve, like so many contemporary playwrights, was indebted to the French romance. See *Hymen's Pradudia: or Cleopatra*, trans. James Webb et al. (London, 1663), II, 94-95 (VII, iii).

5. Congreve may also have taken certain hints for his plot from Otway's *Alcibiades* (1675) and Southerne's *The Loyal Brother* (1682).

6. Thomas Rymer, the most feared critic of the Restoration, followed Scaliger in making the description of night the basis for comparing the merits of various poets. He found Dryden's description from *The Indian Emperor* better than similar passages in such poets as Tasso, Marius, and Chapelain. See Rymer, *Preface to the Translation of Rapin's Reflections on Aristotle's Treatise of Poesie* (1674), in *Critical Essays of the Seventeenth Century*, ed. Joel Spingarn (Oxford, 1908), II, 174-79.

7. Georges Poulet, *Studies in Human Time*, trans. Elliot Coleman (Baltimore, 1956), pp. 19-21.

8. Roland Barthes, *On Racine*, trans. Richard Howard (New York, 1964), pp. 8-10.

9. For Johnson's qualification of his remarks in the "Life of Congreve," see James Boswell, *The Life of Samuel Johnson*, ed. G. B. Hill and L. F. Powell (Oxford, 1934), II, 85-87.

10. John Dryden and Nathaniel Lee, *Oedipus*, in *Dramatic Works*,

by John Dryden, ed. Montague Summers (London, 1932), IV, 382-83.

11. *Ibid.*, IV, 418.

12. John Locke, *An Essay concerning Human Understanding*, ed. Alexander Fraser (New York, 1959), I, 199. See also René Descartes, *Works*, trans. Elizabeth Haldene and G. R. T. Ross (New York, 1955), I, 341, 347.

13. Charles Gildon was probably the first to suggest Congreve's debt to Racine "when he formed his Design." Though attempts to demonstrate verbal borrowings have failed, there are similarities between the situation of the characters in *Bajazet* and *The Mourning Bride* that make Gildon's thesis very likely. See Langbaine, p. 24. For a summary of the debate over this problem, see Katherine Wheatley, *Racine and English Classicism* (Austen, 1956), pp. 57-81. Wheatley is probably correct in judging that "in all essentials Congreve's play is antithetical to the Racinian genre," but in proving that Congreve's play is very English she does not invalidate the case for Racine's influence. The plays of Corneille, Molière, and Racine—after they were adapted and revised for the English stage—would have been almost unrecognizable to their authors.

14. See for example François Hedelin, Abbé D'Aubignac, *The Whole Art of the Stage* (London, 1684), Part I, p. 39.

15. Eric Rothstein has recently praised the "thematic" imagery of *The Mourning Bride*, pointing to the large number of references to water and the sea. See *Restoration Tragedy* (Madison, 1967), pp. 173-80.

Chapter Eight

1. Samuel Johnson, *Lives of the English Poets*, ed. George B. Hill (Oxford, 1905), II, 228.

2. Cf. *Incognita*, II, 19.

3. Puzzles, "Enigmas," and games similar to the kind played by Mirabell and Millamant were a prominent feature of Motteux's *Gentlemans' Journal*, which is an excellent index of contemporary taste. Congreve uses his game in much the same manner as Jane Austen was to do in *Emma*. If he did not actually write the "Allegory on the game of Quadrille," a sexual interpretation of a popular card game, he was certainly capable of this kind of performance. For an analysis of the "play" behind such games, see Johan Huizinga, *Homo Ludens* (Boston, 1962), pp. 105-18, 132-34.

4. *The Social Mode of Restoration Comedy* (New York, 1926), especially pp. 182-217.

5. In this scene Congreve resolves the debate between Mellefont and Cynthia in *The Double Dealer* (II, iii, 2-26) on the side of Mellefont. The distinction between the game of true love and other games is that the first is actually a ritual which resolves contradictions and brings about a union between two initially separate and seemingly

hostile forces rather than a competition in which there must be a winner and a loser. Levi-Strauss points out that in games there is an apparent order and symmetry with the rules the same for both sides and the contest decided by chance or talent; whereas the "reverse is true of ritual. There is an asymmetry, which is postulated in advance between profane and sacred, faithful and officiating, dead and living, initiated etc., and the 'game' consists in making all the participants pass to the winning side by means of events, the nature and ordering of which is genuinely structural." Though both Mirabell and Millamant treat life as a game, they raise their personal relations to a higher plain of meaning. See Claude Levi-Strauss, *The Savage Mind* (London, 1966), p. 32.

6. For a complete misunderstanding of the emotional tone of Congreve and Restoration comedy, see L. C. Knights, "Restoration Comedy: The Reality and the Myth," in *Explorations* (London, 1946), pp. 131-54. The seriousness with which Knights's remarks are still regarded is evidenced by the somewhat defensive tone of Bernard Harris's excellent essay, "The Dialect of those Fanatic Times," *Restoration Theatre,* ed. John Brown and Bernard Harris (London, 1965), pp. 13-17.

7. V, iv, 22-26. That music is evil in itself might seem an absurd exaggeration of the Christian position, but see William Prynne, *Historio-Mastix* (London, 1633), p. 286; and Jeremy Collier, *A Short View of the Immorality and Profaneness of the English Stage,* 4th ed. (London, 1699), pp. 278-80.

8. Quoted in *Biographia Britannica,* 2nd ed. (London, 1789), IV, 80.

9. *Works* (London, 1700), I, 487-88.

Chapter Nine

1. *Poetical Miscellanies* (London, 1704), V, 180.

2. *An Essay upon Pastoral* (London, 1695), Sig. Bi^v. See also *The Mourning Poets* (London, 1695), p. 4.

3. William Pittis, *An Epistolary Poem to N. Tate* (London, 1696), preface.

4. William Melmoth, *The Letters of Sir Thomas Fitzosborne,* 3rd ed. (London, 1750), pp. 270-75.

5. Bateson, ed., *The Works of Congreve* (London, 1930), p. xxvi.

6. *Correspondence,* ed. George Sherburn (Oxford, 1956), III, 29.

7. See *Heraclitus Ridens,* February 26-29, 1704; and *A New Collection of Poems Relating to State Affairs* (London, 1705), p. 567.

Chapter Ten

1. Catherine Cockburn, *Works* (London, 1751), II, 564-65.

2. "Congreve's *Incognita* and the Contrivances of Providence,"

Imagined Worlds, ed. Maynard Mack and Ian Gregor (London, 1968), p. 17. See also Aubrey Williams, "Poetical Justice, the Contrivances of Providence, and the Works of William Congreve," *English Literary History*, XXXV (1968), 540-65.

3. *The Savage Mind* (London, 1966), p. 257.

Selected Bibliography

PRIMARY SOURCES

1. Collected Works

The Works of Mr. William Congreve, 3 vols. London, 1710. The first collected edition of plays and poems. The fifth edition appeared in 1730, and there were many editions throughout the eighteenth century including the well-printed and illustrated Baskerville edition in 1761.

The Complete Works. Ed. Montague Summers. 4 vols. London: The Nonesuch Press, 1923. Text of plays based on the first editions. Includes complete textual notes.

The Comedies, The Mourning Bride, Poems and Miscellanies. Ed. Bonamy Dobrée. 2 vols. London: Oxford University Press, 1925-1928. Text of plays based on the *Works* (1710). Includes some of the doubtful works.

The Works. Ed. F. W. Bateson. London: P. Davies, 1930. The comedies based on the *Works* (1710) and a selection of the poems only. A good introduction and textual notes.

The Complete Plays. Ed. Herbert Davis. Chicago: University of Chicago Press, 1967. Text based on the first editions.

2. Separate Works

Incognita: or, Love and Duty Reconcil'd. London, 1692. Fiction.
————— ed. H. F. B. Brett-Smith. Oxford: B. Blackwell, 1922.

The Satires of D. J. Juvenalis, Translated into English Verse. By Mr. Dryden, and . . . other eminent hands [No. 10 by Congreve]. *Together with the Satires of A. Persius Flaccus.* Made English by Mr. Dryden. [Commendatory verses by Congreve.] London, 1693. Verse.

The Old Batchelor. London, 1693. Comedy.

The Double Dealer. London, 1694. Comedy.

The Mourning Muse of Alexis. A Pastoral Lamenting the Death of Queen Mary. London, 1695. Verse.

Love for Love. London, 1695. Comedy.

A Pindarique Ode, Humbly Offer'd to the King on His Taking Namure. London, 1695. Verse.

An Essay Concerning Humour in Comedy. In *Letters upon Several Occasions,* ed. John Dennis. London, 1696. Criticism.

The Mourning Bride. London, 1697. Tragedy.

The Birth of the Muse. London, 1698. Verse.

181

Amendments of Mr. Collier's False and Imperfect Citations from the Old Batchelour, Double Dealer, Love for Love, Mourning Bride. By the Author of Those Plays. London, 1698. Criticism.

The Way of the World. London, 1700. Comedy.

————. Ed. Kathleen M. Lynch. Regents Restoration Drama Series. Lincoln, Nebraska: University of Nebraska Press, 1965.

The Judgment of Paris: a Masque. London, 1701. Masque.

A Hymn to Harmony, Written in Honour of St. Cecilia's Day. London, 1703. Verse.

The Tears of Amaryllis for Amyntas: a Pastoral on the Death of the Marquis of Blandford. London, 1703. Verse.

A Pindarique Ode, Humbly Offer'd to the Queen, on the Victorious Progress of her Majesty's Arms, Under the Conduct of the Duke of Marlborough. To which is Prefixed a Discourse on the Pindarique Ode. London, 1706. Verse and criticism.

Ovid's Art of Love [Book III translated by Congreve]. London, 1709. Verse.

Ovid's Metamorphoses [Translated by Dryden, Addison, Congreve etc. "Orpheus and Eurydice" and "The Tale of Cyparissus" by Congreve]. London, 1717. Verse.

"Preface." *The Dramatic Works of Dryden.* Ed. W. Congreve. 6 vols. London, 1717. Criticism.

An Impossible Thing. A Tale. London, 1720. Verse. In the same volume: "The Peasant in Search of his Heifer."

A Letter to Viscount Cobham. London, 1729. Verse.

Mr. Congreve's Last Will and Testament, with Characters of his Writings . . . to Which are Added, Two Pieces, viz. I. Of Rightly Improving the Present Time . . . II. The Game of Quadrille. An Allegory. London, 1729. Prose and verse.

3. Letters

William Congreve: Letters & Documents. Ed. John C. Hodges. New York: Harcourt, Brace and World, 1964.

SECONDARY SOURCES

ALLEMAN, GELLERT. *Matrimonial Law and the Materials of Restoration Comedy.* Wallingford: University of Pennsylvania, 1942. Clarifies the relationship between love and marriage in the comedies and the operation of matrimonial law in real life.

Animadversions on Mr. Congreve's Late Answer to Mr. Collier. In a Dialogue between Mr. Smith and Mr. Johnson. Anon. pamph. London, 1698. Witty attack on Congreve in support of Jeremy Collier; contains some interesting details on Congreve's life and some sharp criticism.

ANTHONY, SISTER ROSE. *The Jeremy Collier Stage Controversy 1698-1726*. Milwaukee: Marquette University Press, 1937. Study biased in favor of Collier, inadequate as a critical document and faulty in its facts; but the most detailed study of the Collier controversy.

AVERY, EMMETT. "The Premier of *Mourning Bride*," *Modern Language Notes*, LVII (1942), 55-57. Dates the thirteen night's run of Congreve's tragedy.

————. *Congreve's Plays on the Eighteenth-Century Stage*. Modern Language Association of America Monograph Series, No. 18. New York: Modern Language Association of America, 1951. Excellent study of the reception and reputation of Congreve's plays.

————. *The London Stage. Part 2: 1700-1729*. 2 vols. Carbondale: Southern Illinois University Press, 1960. Invaluable for its list of performances and contemporary comment on the drama. Introduction gives an excellent picture of the actors, theaters, and the types of plays being written.

BALL, F. ERLINGTON. "Congreve as a Ballad-writer," *Notes and Queries*, ser. 12, VIII (1921), 301-3. Ascribes "Jack Frenchman's Defeat" and other ballads to Congreve.

BARNARD, JOHN. "Did Congreve Write *A Satyr Against Love*," *Bulletin of the New York Public Library*, LXVIII (1964), 308-22. Argues convincingly that Congreve did not write this poem included in Dobrée's edition.

BATESON, F. W. "Second Thoughts: II. L. C. Knights and Restoration Comedy," *Essays in Criticism*, VII (1957), 56-67. A reply to L. C. Knights's attack on Restoration comedy defending its comic seriousness. Bateson draws many of his examples from *Love for Love*.

BERKELEY, DAVID. "Préciosité and the Restoration Comedy of Manners," *Huntington Library Quarterly*, XVIII (1955), 109-28. Includes some useful comments on Congreve's parody of the *précieuse* vocabulary.

BERNBAUM, ERNEST. *The Drama of Sensibility*. Harvard Studies in English, No. 3. Boston: Ginn, 1915. Draws a clear distinction between Congreve's anti-sentimentalism and later sentimental comedy. Good antidote to certain modern critics like Rose Zimbardo, who regard Congreve as halfway on the road to sentimentalism.

BROSSMAN, S. W. "Dryden's Cassandra and Congreve's Zara," *Notes and Queries*, N.S. III (1956), 102-3. Parallels drawn by Brossman do not reveal any specific borrowings.

CAMPBELL, JOHN. "Congreve." *Biographia Britannica*. 2nd ed. Rev. Andrew Kippis. London, 1789. Excellent summary of Congreve's literary reputation in the eighteenth century with ample quotations from various critics.

CIBBER, COLLEY. *An Apology for the Life of Mr. Colly Cibber*. Ed. Robert Lowe. 2 vols. London: J. C. Nimmo, 1889. Best contemporary picture of the London stage as Congreve knew it— its playwrights, actors, and theater managers.

COLLIER, JEREMY. *A Short View of the Immorality and Profaneness of the English Stage*. 4th ed. London, 1699. Devastating attack on the morality of Restoration drama, particularly on Dryden, Congreve, Durfey, and Vanbrugh.

————. *A Defence of the Short View of the Profaneness and Immorality of the English Stage etc. Being a Reply to Mr. Congreve's Amendments, etc.* London, 1699. Direct reply to Congreve's and Vanbrugh's counterattacks in which Collier clarifies his critical position.

————. *A Second Defence of the Short View of the Profaneness and Immorality of the English Stage.* London, 1700. Collier's reply to able defenses of the stage by James Drake and John Dennis.

————. *Mr. Collier's Dissuasive from the Play-house.* London, 1704. In a mood of triumph, Collier suggests abolishing the stage entirely.

————. *A Farther Vindication of the Short View.* London, 1708. Reply to Edward Filmer's *A Defence of Plays: or the Stage Vindicated* (1707) arguing that there can be no defense.

A Comparison Between the Two Stages. Ed. Staring Wells. Princeton: Princeton University Press, 1942. Excellent compendium of stage gossip and criticism in 1702 with frequent mention of Congreve.

COOKE, ARTHUR L. "Two Parallels between Dryden's *Wild Gallant* and Congreve's *Love for Love*," *Notes and Queries*, N.S. I (1954), 27-28. "Parallels" are general enough to fit any number of Restoration comedies.

CORRIGAN, BEATRICE. "Congreve's *Mourning Bride* and Cottellini's *Almeria*," *Annali Instituto Universitario Orientale, Napoli, Sezione Romane*, IV (1962), 145-66. Interesting study of the translation into Italian and adaptation of Congreve's play into an opera, first performed at Livorno in 1761.

DEBEER, E. S. "Congreve's Incognita: The Source of its Setting with a note on Wilson's *Belphegor*," *Review of English Studies*, VIII (1932), 74-77. Congreve's debt to John Raymond's *An Itinerary Containing a Voyage Made through Italy, in the Years 1646, and 1647* (London, 1648).

DENNIS, JOHN. *Critical Works*. Ed. Edward Hooker. 2 vols. Baltimore: the Johns Hopkins Press, 1938-1943. Dennis was a fast friend of Congreve and an admirer and defender of his style of comedy.

DOBRÉE, BONAMY. *Restoration Comedy 1660-1720*. Oxford: Oxford University Press, 1924. Probably the first balanced view of

Restoration comedy; contains a suggestive comparison between Congreve and Flaubert.

————. *William Congreve: A Conversation between Swift and Gay.* University of Washington Chapbooks, No. 26. Seattle: University of Washington bookstore, 1929. Amusing re-creation of Congreve's character through the eyes of his friends.

————. *William Congreve. Writers and Their Work,* No. 164. London: British Council, 1963. Useful, brief introduction to Congreve; has a helpful bibliography.

FALLS, CYRIL. "Congreve." *The Critics Armoury.* London: R. Cobden-Sanderson, 1924. Useful as a summary of attitudes toward Congreve at a time when his reputation was on the rise.

FUJIMURA, THOMAS H. *The Restoration Comedy of Wit.* Princeton: Princeton University Press, 1952. Excellent analysis of the meaning of wit for the Restoration and its relevance to Restoration comedy.

GAGEN, JEAN. "Congreve's Mirabell and the Ideal of the Gentleman," *PMLA,* LXXIX (1964), 422-27. Study of the values behind Congreve's creation of Mirabell as an ideal hero.

GENEST, JOHN. *Some Account of the English Stage from the Restoration in 1660-1830.* 10 vols. Bath: H. E. Carrington, 1832. The list of plays has been superseded by *The London Stage,* but many of Genest's comments are personal and critical in nature.

GENTLEMAN, FRANCIS. *The Dramatic Censor.* 2 vols. London, 1770. Contains a general estimate of Congreve as well as a thorough examination of *The Mourning Bride.*

GILDON, CHARLES, ed. *The Lives and Characters of the English Dramatick Poets,* by Gerard Langbaine. London, 1699. Useful in its suggestion of possible sources for Congreve's plays and interesting for its distinctly moderate rapture for Congreve at a time when his reputation was at its height.

GOSSE, ANTHONY C. "The Omitted Scene in Congreve's *Love for Love,*" *Modern Philology,* LXI (1963), 40-42. Argues that the omitted scene was III, ii, not as Summers thought III, xii.

GOSSE, EDMUND. *Life of William Congreve.* New York: C. Scribner's Sons, 1924. First published in 1888 but revised to include new facts; the criticism, however, remains Victorian.

HAZLITT, WILLIAM. *Lectures on the English Comic Writers. The Complete Works.* Ed. P. P. Howe. 21 vols. London: Dent, 1930-1934. Hazlitt regards Congreve's plays as brilliant, realistic descriptions of an artificial society.

HODGES, JOHN C. "William Congreve in the Government Service," *Modern Philology,* XXVII (1929), 183-92. Notes that Congreve's literary production decreased as government sinecures brought him financial independence.

————. "The Ballad in Congreve's *Love for Love,*" *PMLA,* XLVIII

(1933), 953-54. Reinforces Ball's contention that Congreve wrote ballads.

———. "On the Date of Congreve's Birth," *Modern Philology,* XXXIII (1935), 83-85. A rebuttal to Taylor's contention that Congreve was born in 1669.

———. "The Dating of Congreve's Letters," *PMLA,* LI (1936), 153-64. Corrects the arrangement of letters in the editions of Summers and Dobrée.

———. "William Congreve: Confused Signatures," *[London] Times Literary Supplement,* August 15, 1936, p. 664. Warns that there were five William Congreves alive in 1700 whose signatures might be confused with that of the dramatist.

———. "Fresh MSS Sources for a Life of Wm. Congreve," *PMLA,* LIV (1939), 432-38. Outlines the new material that was to be used in his biography.

———. *William Congreve: The Man; A Biography from New Sources.* MLA General Series, No. 11. New York, 1941. Standard biography of Congreve bringing together all the known facts of his life.

———. "The Composition of Congreve's First Play," *PMLA,* LVIII (1943), 971-76. Dates the original composition of *The Old Batchelor* in 1689 and the revision in 1692.

———. *The Library of William Congreve.* New York: New York Public Library, 1955. This list of books in Congreve's library is reprinted from earlier issues of the *Bulletin of the New York Public Library.*

———. "Saint or Sinner: Some Congreve Letters and Documents," *Tennessee Studies in Literature,* No. 3 (Knoxville, 1957), pp. 3-15.

HOLLAND, NORMAN. *The First Modern Comedies.* Cambridge, Mass.: Harvard University Press, 1959. Brilliant study of appearance and reality in Restoration comedy.

HOWARD, EDWARD. *An Essay upon Pastoral.* London, 1695. Contains extravagant praise of Congreve as a writer of pastorals.

HOWARTH, R. G. "The Date of the Old Bachelor," *[London] Times Literary Supplement,* (June 13, 1936), p. 500. Suggests 1689 as the date for the composition of this play.

———. "Congreve's First Play: Addendum," *PMLA,* LXI (1946), 596-97. Reply to Hodges' dating of *The Old Batchelor,* assigning an earlier date for revision.

———. "Congreve and Ann Bracegirdle," *English Studies in Africa,* IV (1961), 159-61. Attack on Hodges' theory that Mrs. Bracegirdle became Congreve's mistress and a far less convincing argument to the same effect concerning the young Duchess of Marlborough.

HUNT, LEIGH. *The Dramatic Works of Wycherley, Congreve, Vanbrugh and Farquhar.* London: E. Moxon, 1840. Introductory section on Congreve attacks his plots as "over-ingenious," his wit as "tiresome," his characters as "heartless."

ISSACS, J. "Congreve and America," *Review of English Studies*, III (1927), 79. Gives some vivid details on the accident at Bath that may have hastened Congreve's death.

————. "Congreve's Library," *Library*, XX (1939), 41-42. List of some of Congreve's books including a fuller account of his volume of Otway than appears in Hodges' catalogue.

JACOB, GILES. *The Poetical Register*. London, 1719. The earliest life of Congreve containing information supplied by Congreve.

JOHNSON, SAMUEL. "Congreve." *Lives of the Poets*. Ed. George B. Hill. 3 vols. Oxford: Clarendon Press, 1905. Many of Johnson's strictures on Congreve reflect his opposition to Congreve's Whig politics and Congreve's low reputation at the time; but, as usual, Johnson's remarks are pertinent.

KAMES, LORD (HENRY HOME). *Elements of Criticism*. 3 vols. Edinburgh, 1762. Contains some interesting criticism of the unity of Congreve's plays.

KENRICK, DANIEL. *A New Session of the Poets, Occasion'd by the Death of Mr. Dreyden*. London, 1700. Apollo dismisses Congreve's petition to become the new laureate.

KNIGHTS, L. C. "Restoration Comedy: The Reality and the Myth." *Explorations*. London: Chatto and Windus, 1946. Most influential attack on Congreve and Restoration comedy in this century.

KOZIOL, HERBERT. "Pope's Sylphen and Congreve's 'Incognita,'" *Anglia*, LXX, (1952), 433-35. Study of attendant cupids from Shakespeare through *Incognita* and to *The Rape of the Lock*.

KRUTCH, JOSEPH WOOD. *Comedy and Conscience After the Restoration*. New York: Columbia University Press, 1961. Originally published in 1924, this study of the moral onslaught upon Restoration drama still commands respect.

LAMB, CHARLES. *Works*. Ed. E. V. Lucas. 7 vols. London: Methuen, 1903-1905. Essay "On the Artificial Comedy of the Last Century" argued that Congreve's comedy and that of his fellow dramatists depicted an unreal, fairy world. Set the tone for much later Congreve criticism and for many productions of his plays.

LEECH, CLIFFORD. "Congreve and the Century's End," *Philological Quarterly*, XLI (1962), 275-93. Judicious attempt to place Congreve in the 1690's with its combination of the old comic tradition and a new seriousness.

A Letter to Mr. Congreve. Anon. poem. London, 1698. More concerned with Congreve's patron, Charles Montague than with Congreve; but praises Congreve as a poet, comparing him to Theocritus, Virgil, and Milton.

LINCOLN, STODDARD. "The First Setting of Congreve's *Semele*," *Music and Letters (London)*, XLIV (1963), 103-11. Some interesting remarks on Congreve's meter in his libretto.

————. "Eccles and Congreve: Music and Drama on the Restoration Stage," *Theatre Notebook*, XVIII (1963), 7-18. Some excellent information and some interesting ideas on elements of parody in Congreve's songs.

LOFTIS, JOHN. *Comedy and Society from Congreve to Fielding*. Stanford Studies in Language and Literature, No. 19. Stanford: Stanford University Press, 1958. Discussion of the social context and content of the drama of Congreve and his contemporaries.

LYNCH, KATHLEEN. *The Social Mode of Restoration Comedy*. New York: Macmillan Company, 1926. Survey of the *précieuse* tradition in England before Congreve and its influence on him.

————. "Congreve's Irish Friend, Joseph Keally," *PMLA*, LIII (1938), 1076-87. Congreve's relationship with the friend to whom he wrote his warmest and most personal letters.

————. *A Congreve Gallery*. Cambridge, Mass.: Harvard University Press, 1951. Study of Congreve's most intimate friends.

————. "References to William Congreve in the Evelyn MSS," *Philological Quarterly*, XXXII (1953), 337-40. Glimpse into the life of Congreve's mistress, Lady Godolphin, suggesting that Lord Godolphin may have admired his wife's lover.

LYONS, CHARLES. "Congreve's Miracle of Love," *Criticism*, VI (1964), 331-48. Interpretation of *Love for Love* as an affirmation of the values underlying love and marriage with some detailed examination of Congreve's imagery.

MALLET, DAVID. "A Poem to the Memory of Mr. Congreve." *The Complete Poetical Works* by James Thomson. Ed. J. Logie Robertson. London: Oxford University Press, 1908. Panegyric on Congreve the man but mild censure of the morality of his comedies.

MAUROCORDATO, ALEXANDRE. *Ainsi Va le Monde*, Archives des Lettres Modernes, No. 76. Paris: Lettres Modernes, 1967. This structuralist interpretation of *The Way of the World* has disappointing results.

MELMOTH, WILLIAM. *The Letters of Sir Thomas Fitzosborne*. London, 1750. Contains a critique of Congreve's translations from Homer.

MEREDITH, GEORGE. *Essays on Comedy and the Uses of the Comic Spirit*. Ed. Lane Cooper. New York: Scribners, 1918. Congreve and Molière as the masters of comedy.

MIGNON, ELISABETH. *Crabbed Age and Youth*. Durham, N.C.: Duke University Press, 1947. Useful in connection with the struggles between Congreve's youthful protagonists and their guardians.

MONK, SAMUEL H. "A Note on Montague Summer's Edition of *The Way of the World*, Corrected," *Notes and Queries*, N.S. VII

(1960), 70. Sir Wilfull is compared with Caliban, not Sycorax.

MOTTEUX, PETER. *The Gentleman's Journal: or the Monthly Miscellany.* 3 vols. London, 1691-1694. Contains comments on Congreve's plays and reprints some of his songs.

The Mourning Poets: or, an Account of the Poems on the Death of the Queen. Anon. poem. London, 1695. Praises Congreve's poetry.

MUDRICK, MARVIN. "Restoration Comedy and Later." *English Stage Comedy.* Ed. W. K. Wimsatt. New York: Columbia University Press, 1955. Reply to L. C. Knights and defence of Restoration comedy on the grounds that it possessed a cogent appeal for the audience for whom it was written.

MUESCHKE, PAUL and MIRIAM. *A New View of Congreve's Way of the World.* University of Michigan Contributions in Modern Philology, No. 23. Ann Arbor: University of Michigan Press, 1958. Detailed analysis of Congreve's play in terms of balance and structure.

MUIR, KENNETH. "The Comedies of William Congreve." *Restoration Theatre.* Ed. John Brown and Bernard Harris. Stratford-upon-Avon Studies, No. 6. London: Shakespeare Institute, 1965.

NICOLL, ALLARDYCE. *History of English Drama 1660-1900.* 6 vols. Cambridge, [England]: University Press, 1959. Record of the changing forms of drama, taste, and the theater.

NORRIS, EDWARD T. "A Possible Source of Congreve's Sailor Ben," *Modern Language Notes,* XLIX (1934), 334-35. Suggests the influence of Edward Ravenscroft's sailor, Durzo, from *The Canterbury Guests* (1694).

NOYES, ROBERT GALE. "Congreve and his comedies in the Eighteenth-Century Novel," *Philological Quarterly,* XXXIX (1960), 464-80. Interesting article on eighteenth-century attitudes toward Congreve and his plays as a measure of contemporary taste.

O'REGAN, M. J. "Two Notes on French Reminiscences in Restoration Comedy," *Hermathena,* XCIII (1959), 63-70. Argues Congreve's borrowing from Thomas Corneille's *Le Baron d'Albrikac* with no acknowledgment of John Harrington Smith's argument that Congreve knew Betterton's adaptation of Corneille's play.

PALMER, JOHN. *The Comedy of Manners.* London: G. Bell and Sons, Ltd., 1913. First effort at defining the term "comedy of manners" and suggesting its social context.

PELTZ, CATHARINE W. "The Neo-classic lyric, 1660-1725," *Journal of English Literary History,* XI (1944), 92-116. Ranks Congreve with Earl of Rochester and Prior as masters of the lyric.

PERRY, HENRY TEN EYCK. *The Comic Spirit of Restoration Drama.* New Haven: Yale University Press, 1925. Divorces the comedies from their subject matter or from any moral concerns to treat them as formal exercises in comedy.

POOL, E. MILLICENT. "A Possible Source of Way of the World," *Modern Language Review*, XXXVI (1938), 258-60. Argues unconvincingly that the proviso scene from *Arlequin Jason* influenced Congreve.

POPE, ALEXANDER. *Correspondence*. Ed. George Sherburn. 6 vols. Oxford: Clarendon Press, 1956. Warns that many of Pope's letters to Congreve may have been fabricated.

POTTER, ELMER B. "The Paradox of Congreve's *Mourning Bride*," *PMLA*, LVIII (1943), 977-1001. Study of the reception and stage history of Congreve's tragedy concluding that its continued popularity depended on the opportunities it afforded for actresses. Potter's view was sharply criticized by Avery.

PROTOPESCO, DRAGOSH. *Un classique moderne: William Congreve; sa vie, son oeuvre*. Paris: Editions La Vie Universitaire, 1924. Some excellent criticism is lost in a maze of indiscriminate and insensitive source hunting.

————. *A Sheaf of Poetical Scraps*. Academia Romôna; Memoriile Sectiunei Literore, serie 3, tomul I (June, 1923). Some of the ascriptions to Congreve are questionable.

ROTHSTEIN, ERIC. *Restoration Tragedy*. Madison: University of Wisconsin Press, 1967. Contains a good discussion of *The Mourning Bride*.

SCOUTEN, ARTHUR. "Notes on Restoration Comedy," *Philological Quarterly*, XLV (1966), 62-70. Treats the last decade of the seventeenth century as "a distinct phase of the comedy of manners."

SMITH, JOHN HARRINGTON. "Thomas Corneille to Betterton to Congreve," *Journal of English and Germanic Philology*, XLV (1946), 209-13. Argues that *The Way of the World* was influenced by Thomas Betterton's *The Amorous Widow* (1670).

————. *The Gay Couple in Restoration Comedy*. Cambridge, Mass.: Harvard University Press, 1948. Study of a particular type of love play in the drama of the period. Particularly relevant to Congreve.

SNIDER, ROSE. *Satire in the Comedies of Congreve, Sheridan, Wilde, and Coward*. University of Maine Studies, Ser. 2, No. 42. Orono: University of Maine Press, 1937. Treatment of satire is seldom enlightening but the writer's strong feminist slant leads to some intelligent conclusions.

SPENCE, JOSEPH. *Observations, Anecdotes, and Characters of Books and Men*. Ed. James Osborn. 2 vols. Oxford: Clarendon Press, 1966. Records some important statements on Congreve's life and writings.

STEELE, RICHARD. *The Occasional Verse*. Ed. Rae Blanchard. Oxford: Clarendon Press, 1962. "To Mr. Congreve Occasion'd by His Comedy Called the *Way of the World*" contains some perceptive remarks on Congreve's craft.

SWAEN, A. E. H. "The Authorship of A Soldier and A Sailor," *Archiv*, CLXVIII (1935), 237-40. Does not eliminate the possibility of Congreve's authorship but points out the existence of such a song in 1693.

SWIFT, JONATHAN. *Journal to Stella*. Ed. Harold Williams. 2 vols. Oxford: Clarendon Press, 1948. Swift gives several accounts of his visits to Congreve.

TAYLOR, D. CRANE. *William Congreve*. New York: Russell and Russell, 1963. Though published originally in 1933, this work, as the *[London] Times Literary Supplement* reviewer suggested, was probably completed by 1923. It is extremely unreliable in both its facts and judgments.

TURNER, DARWIN. "The Servant in the Comedies of William Congreve," *College Language Assoc. Journal*, I (1958), 68-74. Congreve avoided making his servants into mere types. They are diverse in character and Congreve treats them with respect.

UNDERWOOD, DALE. *Etheredge, and the Seventeenth-Century Comedy of Manners*. Yale Studies in English, No. 135. New Haven: Yale University Press, 1957. Brilliant study of the libertine thought which underlay Restoration comedy.

VAN LENNEP, WILLIAM. Ed. *The London Stage 1660-1800: Part I: 1660-1700*. Carbondale: Southern Illinois University Press, 1965. Record of the performances of Congreve's plays with a useful introduction on the conditions of the stage.

VOLTAIRE, FRANÇOIS. *Letters concerning the English Nation*. Trans. John Lockman. London: P. Davies, 1926. Contains Voltaire's famous interview with Congreve.

VORIS, WILLIAM VAN. "Congreve's Gilded Carousel," *Educational Theatre Journal*, X (1957), 211-17. *The Way of the World* as an expression of the ideals of the Whig aristocracy.

————. *The Cultivated Stance*. Dublin: Dolmen P., 1965. Concentrates mainly on Congreve's treatment of time in his plays.

WAIN, JOHN. "Restoration Comedy and its Modern Critics," *Essays in Criticism*, VI (1965), 367-85. In substantial agreement with L. C. Knights's attack on Restoration drama.

WILKINSON, D. R. M. *The Comedy of Habit*. Leiden: Universitaire Pers, 1964. Reading of Restoration comedy in terms of contemporary conduct books. Severe on Congreve in the tradition of L. C. Knights.

"William Congreve," *[London] Times Literary Supplement*, January 17, 1939, 33-34. Panegyric on Congreve, dating his revival with Dobrée's *Restoration Comedy* and the 1924 production of *The Way of the World* at the Lyric Theatre, Hammersmith.

WILLIAMS, AUBREY. "Congreve's *Incognita* and the Contrivances of Providence." *Imagined Worlds*. Eds. Maynard Mack and Ian

Gregor. London: Methuen, 1968. Christian reading of *Incognita;* foreshadows a similar reading of Congreve's plays.

————. "Poetical Justice, the Contrivances of Providence, and the Works of William Congreve," *English Literary History,* XXXV (1968), 540-65. Congreve's plots as intricate examples of God's contrivances, including a general discussion of the relation between Providence and artistic design.

WILSON, CHARLES (pseud?). *Memoirs of the Life, Writings, and Amours of William Congreve.* London, 1730. Disappointing collection of gossip, letters, and some of Congreve's writings.

Index

82012